First World War
and Army of Occupation
War Diary
France, Belgium and Germany

2 CAVALRY DIVISION
Divisional Troops
Royal Army Veterinary Corps
8 Mobile Veterinary Section
4 August 1914 - 30 June 1915

WO95/1126/2

The Naval & Military Press Ltd
www.nmarchive.com
Published in association with The National Archives

Published by

The Naval & Military Press Ltd

Unit 10 Ridgewood Industrial Park,

Uckfield, East Sussex,

TN22 5QE England

Tel: +44 (0) 1825 749494

www.naval-military-press.com

www.nmarchive.com

This diary has been reprinted in facsimile from the original. Any imperfections are inevitably reproduced and the quality may fall short of modern type and cartographic standards.

© Crown Copyright
Images reproduced by permission of The National Archives, London, England, 2015.

Contents

Document type	Place/Title	Date From	Date To
Heading	WO95/1126/2		
Heading	1914-1919 2nd Cavalry Division. No. 8 Mobile Vety Section Oct 1914-Mar 1919		
Heading	War Diary of 8 Mobile Vet. Section 2nd Cavalry Division August-1914 and September-1914		
Heading	No 8 Mobile Vety: Section Capt Denise Vols I & II 4.8-30.9.14		
War Diary	Aldershot	04/08/1914	05/08/1914
War Diary	Bulford	06/08/1914	15/08/1914
War Diary	Tidworth	15/08/1914	15/08/1914
War Diary	Southampton	15/08/1914	16/08/1914
War Diary	Boulogne	16/08/1914	16/08/1914
War Diary	Pont-De-Bruges Camp	17/08/1914	17/08/1914
War Diary	Maubeuge	18/08/1914	18/08/1914
War Diary	Obreiches	19/08/1914	19/08/1914
War Diary	Obreiches	20/08/1914	22/08/1914
War Diary	Vallenciennes	23/08/1914	23/08/1914
War Diary	Solemes	24/08/1914	24/08/1914
War Diary	Le Cateau	25/08/1914	26/08/1914
War Diary	Ham	27/08/1914	27/08/1914
War Diary	Sempigne	28/08/1914	28/08/1914
War Diary	Les-Cloyes	29/08/1914	31/08/1914
War Diary	Leon	01/09/1914	01/09/1914
War Diary	Baron	01/09/1914	02/09/1914
War Diary	Dammarten	02/09/1914	02/09/1914
War Diary	Serrais	05/09/1914	05/09/1914
War Diary	Brie-Comte-Robert	06/09/1914	07/09/1914
War Diary	Crecy	08/09/1914	08/09/1914
War Diary	Rebais	09/09/1914	10/09/1914
War Diary	Marini	11/09/1914	11/09/1914
War Diary	Boussiear	12/09/1914	13/09/1914
War Diary	Marini-En-Oxuis	14/09/1914	14/09/1914
War Diary	Breny	15/09/1914	15/09/1914
War Diary	Braine	16/09/1914	16/09/1914
War Diary	Fere-En-Tendonois	17/09/1914	19/09/1914
War Diary	Chateau-Theiry	20/09/1914	22/09/1914
War Diary	Braine	23/09/1914	30/09/1914
War Diary	Mont-Notre-Dame	30/09/1914	30/09/1914
Heading	War Diary of 2nd Cavalry Division August-1914		
Heading	No. 9 Mobile Vet. Sect. Vol I.		
War Diary		16/08/1914	01/09/1914
Heading	War Diary of No 8 Section A V C Volume I 914 Aug To Sep		
Miscellaneous			
War Diary	Aldershot	04/08/1914	05/08/1914
War Diary	Bulford	06/08/1914	15/08/1914
War Diary	Tidworth	15/08/1914	15/08/1914
War Diary	Southampton	15/08/1914	16/08/1914
War Diary	Boulogne	16/08/1914	16/08/1914
War Diary	Pont-De-Bruges Camp	15/08/1914	15/08/1914

War Diary	Obreiches	20/08/1914	22/08/1914
War Diary	Vallenciennes	23/08/1914	23/08/1914
War Diary	Sulemes	24/08/1914	24/08/1914
War Diary	Le Cateau	25/08/1914	26/08/1914
War Diary	Ham	27/08/1914	27/08/1914
War Diary	Sempigne	28/08/1914	28/08/1914
War Diary	Les-Cloyes	29/08/1914	31/08/1914
War Diary	Leon	01/09/1914	01/09/1914
War Diary	Baron	01/09/1914	02/09/1914
War Diary	Dammarten	02/09/1914	02/09/1914
War Diary	Serrais	05/09/1914	05/09/1914
War Diary	Brie-Comte-Robert	06/09/1914	07/09/1914
War Diary	Crecy	08/09/1914	08/09/1914
War Diary	Rebais	09/09/1914	10/09/1914
War Diary	Marini	11/09/1914	11/09/1914
War Diary	Boussiear	12/09/1914	13/09/1914
War Diary	Marini En Oxuis	14/09/1914	14/09/1914
War Diary	Breny	15/09/1914	15/09/1914
War Diary	Braine	16/09/1914	16/09/1914
War Diary	Fere-En-Tendonois	17/09/1914	19/09/1914
War Diary	Chateau-Theiry	20/09/1914	22/09/1914
War Diary	Braine	23/09/1914	30/09/1914
War Diary	Mont-Notre-Dame	30/09/1914	30/09/1914
Heading	2nd Cavalry Division October-1914 To March 1919		
Heading	No.8 Mobile Veterinary Section Vol III 1-31.10.14		
War Diary	Mont-Notre-Dame	01/10/1914	03/10/1914
War Diary	Vauciennes	04/10/1914	04/10/1914
War Diary	Estrees-St-Denis	05/10/1914	05/10/1914
War Diary	St Just	06/10/1914	06/10/1914
War Diary	Ailly-Sur-Noie	07/10/1914	07/10/1914
War Diary	St Just	08/10/1914	08/10/1914
War Diary	Hiermont	09/10/1914	09/10/1914
War Diary	Fleury	10/10/1914	10/10/1914
War Diary	Fabvin-Palaert	11/10/1914	11/10/1914
War Diary	Fabvin	12/10/1914	12/10/1914
War Diary	Aire	13/10/1914	13/10/1914
War Diary	Hazebrouck	14/10/1914	14/10/1914
War Diary	Kemmel	15/10/1914	15/10/1914
War Diary	Messines	16/10/1914	17/10/1914
War Diary	Kemmel	18/10/1914	18/10/1914
War Diary	St Razeele	19/10/1914	19/10/1914
War Diary	Kemmel	20/10/1914	20/10/1914
War Diary	Holebecke	21/10/1914	21/10/1914
War Diary	Dickebusch	22/10/1914	29/10/1914
War Diary	St Eloi	30/10/1914	30/10/1914
War Diary	Dickebusch	31/10/1914	31/10/1914
Heading	War Diary of 2nd Cavalry Division November-1914		
Heading	No 8 Mobile Vety: Section 1-30.11.14		
War Diary	Dickebusch	01/11/1914	01/11/1914
War Diary	Locre	02/11/1914	02/11/1914
War Diary	Berthen	03/11/1914	07/11/1914
War Diary	Hazebrouck	08/11/1914	08/11/1914
War Diary	Berthen	09/11/1914	12/11/1914
War Diary	Hazebrouck	13/11/1914	13/11/1914
War Diary	Berthen	14/11/1914	14/11/1914
War Diary	Noote-Boom	15/11/1914	25/11/1914

War Diary	Blev-Tour	26/11/1914	30/11/1914
Heading	War Diary of 2nd Cavalry Division December-1914		
Heading	No 8. Mobile Vety: Section Vol V.		
War Diary	Bleve-Tour	01/12/1915	31/12/1915
Heading	2nd Cavalry Division No 8. Mobile Vety: Sect. January And February 1915 Vol VI		
War Diary	Bleve-Tour	01/01/1915	16/01/1915
War Diary	Dohem	17/01/1915	31/01/1915
War Diary	Sec-Bois	01/02/1915	28/02/1915
Heading	2nd Cavalry Division No. 8. Mobile Vety: Section Vol VII March 1915		
War Diary	Clety	01/03/1915	03/03/1915
War Diary	Inghem	04/03/1915	11/03/1915
War Diary	Sec-Bois	12/03/1915	31/03/1915
War Diary		01/04/1915	30/04/1915
War Diary		01/05/1915	31/05/1915
Heading	2nd Cavalry Division No 8. Mobile Vety Section Vol VIII 16-30.6.15		
War Diary		01/06/1915	12/06/1915
Miscellaneous	Army Book 152		
Heading	Opened on July 8 1915 Closed on July 31-1916		
War Diary		08/07/1915	31/07/1916
Heading	2nd Cavalry Division No 8. Mobile Vety: Section Vol IX 1-31.7.15		
Miscellaneous	No.8 Mobile Veterinary Section.		
War Diary	Hondighem	01/07/1915	14/07/1915
War Diary	Volkerinckhove	15/07/1915	31/07/1915
War Diary	2nd Cavalry Division No 8. Mobile Vety Section Vol X August. 15		
War Diary	St Quentin	08/08/1915	13/08/1915
War Diary	Volkerinckhove	01/08/1915	05/08/1915
War Diary	Volkerinckhove	06/08/1915	07/08/1915
War Diary	St Quentin	14/08/1915	31/08/1915
Heading	2nd Cavalry Division No 8. Mobile Vety: Section Vol XI Sept 15		
War Diary	St Quentin	01/09/1915	20/09/1915
War Diary	Mametz	21/09/1915	23/09/1915
War Diary	Monchy	24/09/1915	24/09/1915
War Diary	Lozingham	25/09/1915	28/09/1915
War Diary	Ferfay	29/09/1915	30/09/1915
Heading	2nd Cavalry Division 8th M.V.S. Oct: 15 Vol XII		
War Diary	Ferfay	01/10/1915	02/10/1915
War Diary	Norrent Fontes	03/10/1915	16/10/1915
War Diary	Rombly	17/10/1915	23/10/1915
War Diary	St Quentin	24/10/1915	31/10/1915
Heading	2nd Cavalry Division No. 8. Mob. Vet. Sec. Nov. 1915 Vol XIII		
War Diary	St Quentin	01/11/1915	16/11/1915
War Diary	Campaignette	17/11/1915	20/11/1915
War Diary	Grand Manillet	21/11/1915	30/11/1915
Heading	8. Mob. Vet. Sec. Dec 1915. Vol. XIV		
War Diary	Grand Manillet	01/12/1915	31/12/1915
Miscellaneous	Officer Commanding		
Heading	8 Mobile Vety Sec Jan 1916 Vol XV		
War Diary	G.D. Manillet	01/01/1916	28/01/1916
War Diary	Grand Manillet	29/01/1916	28/04/1916

War Diary	Recquebrecq Ouvre Wirqvin	01/06/1916	07/06/1916
War Diary	Recquebreucq	08/06/1916	19/06/1916
War Diary	St Razeele	20/06/1916	30/06/1916
Heading	War Diary of. 8th Mobile Veterinary Section-2nd Cav. Div. From 1st July. To 31st July. 1916. Volume		
War Diary	St Razeele	01/07/1916	07/07/1916
War Diary	Wallon Capel	08/07/1916	15/07/1916
War Diary	Merris	16/07/1916	31/07/1916
Heading	War Diary of 8th Mobile Vety. Section For August, 1916 Vol. 22		
War Diary	Merris	01/08/1916	31/08/1916
Heading	War Diary of No.8 Mobile Veterinary Section For September, 1916. Vol 23		
War Diary	Merris	01/09/1916	05/09/1916
War Diary	Robecq	06/09/1916	06/09/1916
War Diary	Conteville	07/09/1916	07/09/1916
War Diary	Wail	08/09/1916	09/09/1916
War Diary	Outrebois	10/09/1916	10/09/1916
War Diary	Wargnies	11/09/1916	11/09/1916
War Diary	Bonnay	12/09/1916	14/09/1916
War Diary	Dernancourt	15/09/1916	30/09/1916
Heading	War Diary of 8th Mobile Veterinary Section October, 1916. Vol. 24		
War Diary	Dernancourt	01/10/1916	31/10/1916
Heading	War Diary of 8th Mobile Veterinary Section. November, 1916. Vol. 25		
War Diary	Dernancourt	01/11/1916	07/11/1916
War Diary	Bussy	08/11/1916	08/11/1916
War Diary	Bourdon	09/11/1916	09/11/1916
War Diary	Le Titre	10/09/1916	10/11/1916
War Diary	Torte Fontaine	11/11/1916	30/11/1916
Heading	War Diary of 8th Mobile Veterinary Section. December, 1916. Vol. 26		
War Diary	Torte Fontaine	01/12/1916	31/12/1916
Heading	War Diary of 8th Mobile Veterinary Section. January 1917- Vol. XXIX.		
War Diary	Torte Fonteine	01/01/1917	31/01/1917
Heading	War Diary of 8th Mobile Veterinary Section. February, 1917. Vol. XXX.		
War Diary	Torte Fonteine	01/02/1917	28/02/1917
Heading	War Diary of 8th Mobile Veterinary Section March 1917 Vol. XXXI.		
War Diary	Torte Fonteine	01/03/1917	31/03/1917
Heading	War Diary of 8th Mobile Veterinary Section. April, 1917. Vol. XXXII.		
War Diary	Torte Fonteine	01/04/1917	04/04/1917
War Diary	Macfer Occoches	05/04/1917	07/04/1917
War Diary	Gubeaumpre	08/04/1917	08/04/1917
War Diary	Riviere	09/04/1917	09/04/1917
War Diary	Ronville	10/04/1917	11/04/1917
War Diary	Gaudiempre	12/04/1917	18/04/1917
War Diary	Frohen Le Grand	19/04/1917	19/04/1917
War Diary	Le Planty Ferm Auxi Le Chateau	20/04/1917	30/04/1917
Heading	War Diary of No. 8 Mobile Veterinary Section. May, 1917- Vol. XXXIII.		
War Diary	Le Planty Ferme Auxi Le Chateau	01/05/1917	08/05/1917

War Diary	Auxi Le Chateau	09/05/1917	11/05/1917
War Diary	Frohen Le Grand	12/05/1917	12/05/1917
War Diary	Warnies	13/05/1917	13/05/1917
War Diary	Quaerieu	14/05/1917	14/05/1917
War Diary	Suzannie	15/05/1917	15/05/1917
War Diary	Hamel	16/05/1917	18/05/1917
War Diary	Boucly	19/05/1917	31/05/1917
Heading	War Diary of 8th. Mobile Vet. Section. From 1st. June-30th. June, 1917 (Volume XXXIV)		
War Diary	Boucly	01/06/1917	30/06/1917
Heading	War Diary of No.8 Mobile Vety Section From 1/7/17 To 31/7/17 (Volume XXXV)		
War Diary	Bucley	01/07/1917	25/07/1917
War Diary	In the Field	26/07/1917	31/07/1917
Heading	War Diary of 8th Mob. Veterinary Section From 1st Aug. 1917 To 31st Aug. 1917 Volume XXXVI		
Heading	War Diary of 8th Mobile Veterinary Section For Month of August 1917 (Vol. XXXVI)		
War Diary	In The Field	01/08/1917	31/08/1917
Heading	No 8 Mobile Vety Section War Diary For Month Of September 1917 Volume Number XXXVII		
War Diary	Field	01/09/1917	30/09/1917
Heading	War Diary of 8th Mobile Vet. Section From 1st Oct 1917 To 31st Oct 1917 (Volume XXXVIII)		
Heading	War Diary Volume (Ns XXXVIII)From 1st October 1917 To 31st October of No 8 Mobile Veterinary Section		
War Diary		01/10/1917	27/10/1917
War Diary	Field	28/10/1917	31/10/1917
Heading	War Diary of 8th Mobile Vety Sect From 1st Nov 1917 To 30 Nov 1917 (Vol XXXIX)		
War Diary	Field	01/11/1917	30/11/1917
Heading	War Diary of 8th M.V. Section From 1st Dec 1917 To 31st Dec 1917 (Volume XL)		
Miscellaneous	Cover for Documents. Nature of Enclosures.		
War Diary	Field	01/12/1917	31/12/1917
Heading	8th Mobile Veterinary Section War Diary January-1918 Vol 41		
Miscellaneous	Inter-Office Minutes		
Miscellaneous	Not To Be Written On.		
War Diary		01/01/1917	31/01/1917
Heading	8th Mobile Veterinary Section War Diary February-1918 (Volume 42)		
Miscellaneous	Inter-Office Minutes		
Miscellaneous	Not To Be Written On.		
War Diary		01/02/1918	27/02/1918
Heading	No 8 Mobile Vety Section War Diary Of.March 1918 Volume 43		
Miscellaneous	Inter-Office Minutes		
Miscellaneous	Not To Be Written On.		
War Diary		01/03/1918	31/03/1918
Heading	War Diary Vol 44 8th Mobile Vety in 3 Cav Bde Reference No.6 Records Letter 17.259.18 Dated 3rd April 1918 Dale of Mobilisalion 5th Aug 1918 Arrived in France 16th Aug 1918		
War Diary		01/04/1918	30/04/1918

Heading	War Diary May 8th Mobile Vety. Sec From 1st May 1918 To 31st May 1918 Volume 45		
War Diary		01/05/1918	09/05/1918
War Diary	Le Faux	10/05/1918	20/05/1918
War Diary	Field	21/05/1918	31/05/1918
Heading	War Diary of 8th. Mobile Veterinary Section From 1st. June, 1918.-To-30th. June, 1918. (Volume 46).		
Heading	8th Mobile Vety in War Diary. Volume 46 June		
Miscellaneous	Inter-Office Minutes		
War Diary	Lefaux	01/06/1918	30/06/1918
Heading	No 8 Mobile Vety War Diary For.July 1918 Volume 47		
Miscellaneous	Inter-Office Minutes		
Miscellaneous	Not To Be Written On.		
War Diary	Lefaux	01/07/1918	31/07/1918
Heading	War Diary Volume 48 8th Mobile Vety Section August 1918		
Miscellaneous	Inter-Office Minutes		
Miscellaneous	Not To Be Written On.		
War Diary		01/08/1918	27/08/1918
War Diary	Coullemont	28/08/1918	31/08/1918
Heading	War Diary of 8th Mobile Veterinary Section From 1st To 30th September 1918 Vol. No.49		
Miscellaneous	Inter-Office Minutes		
Miscellaneous	Not To Be Written On		
War Diary	Coullemont	01/09/1918	07/09/1918
War Diary	Lattre St Quentin	08/09/1918	10/09/1918
War Diary	Dieval	11/09/1918	28/09/1918
War Diary	Mailly	29/09/1918	29/09/1918
Heading	Inchy	30/09/1918	30/09/1918
Heading	War Diary of 8th Mobile Vety Sec. Volume 50 October 1918		
Miscellaneous	Inter-Office Minutes		
Miscellaneous	Not To Be Written On.		
War Diary	Inchy	01/10/1918	26/10/1918
War Diary	Baralle	27/10/1918	31/10/1918
Heading	War Diary Volume 51 Nov.1918 8th Mobile Veterinary Section Volume 51		
War Diary	Baralle	01/11/1918	15/11/1918
War Diary	Field	16/11/1918	30/11/1918
Heading	War Diary Volume 52 8th Mobile Veterinary Section 3rd Cavalry Bde. December 1918		
War Diary	Menil Favay	01/12/1918	16/12/1918
War Diary	Awan	17/12/1918	31/12/1918
Heading	War Diary No.8 Mobile Vety Section Month of January 1919 Volume. 5.3.		
War Diary	Awan	01/01/1919	31/01/1919
Heading	War Diary No 8 M V S Volume 54 Month of February 1919		
War Diary	Awan	01/02/1919	28/02/1919
Heading	War Diary Volume No 56 1/3/19-31/3/19 No. 8 Mobile Vety Section		
War Diary	Awan	01/03/1919	10/03/1919
War Diary	Ensival	11/03/1919	31/03/1919
War Diary		13/06/1915	30/06/1915

WO 95/1126/2

1914-1919
2ND CAVALRY DIVISION

NO.8 MOBILE VETY SECTION

OCT 1914 - MAR 1919

War Diary

of

8 Mobile Vet. Section

2nd Cavalry Division

August – 1914
and September – 1914

2c

aos

121/1966

No P. hostile Vilg: Lectiora: Copt Senior

Jols I & II. 4.8. — 30.9.14

Army Form C. 2118.

WAR DIARY
or
INTELLIGENCE SUMMARY.
(Erase heading not required.)

Instructions regarding War Diaries and Intelligence Summaries are contained in F.S. Regs., Part II. and the Staff Manual respectively. Title pages will be prepared in manuscript.

Hour, Date, Place	Summary of Events and Information	Remarks and references to Appendices
Aldershot 4th August 5.30 pm	Received orders to mobilize and proceed to BELFORD I/c Command of No 8 Mobile Veterinary Section	1D
5th August	Proceeded to BELFORD by 11.30 a.m. train from Farnborough Station arriving 5.20 p.m.	
BELFORD. 6th August to 15th August	Took over equipment & two horses of the Section. The men of the Section consisted of the following viz:— One Sergeant:— three Corporals (One man of the Army Veterinary Corps. The Remaining N.C.O's were 14th Hussars (Infantry) One Reservist A.S.C. (Driver) No Cattle Killer and only 12 rounds of Revolver ammunition were received, only 4 2nd reserve horses which I consider to have been enough. No horse ever came in	

Army Form C. 2118.

WAR DIARY
or
INTELLIGENCE SUMMARY.
(Erase heading not required.)

Instructions regarding War Diaries and Intelligence Summaries are contained in F.S. Regs., Part II. and the Staff Manual respectively. Title pages will be prepared in manuscript.

Hour, Date, Place	Summary of Events and Information	Remarks and references to Appendices
BULFORD 15th August 8 am	Parade & got all regiment Shooting, then went to Showers bath in the Station	
TIDWORTH 6.30 am	Left BULFORD and marched to TIDWORTH & catch 10 am train for SOUTHAMPTON	
	Entrained Sudden Losses report and arr. Tidworth and reached SOUTHAMPTON arrived 4pm	
SOUTHAMPTON 15th Aug Aug 16th	Embarked on S.S. Wheelman arr. 4 pm	
	Left SOUTHAMPTON at 5 pm, then went into 92nd of the 2nd Cav Bde under command of Gen'l De Lisle, our destination not known but in view, See Convoy got	
Boulogne 16th Aug	Arrived at 5.45 pm disembarked and marched three miles to Camp at Pont-du-Briche, G.S. where we camped for night	

Army Form C. 2118.

WAR DIARY
or
INTELLIGENCE SUMMARY.
(Erase heading not required.)

Instructions regarding War Diaries and Intelligence Summaries are contained in F.S. Regs., Part II. and the Staff Manual respectively. Title pages will be prepared in manuscript.

Hour, Date, Place	Summary of Events and Information	Remarks and references to Appendices
PONT-DE-BRIQUES CAMP 17th August	All the Horses on disembarkation were looked up and fed.	
4 P.M.	Entrained Horses, drew rations and forage	
	Received orders from H.Q. Quartier II Car Bouger to entrain the Section at Boulogne at 8 P.M. for a journey up country. These orders were carried out, the train leaving at 12 midnight. Watered and fed on the journey.	
Hautmont Aug 18th 10 h.	Arrived at Hautmont next morning, watered and fed horses, and prepared under orders from II Car Bouger to O BREICHES. Inches where we arrived. The battalion. Inspected by H A.D.V.S. 1st Division. overious etc.	
O BREICHES August 19th		
O BREICHES August 20th	Received orders from A.D.V.S. II Division to Landown the eighteen of the Cavalry Recent to H O.C. 1st D. before entrainy.	
	Left by rail Railhead DOUZIES.	

Forms/C. 2118/10.

Army Form C. 2118.

WAR DIARY
or
INTELLIGENCE SUMMARY.
(Erase heading not required.)

(4)

Instructions regarding War Diaries and Intelligence Summaries are contained in F. S. Regs., Part II. and the Staff Manual respectively. Title pages will be prepared in manuscript.

Hour, Date, Place	Summary of Events and Information	Remarks and references to Appendices
OBREICHES August 20th	Continued main manoeuvres 6-2nd Them 6-III O.T. 10.5 S.E. Wing Section air at the Base. Admitted 3 horses sick from the II Cavalry Brigade. No 4 hostile Section arrived in Camp.	
OBREICHES Aug 21st	Admitted 25 horses sick from II Cav Bde and marched 6-DOUZIES which were informed was rail head Section Horse Company will be in great condition. Cavalry at-DOUZIES for the night. Was unsure our entraining as it was not railhead, also supplies here Section arrived with 10 sick horses.	
August 22nd	Marched to Maubeuge and entrained 30 sick horses 6 [crossed out] here, marched to VALENCIENNES 25. to the away and camped outside the Town.	
VALENCIENNES Aug 23rd	Marched to SOLESMES which was a without billets for the night. Horses good but tired.	

WAR DIARY
or
INTELLIGENCE SUMMARY.
(Erase heading not required.)

Army Form C. 2118.

Hour, Date, Place	Summary of Events and Information	Remarks and references to Appendices
SOLESMES August 24th	Marched to LE CATEAU 10 miles away, horses good condition this can arrived in camp at 4 AM went on to AMIENS for orders	
LE CATEAU Aug 25th	Were received for DES of MIENS ordering Section to proceed to ST QUENTIN to 1st miles away to billet not available so have to camp in a street, nearly were killed	
Aug 26th	Marched 15 miles to HAM, lots of troops on the road delaying arrived at 11 AM 10 P.M., Camped inside the Station in the street hay not beaver, meals very bad, no returns obtainable from men started to town rear.	
HAM August 27th	Marched to SEMPIGNE, had a medium train on NOV on interior waited here, Camped in a large field, no orders or further Signal the Section almost join, alone entering towns for Duvall.	

Army Form C. 2118.

WAR DIARY
or
INTELLIGENCE SUMMARY.
(Erase heading not required.)

Instructions regarding War Diaries and Intelligence Summaries are contained in F. S. Regs., Part II. and the Staff Manual respectively. Title pages will be prepared in manuscript.

Hour, Date, Place	Summary of Events and Information	Remarks and references to Appendices
SEA PIGNE August 28th	Received orders from Col. Buttler to join the III Cavalry Brigade at gun opposition, sent on two men to the town with convoy of E Sector.	
LES-CLOYES August 29th	Marched over hes. 1 & 9 Autumn about 4 miles and camped for the night, can find no information as to the location of the Cav Bde which is supposed to be any large distance away, meeting have with the 4th Division.	
August 30th	Marched to TRACY-LE-MENT Remained in a great field for the night, no return attempts.	
August 31st 9 am	Marched out to LEON twenty miles away, took 12½ hours to fires allowed, as the enemy are very near frightening our right. Close river camp.	

Army Form C. 2118.

WAR DIARY
or
INTELLIGENCE SUMMARY.
(Erase heading not required.)

Hour, Date, Place	Summary of Events and Information	Remarks and references to Appendices
LEON September 1st	Moved off at 5 AM in a great hurry. Capt. Ponsonby to the convoy. So we left "L" Battery R.H.A. reported enemy in Section approx 5 miles outside LEON by a General and went for reconnaissance duties and "L" Batt Section came in — the 4th Dragoon Guards Column	
BARON	Marched to BARON and halted for 4 hours, watered and fed. When supplies arrived at 5 PM and camped for the night – 6 miles away, — broke camp, marched for camp at 2.30 AM feeding of 3 abandoned horses and	
September 2nd DAMMARTEN	Camped 15 miles away at DAMMARTEN, about 3 forms of the Station. Some trust, tore lookings valise. Marched all night – forced through LANGY at 6 AM and camped. Watered outside it. A man and horse very tired. No sleep for 5 days. Supplies very short – arrived morning of 3rd Sept. Camped & tented morning of 5.30 Sept Q	

Army Form C. 2118.

WAR DIARY
or
INTELLIGENCE SUMMARY.
(Erase heading not required.)

Instructions regarding War Diaries and Intelligence Summaries are contained in F. S. Regs., Part II. and the Staff Manual respectively. Title pages will be prepared in manuscript.

Hour, Date, Place	Summary of Events and Information	Remarks and references to Appendices
SERRAIS Sept 5th	Took over one man of 4th Hussars wounded in hand, left Camp at 4.30 A.M. and arrived at BRIE-COMTE-ROBERT at 3 P.M. Incident at Lozin & the Rome most 30 rolls of hot soden.	
BRIE-COMTE-ROBERT Sept 6th	Left Camp at 6 A.M. and marched to FERRIERES 10 miles away. Camped in Barn in Rothschilds estate until 10 P.M. when we struck camp and marched 10 miles to camp water supply very good, plenty of grazing, broke up camp at 10.0 P.M. and marched to SERRAIS.	
September 7th 10 A.M.	Marched to CRECY, about 18 miles away, roads fairly beaten fine, still under 4th Division.	

Army Form C. 2118.

WAR DIARY
or
INTELLIGENCE SUMMARY.
(Erase heading not required.)

Instructions regarding War Diaries and Intelligence Summaries are contained in F. S. Regs., Part II. and the Staff Manual respectively. Title pages will be prepared in manuscript.

Hour, Date, Place	Summary of Events and Information	Remarks and references to Appendices
CRECY September 8th	Marched to REBAIS when B echelon of 1st & 2nd Cavalry Brigade are in camp, and joined them. Horses very tired, not in trim since supplies, shoes and harness for a fortnight back	
REBAIS Sept 9th Sept 10th	Marched at 10 a.m. to SACY. Rested at our horses in the road there was report by the Station no fire transport north. Marched to MARIGNY en OXOIS, took over 16 horses (cobs) from 3rd Cav. Bde. Camped for the night, no supplies, but had enough to carry on until	
MARIGNY Sept 11th	Took over 10 more horses from 3rd RHA. Remainder of entries are requisitioned for return to Just horses between Q.S.O. and then returning to the base, marched to the RUSSIANS where we halted for the night. Our orders were later went.	General PENBURG

Army Form C. 2118.

WAR DIARY
or
INTELLIGENCE SUMMARY.
(Erase heading not required.)

Instructions regarding War Diaries and Intelligence Summaries are contained in F. S. Regs., Part II. and the Staff Manual respectively. Title pages will be prepared in manuscript.

Hour, Date, Place	Summary of Events and Information	Remarks and references to Appendices
BOUSSIEAR September 12th	Arrived at 9.30pm. Took on horses of No 7 Field Ambulance for conveyance my men. In turn, join the Section, marched with No 7 Section to St Souson and entrained 42 Reck Horse to the trot at VILLENEUVE-LA-FERTE, unload and fed, then saddle and retired to BUSSIERS arriving every evening at 9.30pm. bivalled for night.	
September 13th	Marched to MARINI-EN-OXOIS 15 miles away and bivalled for night, terrific hot road, road off feet, weather fine, roads good.	
MARINI-EN-OXOIS Sep 14th	Marched north to 7 Section 6 BRENY. On reaching No 7 Section 6 BRENY the Brigade down arms and camped in a field for the night. Short two horses of Section.	
BRENY Sep 15th	Marched 22 miles away to BRAINE and joined the 13th echelon of 3rd Cavalry Brigade camped in the grounds of a Large Chateau, weather fine.	

WAR DIARY
or
INTELLIGENCE SUMMARY.

(Erase heading not required.)

Army Form C. 2118.

Hour, Date, Place	Summary of Events and Information	Remarks and references to Appendices
BRAINE September 16th	Reported to A.O.V.S. 2nd Cavalry Brigade. Dismounted collected 124 Rob horses from 3rd Cavalry Brigade at LIME his mules away 25 men were taken over with the horses & found to the tree, marched to railwhd at —	
FERE-EN-TERDONOIS Sept 17th	FERE-EN-TERDONOIS and camped for night – requisitioned supplies for the next three.	
" Sept 18th	Could not procure any trucks at the station & sent the horses away. Inspected by Col. Bullen, we note good review 6 clean faces.	
Sept 19th	Lazy but busy day, 12 trench ambulances. Ordered by AH Col. Bull Rich turned to CHATEAU-THIERRY 15 miles away, and entrain the horses to the Tree as horses were shot two, left than behind over 67 horses.	

Army Form C. 2118

WAR DIARY
or
INTELLIGENCE SUMMARY.
(Erase heading not required.)

Instructions regarding War Diaries and Intelligence Summaries are contained in F. S. Regs., Part II. and the Staff Manual respectively. Title pages will be prepared in manuscript.

Hour, Date, Place	Summary of Events and Information	Remarks and references to Appendices
CHATEAU-THIERRY September 20th	Entrained for next town to file trol, plenty of trucks & ammunition	
September 21st	Very wet and cold. Marched out 7.30 a.m. on the road to BRAINE, halted at FERE-EN-TARDENOIS, from here I were ordered out first and shot 3 horses, we camped on the Marne 6 BRAINE and arrived there at 6.0 m. to new not camp	
Sept 22nd BRAINE	Reported to Brigade Major 3rd Cav Brigade shot 3 horses sick.	
Sept 23rd	" " "	
Sept 24th	Selected a new and better camp. admitted 3 horses sick Indin potin. withdrawn from the Section. Paid the men of Section, collected 25 horses from 3rd Brigade and entrained to Vile Farré, ordered attached from the Supply between shot out horse too valuable to more.	

Army Form C. 2118

WAR DIARY
or
INTELLIGENCE SUMMARY.
(Erase heading not required.)

Instructions regarding War Diaries and Intelligence Summaries are contained in F. S. Regs., Part II. and the Staff Manual respectively. Title pages will be prepared in manuscript.

Hour, Date, Place	Summary of Events and Information	Remarks and references to Appendices
BRAINE September 25th	Collected 6 teams from 3rd Cavalry Brigade, horses and mules of the Army transport.	
September 26th	Rode 61 teams Brtn tent rein Cav of "H" Section.	
" 27th	Admitted 19 horses and evacuated them to the horse standing.	
" 28th	2id 67 Bh Sections to entrain 194 teams to the Front.	
" 29th	Admitted 23 teams from 3rd Cav. Brigade, horse atmn.	
" 30th	Received one horse, making our total in Camp 24 sick.	
MONT-NOTRE-DAME September 30th	Admitted two teams from L/7 Section, one from D Battery RHA. Unit two teams that marched to MONT-NOTRE-DAME and billeted in a farm which was vacant.	

WAR DIARY

of

No. 9 MOBILE VET. SECTION

2nd CAVALRY DIVISION

AUGUST - 1914

121/1096

Geo. G. Mobile City Lot.

Vol I.

War Diary.
No 9 Mobile Veterinary Section

16th Aug. Sunday - Entrained Woolwich Arsenal Station for Southampton 12.30 PM. Arrived latter place about 5 PM. Embarked SS. Californian.

17th Aug. Disembarked LE HAVRE about 4.30 PM. Proceeded No 2 Rest Camp arriving about 10.30 PM. Had great difficulty picketting horses. Pegs issued, no use on this soil as ground line soon pulled up. Tried picketting each horse separately; pegs again soon pulled up. Must have air line in future.

18th Aug. Remained in camp LE HAVRE. Received orders during morning to entrain 19th at GARE. DES. MARCHANDISES. station at 3 PM with Section. Went to base head quarters to hand in base rolls of men. Also went to Ordnance Depot to draw halters and rope for lines, none available.

19th Aug. Entrained during afternoon. Orders received at Station, said BUSIGNY. Station. Then other orders received there as to destination.

20th Aug. Train arrived BUSIGNY about 11 AM. Orders handed to me to disentrain at MAUBEUGE and proceed to WATTIGNES by road. Arrived latter place about 3.30 PM. Country fairly hilly on the journey. One thing quite evident at this early stage viz: The two wheeled cart for the section is much too heavy, although very little kit on it and no forage or provisions yet.

draught-horses had great difficulty in mounting the slopes. WATTIGNES about 6 miles from MAUBEUGE. Went into billets. No orders received by me beyond those saying proceed to WATTIGNES. Found 2 Squadrons of 3rd Hussars here; also saw Brigade Major who said he knew nothing of me.
Received orders 10PM to collect sick horses of 4th Cavy Bde at 7AM next morning.

21st Aug. Went to cross roads mentioned in previous night's orders, at 7AM. Saw nothing. No sick horses. No orders sent to me. Went to SOLRE-LE-CHATEAU during the morning to see if could get orders. Saw only French troops. Sent men of a Section to other places around to see if I could get orders, or any information. All came back not having seen any signs of British troops.
Sent one Sergeant during afternoon to MAUBEUGE to try and get into touch with troops. No British troops there. Decided to stay the night at WATTIGNES and move to MAUBEUGE early next morning. No orders received by me up to late at night. Original orders received by me were very vague. Simply said proceed to WATTIGNES. Did not mention any Brigades or Divisions to report to.

22nd Aug. No orders received. So decided to try and find Cavalry Division. Went by road to MAUBEUGE during morning. There found 1st Division passing through, going northwards.

Decided to foll on in rear of their baggage.
At 11AM 1st Division halted. I learned approximate position of Cavalry Division, so pushed on with Section towards MONS. On the way met A.D.V.S. Cavalry Division who said Head quarters were going to QUIVERAIN Section got as far as BOUSSU where one of the draught horses was found to be exhausted. Had to halt here for the night. We had come about 25 miles. Roads mostly stones & country fairly hilly & rough going. Bivouacked in field. Had very little rations or forage.

23rd Aug. Left at 7AM for VALENCIENNES, this being Cavalry Division railhead, where I was informed Mobile Sections ought to be.
Passed thro QUIVERAIN on the way & reported to ADVS Cavalry Division. Arrived at first place about 11.45AM and was informed that railhead was at SOLESMES. Moved on to latter at 1.30 after watering and feeding. Same difficulty with cart to-day - nearly exhausted both horses. Can only go at slow pace. Cart delays Section considerably. Roads still paved with cobble stones. Arrived SOLESMES at 5 PM. Billeted in large farm yard in town. Drew forage and rations for 2 days.

24th Aug. Railhead for to-day LE CATEAU.
So proceeded arriving at 11AM. If mobile sections auto move with each movement of railhead I stay there until orders are received to collect horses

little of latter will be done as it will take Sections all their time to keep pace with daily movement of railhead without collecting sick horses.
Bivouacked in good field, with Sections commanded by CAPTAINS - WADLEY. BLACK. DEVINE & LECKIE. Late at night orders were received from the D.D.V.S. General Head Quarters at LE CATEAU for No 9 Mobile Section to proceed by road to ST. QUENTIN in the morning. Have not seen any signs of the Cavalry Division since leaving QUIVERAIN therefore no sick horses collected up to now. So far Section has been moving along from railhead to railhead by road of no use to anyone. As we seem to be retiring each day there is a great difficulty about collecting sick animals.

25th Aug Arrived ST. QUENTIN by road. Went into billets during evening. Had long march to-day. Draught horses again done up. Cart is useless to a mobile section. Requires something much lighter

26th Aug Ordered by Camp Commandant to join details of 4th Division on the CAMBRAI road. Left billets at 1.15PM, joined details at time stated, 1 mile from ST. QUENTIN. route latter to ROUPY. HAM. Starting point GARE. ST. JEAN at 3.15PM. Column arrived at HAM at 10PM. Rained very hard. Had to keep horses saddled all night. Men held their horses and slept along roadside with reins fastened around themselves.

27th Aug. Column moved on by road at 7AM to NOYON, thence to SEMPIGNY. Arrived at latter at 4 PM. and bivouacked in field

Up to now had mostly been in billets so no difficulty with picketting horses. In this field had to adopt air line, one end tied to cart wheels, and other end across two large stakes fastened together and driven in ground. Only method of any use as far as I can see at present.

28th Aug. Rested all day. Ordered by DDVS Gng to report to 4th Cav Bde Scrap at present

29th Aug. Left SEMPIGNY at 4 PM with 4th Divnl baggage column passed thro small forest to CARLEPONT & bivouacked the night in a field

30th Aug. Left CARLEPONT, still with 4th Divisional baggage train. No information as to whereabouts of 4th Cavy Bde. Got to MONTIGNY, bivouacked the night. No maps yet been issued to Mobile Section.

31st Aug. Left latter place with Section still with above Divisnl column: passed all day thro' FOREST OF COMPEIGNE. Bivouacked at 11PM in small field on outskirts of forest. Have not yet seen any sick animals. Even if any had been collected up to this there would have been no opportunity of getting them away by train.

1st Sept. About 4 AM. firing (rifle) commenced all around us & continued for at least twenty minutes. This first brought home to us the utter helplessness of a Mobile Vety Section without arms of any sort except the old pattern cavalry sword

AVC / M

Major Edwards

WAR DIARY.

121/606

No 8 Section. AVC.

Volume I

1914 AUG & SEP

Maj W B Edwards AVC
O/C No 8 Sec. AVC

4.8. Received the mobilisation order & arrived at Euston about 12 p.m.

5.8. Arrived at Curragh about 8 p.m.

6.8. Reported arrival to A.D.V.S. & started work with No 8 Sect. AVC. Resumed arriving, allotted quarters, fetched remounts, clothed recruits etc.

7.8 Mobilisation proceeding. In addition was placed in charge of Curragh Station Vety. Hospital & details without a proper handing over, owing to hurried departure of officer handing over.

8.8. Mob. satisfactory. Horses shod & harness fitted. Ordered to return to Store reservist spare suit of clothing & boots. Notified O.C. Records own deficiency in horse keepers.

9-10-11 Completed details of mobilisation.

12. Handed over charge of details etc to Capt A Edgar AVC. including books cash & equipment. The reservists joining already equipped had their rifles with them. These were handed in.

13.8. Left Curragh to embark on S.S. Lismore at North Wall. A. Corps, though having received daily notice by a visit of an officer, were very late with their transport but motor lorries being sent no delay to the train occurred. Reported all correct to A.D.V.S. At North Wall the mobilisation staff apparently were at fault for no one had considered the question of transport from yard to train, consequently embarkation was delayed 5 hours.
Onboard men & horses were quite comfortable though the head room for the horses was dangerously limited.

14.8. A quiet passage & all well.

15.8. Arrived Havre & disembarked, proceeded outside Havre to L'Usine Bindu where the Base Vety Hospital was in process of formation. Raining. The factory gave excellent accommodation. Interview with D.D.V.S.

17. Settled in. No complaints.

18.8. Waiting orders to move.

19.8. Lt. Smith sent to Boulogne with two dressers. Several grooms & horses. Replaced lame chargers from Remounts.

20.8. No orders. Paid sections. King's message to troops read. Reservists posted to troops under charge of their own elected Lce Cpl.

21.8. Still waiting orders to move.

22.8. Have no orders. Fatigues for Base Vety. Stores

23.8. " " " " " " "

24.8. Orders arrived at 9 pm. to entrain for Amiens at 11 next morning.

25.8 Arrived Amiens 11 pm.

26.8. Moved from Station to Vety Hospital. No 7 Sect AVC had preceded us 2 or 3 hrs. Lt. J Smidt rejoined from Boulogne & handed over 100 pds. the price of blk horse 3rd Div Ammun. Column. 3 pm. orders received to pack - be in readiness to move on. No 6 Mobile Vety Sect took over all horses & marched off at 8 pm. by road for Rouen. 7 horses destroyed. Received frs 1050 for these from Capt Lake, AVC.

27.8. Entrained at St Roche station at 3.30 pm after having reported all arrival to R.T.O. there at 10.45 am.

28.8 Arrived Rouen at 1 am. Reported to Base Commandant ordered to Rue Cauen Petit Quevilly - reported all arrival to D.V.S. (Wound) & OC. Base Vety Hospital.

29.8 Fatigues for Hospital. Paid members those detached. Paid in to Maj. Arnold Base Paymaster 1150 francs for 8 horses destroyed. 10 pm. D.V.S. gave orders to pack & hold ourselves in readiness to move to Le Mans.

30.8 Lt. Smith detached with 1 troop A.V.C. to conduct to Le Mans 183 Remounts.

31.8 Took over all sick from Vety Hospital Rouen & with Sections entrained for Le Mans - Finished entrainment at 2 a.m. (1 horse shot) Arthritis Elbow
gun shot.

Army Form C. 2118.

WAR DIARY
or
INTELLIGENCE SUMMARY.
(Erase heading not required.)

Instructions regarding War Diaries and Intelligence Summaries are contained in F. S. Regs, Part II. and the Staff Manual respectively. Title pages will be prepared in manuscript.

Hour, Date, Place	Summary of Events and Information	Remarks and references to Appendices
Aldershot - 4th August 5.30 P.m.	Received orders to mobilise and proceed to BULFORD to take command of No 8 Mobile Veterinary Section.	
5th August	Proceeded to BULFORD by 10.30 am train from Farnborough Station arriving 2.5.30 P.m.	
BULFORD. 6th August to 15th August	Took over equipment and horses of the Section. 24 men of the Section consisted of the following, vz :— One Sergeant. Three Corporals Three men of the Army Veterinary Corps The Remainder A.V.C. Tns Reservists 14th Hussars (instructors) One Reservist - A.S.C. (driver) No cattle killer and only 12 rounds of revolver ammunition was received, only 4 feet rope which I consider is not near enough 24 horses taken over were	

Army Form C. 2118.

WAR DIARY
or
INTELLIGENCE SUMMARY.
(Erase heading not required.)

Instructions regarding War Diaries and Intelligence Summaries are contained in F.S. Regs., Part II. and the Staff Manual respectively. Title pages will be prepared in manuscript.

Hour, Date, Place	Summary of Events and Information	Remarks and references to Appendices
BULFORD 15th August 8:15 a.m.	Fairly good. All regiment shoeing. Then went to sheeings smith in the Section	
TIDWORTH 9.30 a.m.	Left BULFORD and marched to TIDWORTH to catch 10.40 a.m. train for SOUTHAMPTON. Entrained Section horses without any difficulty. Train left at 10.46 p.m. and arrived at SOUTHAMPTON at 12.40 p.m.	
SOUTHAMPTON 15th Aug. Aug. 16th	Embarked on S.S. Welshman at 4. P.m. Left SOUTHAMPTON at 5 p.m. the unit ads 9.2s. of the 2nd Cav Bde under command of Lance De Linle, our destination not known. Weather fine, sea passage good.	
BOULOGNE 16th Aug	Arrived at 6.45 P.m. Disembarked and marched three miles to Camp at PONT-de-BRIGUES where we camped for night	

(0 20 6) W 3382—1107 100,000 10/13 H W V Forms/C. 2118/10.

Army Form C. 2118.

WAR DIARY
or
INTELLIGENCE SUMMARY.
(Erase heading not required.)

Instructions regarding War Diaries and Intelligence Summaries are contained in F.S. Regs., Part II. and the Staff Manual respectively. Title pages will be prepared in manuscript.

Hour, Date, Place	Summary of Events and Information	Remarks and references to Appendices
PONT DE BRYGES CAMP 13th August	All the Troops on this unit who were lectured will ...	
4 P.M.	Received orders from N.O.G. to ... the Division at Boulogne at 8 P.M. for a journey up Country. Three trains were sent out of the town leaving at 12 midnight	

WAR DIARY
or
INTELLIGENCE SUMMARY.
(Erase heading not required.)

Army Form C. 2118.

Hour, Date, Place	Summary of Events and Information	Remarks and references to Appendices
OBREICHES August 20th	Continued with instructions to divert them to H.Q. of hs S & 6 Vty before arr: at St Pues Admitted 3 horses sick from the 16 Cavalry Brigade to 4 horses sick arrived in Camp.	
OBREICHES Aug 21st	Admitted 25 horses sick, from the Cav B/s and dismissed 6 - 10 v 2/6.5 which were unfit for service. were marked and Action Horse Company with two Great Coveralls, camped at - 10 v 2/6.5 for the night, but Convoy was in return home as it was not unloaded, drew supplies but before moved with 10 sick horses	
August 22nd	Marched to Maubeuge and entrained 30 sick horses to the from, Marched to VALENCIENNES	
VALENCIENNES Aug 23rd	into camp and Camped outside the Town Marched to SOLESMES where were a mobbed whitting from the marker	

WAR DIARY
or
INTELLIGENCE SUMMARY.
(Erase heading not required.)

Army Form C. 2118.

Instructions regarding War Diaries and Intelligence Summaries are contained in F. S. Regs., Part II. and the Staff Manual respectively. Title pages will be prepared in manuscript.

Hour, Date, Place	Summary of Events and Information	Remarks and references to Appendices
SOLESMES August 24th	Trekked to Le CATEAU 10 miles away, roads good, weather fine, on arrival in camp ourselves for orders.	
Le CATEAU Aug 25th	D.S. AMIENS for orders. Were ordered for D.S. AMIENS outside of district 6th. Found to St QUENTIN to 15 miles away in billets no available, no tents to camp in a street, weather very bad.	
Aug 26th	Marched 15 miles to HAM, E.i. of troops on the road retiring, arrived at HAM 2 P.M., camped beside the Station in the street very much beyond, roads very bad, no water obtained, weather reported to the next rev.	
HAM August 27th	Trekked to St. ..... , had a marching ..... on a large force, no ..... no orders or ..... received, the bridge blown down, troops retiring .... the street	

Forms/C. 2118/10.

Army Form C. 2118.

WAR DIARY
or
INTELLIGENCE SUMMARY.
(Erase heading not required.)

Hour, Date, Place	Summary of Events and Information	Remarks and references to Appendices
SEN P.19 N12 August 28th	Recd. orders from Col Briggs to join the III Cavy Bgde at Montdidier, sent an advance party to the wood S.E. of St Sauveur	
1.E.8 O'CLOCK August 29th	Marched into hop. 1 + 9 Autheuil about 4. No fires used except for the night. Can find no information as to the location of the III Cav Bde which is reported to be very large distance away, marching now even to 4th Division.	
August 30th	Marched to TRACY-LE-MONT rearranged in a great jam for the night, no return obtainable	
August 31st 9 a.m.	Marched out to LEON twenty miles away, took 12½ hours to do the journey, couldn't embark as the village, thrown up [?] to fire ahead, as the enemy aircraft was frightening all after [?] blew horse camp.	

WAR DIARY
or
INTELLIGENCE SUMMARY.

Army Form C. 2118.

(Erase heading not required.)

Hour, Date, Place	Summary of Events and Information	Remarks and references to Appendices
LEON September 1st	Marched off at 5 am on a journey. Cap. found on by the enemy, as on Sept 1st Booting. R.H.A. reported enemy on Section disposed 5 miles outside LEON by a General and sent for reinforcements etc., and the same Section came in now the 4th Queen's Regt. By Column	
BARON	Marched to BARON and halted for 4 hours, watered and fed. Return dept. 6 in. mounted on S.P.G. and camped for the night. 6 in. av. camp, wrote good, water fair	
Sebastian Dr	Marched from camp at 2.20 am. Joined up 3 armoured hours and camped 5 miles away at DAN MARTEN. Went 3 hours by the station	
DAN MARTEN	LANSY of 6 am and camped 4 miles outside in, armed through no sleep for 5 days. suffered my shoots. Received message 2½ 1st Sept Q. camped + until morning of 5th Sept.	

Army Form C. 2118.

WAR DIARY
or
INTELLIGENCE SUMMARY.
(Erase heading not required.)

Instructions regarding War Diaries and Intelligence Summaries are contained in F. S. Regs., Part II. and the Staff Manual respectively. Title pages will be prepared in manuscript.

Hour, Date, Place	Summary of Events and Information	Remarks and references to Appendices
SERRAIS Sept 5th	Took over as men of 4th Hussars came out lines, Sept- Camp at 4.10 A.M. and arrived at BRIG-CUNTS-ROBERT at 5 P.M., distance 12 miles to the Rear about 20 column of her Reston	
BRIG-CUNTE-ROBERT Sept 6th	Left Camp at 6 A.M. and marked to FERRIERES 10 miles away. Camped in Room in Ruethiller estate and 5 P.M. when we struck camp and marched 10 miles & Crop water supply very poor. Plenty of grazing. Left new Camp at 10.10 P.M. and marched to SERRAIS	
September 7th 10 A.M.	Marched to CROUY, about 15 miles away were good water fair, stau with 4th Division	

Forms/C. 2118/10.

Army Form C. 2118.

WAR DIARY
or
INTELLIGENCE SUMMARY.
(Erase heading not required.)

Instructions regarding War Diaries and Intelligence Summaries are contained in F. S. Regs., Part II. and the Staff Manual respectively. Title pages will be prepared in manuscript.

Hour, Date, Place	Summary of Events and Information	Remarks and references to Appendices
CRECY September 8th	Marched to REBAIS where Battalion of the 3rd Cavalry Brigade are in Camp and joined them, horses very tired not in condition received supplies, ration and stores for a fortnight took	
REBAIS Sept 9th	Marched at 10 a.m. to SACEY finished up our stores on the road there was hoped by the future as far transport work	
MARIUS Sept 10th	Marched to MARIUS on orders from 3rd Cav Bde. Camped for the night, over 16 horses cases, enough to keep in order, no expert, but had	
	Sent one 10 man Force to 3rd R.I. Beauchesne to when we requisitioned for rations to find army Genls. Q.D.D. demonstrated were retiring to the base, marched to PEMBRUR to IV after odds on has on arter topes.	RENEURR

Forms/C. 2118/10.

WAR DIARY
or
INTELLIGENCE SUMMARY.

(Erase heading not required.)

Army Form C. 2118.

Hour, Date, Place	Summary of Events and Information	Remarks and references to Appendices
BOISSIEUR Septr 12th	Arrived at 7:15am when at 7.20 the 3 July Ambulance from Breville reporting 2 to/from from at the Section, marched until L.7 Section & O. Simon and entrained at 4.2 Rest, then to the tete at VILLENEUVE-ST-GEORGE, watered and fed, shell 20/1/los and entrained at BOISSIERS Road camping arriving at 9.30 PM. Settled for night.	
Septr 13th	Marched to MARINI EN OXUIS 18 miles away and settled for night. Crossing very bad road up-keep off feet, weather fine, roads good.	
MARINI EN OXUIS Septr 14th	Marched with L.7 Section & BRENY the ambulance being 6 kgm on Brigade, ambulance and carried on a journey for the night, 2 hrs to leave of Section.	
BRENY Septr 15th	Marched 22 miles away to BOINE and joined 13 cables of 3d Cavalry Brigade, carried on the journey to within 7¼ [illegible] reactions from [illegible]	

Army Form C. 2118.

WAR DIARY
or
INTELLIGENCE SUMMARY.
(Erase heading not required.)

Instructions regarding War Diaries and Intelligence Summaries are contained in F. S. Regs., Part II. and the Staff Manual respectively. Title pages will be prepared in manuscript.

Hour, Date, Place	Summary of Events and Information	Remarks and references to Appendices
BRAINE September 16th	Reported to A.D.V.S. 2nd Cavalry Brigade Division, collected 124 sick horses from 3rd Cavalry Brigade at LIME but miles away 25 men were taken over with the horses to proceed to the train, marched on —	
FERE-EN-TEDENOIS Sept 17th	FERE-EN-TEDENOIS and camped for night, requisitioned supplies for the sick horses. Could not procure any trucks on the Station & sent the horses away. Reported by Cpt Butler, no note given orders	
" Sept 18th "	by him but decided, to twelve indicates.	
Sept 19th	Ordered by A/H Col, Butler march to CHATEAU-THIERRY 15 miles away, and entrain the horses to the Ford on horses class that was left than retired near to ? Section	

WAR DIARY
or
INTELLIGENCE SUMMARY.
(Erase heading not required.)

Army Form C. 2118.

Instructions regarding War Diaries and Intelligence Summaries are contained in F. S. Regs., Part II. and the Staff Manual respectively. Title pages will be prepared in manuscript.

Hour, Date, Place	Summary of Events and Information	Remarks and references to Appendices
CHATEAU-THIERRY September 20th	Entrained the sick horses (with hair, plenty of truck) available	
September 21st	very wet and cold	
	Marched out 7.30 a.m. on the way to BRAINE, halted at FERE-EN-TARDENOIS for two hours, watered and fed and shod 3 horses, men resumed the march to BRAINE and arrived there at 6.0 p.m. to new wet camp	
Sep 22nd	Regiment to Brigade horses 2d Cav Brigade, shod 3 horses, Show return	
BRAINE Sep 23rd	Selected a new and better camp, admitted 3 horses sick, Interi/plan was drawn from the Section.	
Sep 24th	Part the men off Section, collected 25 horses sick and entrained with them, no mission attended from the Supply Column	

Army Form C. 2118.

WAR DIARY
or
INTELLIGENCE SUMMARY.
(Erase heading not required.)

Instructions regarding War Diaries and Intelligence Summaries are contained in F. S. Regs., Part II. and the Staff Manual respectively. Title pages will be prepared in manuscript.

Hour, Date, Place	Summary of Events and Information	Remarks and references to Appendices
BRAINE September 25th	Collected to Town Jn. 3rd Cavalry Brigade, these horses after a day of twelve.	
" September 26th	Rested at Town both hors. with Jones & hill Section.	
" 27th	Admission 19 horses and embarked them to the horse, probably his 67th Section to entrain 1914 horses to the front.	
" 28th	Admitted 23 horses from 3rd Car. Brigade, case unknown	
" 29th	Remained in town, making our tent in Camp 24 sick	
" 30th	Admitted one horse from L7 Section, one from D Battery RHA two horses shop, marched to MONT-NOTRE-DAME and	
MONT-NOTRE-DAME September 30th	billeted in a farm which was bearing	

WAR DIARY

of

No 8 MOBILE VET. SECTION

2nd CAVALRY DIVISION

OCTOBER - 1914.

Mar 1919

$\frac{121}{2186}$

C.S. Mostt Veterinary Section.

Vol III. 1 – 31.10.14

Army Form C. 2118.

WAR DIARY
or
INTELLIGENCE SUMMARY.
(Erase heading not required.)

Instructions regarding War Diaries and Intelligence Summaries are contained in F. S. Regs., Part II. and the Staff Manual respectively. Title pages will be prepared in manuscript.

Hour, Date, Place	Summary of Events and Information	Remarks and references to Appendices
MONT-NOTRE-DAME 1st October 1914.	Orders issued during the great difficulty in relieving the Horses. Attend a camp of Corps Hdqrs, by water and grazing. Handed over two Horses to No.6 Section as they were very short of Horses from this Section.	
MONT-NOTRE-DAME 2nd October	Railed 22 sick Horses to the Base Hospital at Villeneuve-Tunnel. very heavy entrainment and harness lifts very obliging. Received orders from A.D.V.S. to Convoy Division at 6 P.m. but without delay to [ ] VERBERIE 42 miles away as the Division has changed its position & Hd....	
3rd October	Marched from NOTRE-DAME at 6.30 a.m. to FAUCIENNES 31 miles. Horses tired and hungry, collected 3 Horses on the way. a few [ ] — Joined the Section. Colonel Gen. Fanshawe Kenyon, no difficulties experienced obtained adequate feeding, fair in a.m. turned very grand, weather fine	

Army Form C. 2118.

WAR DIARY
or
INTELLIGENCE SUMMARY.
(Erase heading not required.)

Instructions regarding War Diaries and Intelligence Summaries are contained in F. S. Regs., Part II. and the Staff Manual respectively. Title pages will be prepared in manuscript.

Hour, Date, Place	Summary of Events and Information	Remarks and references to Appendices
VAVEREMIES 4th October	Halted at 6.45am. WESTREES-ST-DENIS 30 miles away and bivouacked in a village for the night; collected 11 horses on the way. Reparations for sore lh. of Horse (our) feeling forlorn. water as far away. dangers been very trust.	
ESTREES-ST-DENIS 5th October	Hauled off at 6.30am. Received orders from Captain R.O. & 11 Car. Brain for a report to general of any Lores at TRICOT which was supposed to be retaken on arrival. Then found it was not and marched to MAIGNELAY where we awaited them in charge of 3 men. Hauled them to LE PLOYRON under orders from R.O.S.C., and on arrival Then found a horse eyeing. Looking for the Serbian escort, orders from R.O.S. 6/ escort to SR-JUST 12 miles away where we halted for the night, meeting supply train, received forage and supplies for the mess from the 3rd Cav Bde Supply Column at the Railway Station. Horses very tired. Lame, travelled long distances for the train few days.	

Forms/C. 2118/10.

Army Form C. 2118.

WAR DIARY
or
INTELLIGENCE SUMMARY.
(Erase heading not required.)

Instructions regarding War Diaries and Intelligence Summaries are contained in F. S. Regs., Part II. and the Staff Manual respectively. Title pages will be prepared in manuscript.

Hour, Date, Place	Summary of Events and Information	Remarks and references to Appendices
ST JUST 6th October 1914	Marched off at 7.45 am to AILLY-SUR-NOIE a 25 mile journey and halted for the night. Men tired, roads good, wet weather fine.	
AILLY-SUR-NOIE 7th October	Marched off at 7.45 am halted at AMIENS and sent patrols from 3rd Cavalry Bde Supply Column at the Station, marched on to ST-VAST-EN-CHAUSSIE and billeted for the night. Learn that our Brigade is only a short distance in front.	
ST VAST-EN-CHAUSSIE 8th October	Marched at 8 am to HIERMONT where we bivouac. 9200 horses from the Brigade. Sisters for the night, dawn raining. Zero a little bit too bearing for a rest well, great trouble in horse Lines. Camps for dispatches & supplies on wagons.	

Army Form C. 2118.

WAR DIARY
or
INTELLIGENCE SUMMARY.
(Erase heading not required.)

Instructions regarding War Diaries and Intelligence Summaries are contained in F. S. Regs., Part II. and the Staff Manual respectively. Title pages will be prepared in manuscript.

Hour, Date, Place	Summary of Events and Information	Remarks and references to Appendices
HIERMONT 9th October	Collected 32 sick horses from II Cavalry Brigade and marched to FLEURY under the Section orders. Halted for the night. Another attempt 25 miles, some of the sick were hard to get along. They were 28 horses written from two trips west.	
FLEURY 10th October	Tpr. Capt. at 8 AM received 8 horses from W.F. Section making total number of sick 48. Lieuts. CM FABVIN - PALMERT from the ship. Stables very good. Received orders from A.D.V.S. at 4 PM to proceed next day to HELLEOT at ANVIN 14 miles in convoy and entrain there consigned for Havre to put to Remounts.	

Army Form C. 2118.

WAR DIARY
or
INTELLIGENCE SUMMARY.
(Erase heading not required.)

Instructions regarding War Diaries and Intelligence Summaries are contained in F. S. Regs., Part II. and the Staff Manual respectively. Title pages will be prepared in manuscript.

Hour, Date, Place	Summary of Events and Information	Remarks and references to Appendices
FABVIN-PALBERT 11th October	Orders came from A.D.M.S. 1st Cavalry Division marched to ANVIN - via 48 Pick Lorries, and on arrival there found we were now railhead and proceeded then to BLANGY-SI-TERNOISE when we evacuated 18 cases in an empty supply train. Returned to 7 FR 13 DIV.	
FABVIN 12th Oct	Remain on 7 AM and travelled at 7 AM moved to AIRE where the Section was camped for the night. Had over 3 lorries from the Division ammunition column horses.	
AIRE 13th Oct	Marched off at 6 AM to HAZEBROUCK, drew rations and filled for the night in a farm. Weather very wet and cold.	

Army Form C. 2118.

WAR DIARY
or
INTELLIGENCE SUMMARY.
(Erase heading not required.)

Instructions regarding War Diaries and Intelligence Summaries are contained in F. S. Regs., Part II. and the Staff Manual respectively. Title pages will be prepared in manuscript.

Hour, Date, Place	Summary of Events and Information	Remarks and references to Appendices
HAZEBROUCK 14th Oct.	We started at 7:15 A.M. Held meeting at BETHUNE for an hour, marched to GODEWAERSVELDE where we joined the Brigade, marched in with B" Echelon to KEMMEL where we camped for the night down returns, with supply good, night fine.	
KEMMEL 15th Oct.	Orders to move from the Cavalry Brigade, marched to MESSINES and camped for the night. Down returns, munitions not arrived.	
MESSINES 15th Oct.	Received 10 horses from 16th Lancers, also 1 step in rank when the total of 2nd Lieut. turns to one strong 21 guns. Two men in Field hospital, two horses. One man of 6th Inskillian Fusiliers arrived by the D.G A.F. Echelon for inquiry to the Producers of local orders & the MGun W'ckshed.	

Forms/C. 2118/10.

WAR DIARY
or
INTELLIGENCE SUMMARY.
(Erase heading not required.)

Army Form C. 2118.

Hour, Date, Place	Summary of Events and Information	Remarks and references to Appendices
MESSINES 17th Oct.	The men of the Section just under arrest upon a Corporal Bateman were signed to be dealt with by the O.C. Section and were remanded for a Court Martial. He was tried the same day and was sentenced to 6 months H.L. Shop on fire at 4.5 Armours for enemy injuries. Took over 1 suit charger. Handed 6 R.E. mules at 5 p.m. and camped for the night. Passing B4e; HLS; clear interno. Frame Crossing well and fit.	
KEMMEL 18th Oct.	Drove over 13 times from the Damms mending one flat tire. 32 Shots on Keep took for minutes. Passed orders from A.D.S. to return our sick at STRAZEELE. Worked the evening and at 8.30 p.m. entrained sick next day without any trouble.	

WAR DIARY
or
INTELLIGENCE SUMMARY.
(Erase heading not required.)

Army Form C. 2118.

Instructions regarding War Diaries and Intelligence Summaries are contained in F.S. Regs., Part II. and the Staff Manual respectively. Title pages will be prepared in manuscript.

Hour, Date, Place	Summary of Events and Information	Remarks and references to Appendices
STRAZEELE 19th Oct	Entrained 31 Bde Trans to Entrain at LE-HAVRE and returned to KEMMEL arriving at 4.45 P.M. when orders for the nights disposition to the A.D.V.S. were given. Orders to form B.'s Echelon as soon as possible.	
KEMMEL 20th Oct	MOVEMENTS. Headed attack 7.15am reported 6 TANKS at STEEN-EL, which were on our way. Then we were proceeding to StE401 when we saw B's Echelon in Jackets, joined the Echelon at StE401 and marched with them to THIESCHIE when an order to all ryles came in for pushing on, troops kept that position in the center, withdrawn in the times there.	

Army Form C. 2118.

WAR DIARY
or
INTELLIGENCE SUMMARY.
(Erase heading not required.)

Instructions regarding War Diaries and Intelligence Summaries are contained in F. S. Regs., Part II. and the Staff Manual respectively. Title pages will be prepared in manuscript.

Hour, Date, Place	Summary of Events and Information	Remarks and references to Appendices
HOLEBEKE 21st Oct.	In accordance out of camp at 7 A.M. and started in archery on CA-6401, received mark to DICKEBUSCH where we camped within the II Echelon in a large field. Capt. spent five times, motor supply by Govt., plenty of ration attacked	
DICKEBUSCH 22nd Oct.	Orders drawn from A.P.S. office an expect accommodation this First Payment II Col. Denison for Fr 5000. given pay for the town of the Soldier, temple 100 Kilos of pay.	
23rd Oct.	Remained in Camp at DICKEBUSCH, weather very dry	
26th Oct.	Some Enemy will. Heavy firing very close.	
27th Oct.	Took over 27 horses from the Brigade and entrained them from YPRES to the 7 Base Hospital at ABBEVILLE.	

Army Form C. 2118.

WAR DIARY
or
INTELLIGENCE SUMMARY.
(Erase heading not required.)

Instructions regarding War Diaries and Intelligence Summaries are contained in F. S. Regs., Part II. and the Staff Manual respectively. Title pages will be prepared in manuscript.

Hour, Date, Place	Summary of Events and Information	Remarks and references to Appendices
DICKEBUSCH 28th Oct.	Reveille at 6 A.M. exercised the horses and many of the sick horses and were sent to the 4th Field Hospital.	
29th Oct.	Marched to ST. ELOI and took over 10 horses from the Brigade, Brought 100 kilos of Hay. Forage very close. Enemy reported between HOLEBEKE, which is 3 miles away.	
ST. ELOI 30th Oct.	Ordered down to DICKEBUSCH, marched to YPRES and obtained 10 horses to the Base at ABEEVILLE. Marched back to DICKEBUSCH and went into Camp, tonight in Rats of hay.	
DICKEBUSCH 31st Oct.	Collected 18 tons horse from the Brigade and under the to the Base from YPRES. Bought 100 kilos of hay, which is found sufficient to from 16 horses of section for one day.	

WAR DIARY

of

N° 8 MOBILE VET. SECTION

2ND CAVALRY DIVISION

NOVEMBER - 1914.

121/2671

L. B C
6. S. mobile Vetq: Sector.
1 — 30. 11. 14

WAR DIARY or INTELLIGENCE SUMMARY.

(Erase heading not required.)

Army Form C. 2118.

Hour, Date, Place	Summary of Events and Information	Remarks and references to Appendices
DICKEBUSCH 1st Nov 1914.	Trecked to LOCRE at 7.30 a.m. and camped, brought 120 kilos of hay for feeding for the horses.	
LOCRE 2nd Nov.	Slept the all day, marched off at 5:30 p.m. and camped outside BERTHEN which is 15 kilom. in 2.00 a.m. the Section watered our mules and made my camp.	
BERTHEN 3rd Nov.	Marched away from camp at 10 a.m. and camped 2½ miles away in the BERTHEN district.	
" 4th Nov.	Sent over 9 sick horses from the Brigade and entrained them to ABBEVILLE from BAILLEUL in charge of two men. The horses were supplied with ration forage for two days. Marched the whole troop at BERTHEN.	

WAR DIARY
or
INTELLIGENCE SUMMARY.
(Erase heading not required.)

Army Form C. 2118.

Hour, Date, Place	Summary of Events and Information	Remarks and references to Appendices
BERTHEN 5th Nov.	On the arrival of the NCOs & Cavalry Division I bought a light cart for the use of the Section. The cart was in good repair and only cost Francs 30/-. Marched off at 2.30 p.m. and camped at BERTHEN with "B" Echelon Head Q'rs. Conf. of my sent, plenty of hay available, water supply good.	
6th Nov.	Took over 6 horses from the 1st Cavalry Division, all Govt. Coves. Roughs two Riding Horses.	
7th Nov.	Took over 14 Cart Horses from the 1st Cavalry Brigade making a total of 20 under the Section. Marched to STRAZEELE and on arrival the Park at ASHBY was in charge of 3 men. Food supply laid for two days for our own horses.	

Army Form C. 2118.

WAR DIARY
or
INTELLIGENCE SUMMARY.
(Erase heading not required.)

Instructions regarding War Diaries and Intelligence Summaries are contained in F. S. Regs., Part II. and the Staff Manual respectively. Title pages will be prepared in manuscript.

Hour, Date, Place	Summary of Events and Information	Remarks and references to Appendices
7th (continued)	After interviewing Farrier Sergeant Major Sergeant and one man to HAZEBROUCK and purchased a warm Lamm for the Major cost for Francs 80/-, billeted for the night.	
HAZEBROUCK 8th inst.	Returned to Camp at BERTHEN, raining very hard, bought hay for horses.	
BERTHEN 9th inst.	Exercised horses, section admitted one horse to the Care Division was very bad.	
10th inst.	Stuck in Camp, no sign of Brigade moving.	
11th "	Received 1 horse from Divisional Ambulance making total Ries 2	
12th "	Took over 15 Field horses from the Brigade, sent on horse for eye injury. Orders that note 16 horses marched to HAZEBROUCK and entrained. From there to ABBEVILLE in charge of 4 men. Lieutenant for the night.	

Forms/C. 2118/10.
(1 29 6) W 3332—1107 100,000 10/13 H W V

Army Form C. 2118.

WAR DIARY
or
INTELLIGENCE SUMMARY.
(Erase heading not required.)

Instructions regarding War Diaries and Intelligence Summaries are contained in F. S. Regs., Part II. and the Staff Manual respectively. Title pages will be prepared in manuscript.

Hour, Date, Place	Summary of Events and Information	Remarks and references to Appendices
HAZEBROUCK 13th hr.	Regiment to BERTHEN at 7 a.m., took over the sick from Cavalry Corps, hospital kept for horses, which on looking very well.	
BERTHEN 14th hr.	Marched to NOOTE-BOOM 5 miles away and settled in two farm houses, fields not good, and very small water supply (1 tap 1 pump).	
NOOTE-BOOM 15th hr. 16th hr.	Reported to A.D.V.S., received horses etc. Took over 33 sick horses from different units, slept 1 horse for incurable injuries, almost cases beginning dressing. Picture at Rest in a good field. Plenty of water and hay available in a farm & mile away.	
17th hr.	Took over 5 horses from 111 Brigade, slept 2 horses in incurable injuries, making total sick 36 cases.	

Army Form C. 2118.

WAR DIARY
or
INTELLIGENCE SUMMARY.
(Erase heading not required.)

Instructions regarding War Diaries and Intelligence Summaries are contained in F. S. Regs., Part II. and the Staff Manual respectively. Title pages will be prepared in manuscript.

Hour, Date, Place	Summary of Events and Information	Remarks and references to Appendices
MONTE-ROOM 17th Nov (continued)	Handed over 36 sets + B.W.S.V6 and established three LP B.T.S M6 & in charge of one NCO and 3 men of the Section. Two days rations given for each man and horse. Instruction given to the NCO how to prevent track the construction.	Up to the 19th Nov Pte Warren and Lcpl Pigram in the absence of Shoeing Smith Gunn every Saturday.
NOVE-ROOM 18th Nov	Received a visit from D.D.V.S. 12 horses evacuated arrived from 7.6 9g Section. The animals ill and were accommodated for the night by the Section stable night.	
19th Nov	Six men and 4 horses returned from our Section, the Rear marshal horse Section. Took over 3 horses and shot them for incurable injuries. To Coedeulerg Ruclin, Ruston returned from the Rear Marching Welcome for Different Units.	

Army Form C. 2118.

WAR DIARY
or
INTELLIGENCE SUMMARY.
(Erase heading not required.)

Instructions regarding War Diaries and Intelligence Summaries are contained in F. S. Regs., Part II. and the Staff Manual respectively. Title pages will be prepared in manuscript.

Hour, Date, Place	Summary of Events and Information	Remarks and references to Appendices
NOOE - 13.0 P.M. 20th Nov.	Took over 16 sick horses from the Brigade, marched them to STEENWERELE and entrained them to ABBEVILLE in charge of an N.C.O. and 2 men of the Section. Some supplies for our days journey, as horses short on the march for enroute anyways.	
NOOTE - 13.00 M 21st Nov.	The chamamulet man joined the Section, on my return from Hazebrouck was informed that an Officer of the 16th Lancers had taken away one of the Section horses, claiming to act in own. Inquired at return to the H.QS. was told action because an apology from the Officer and a new horse.	
22nd Nov.	Examined horses, the 11 new ones former Officers nothing abnormal, started a course of daily instruction for standing to.	

Army Form C. 2118.

WAR DIARY
or
INTELLIGENCE SUMMARY.
(Erase heading not required.)

Instructions regarding War Diaries and Intelligence Summaries are contained in F. S. Regs., Part II. and the Staff Manual respectively. Title pages will be prepared in manuscript.

Hour, Date, Place	Summary of Events and Information	Remarks and references to Appendices
NOON E - 13.00 M 23rd hrs	Instruction of new men in the handling of horses. Admitted 1 horse of W.G. Duncan Corps Column.	
24th	Admitted 9 horses from the Brigade and entrained 10.5.14. two at ABBEVILLE in charge of an NCO and two men of it's Section horse and mule supplied with two days rations. Hurried to BLEU-TOUR and billeted in a small farm. Loose the Brigade Head Qrs, Loan from Wm. Bergur Staff as an Edwin Foreman. Saw for some Ememerts Turk. Water supply erg. Find from India. Good work from the Indian horsemen. Two on knew Ellen Foot teams loan inspect the lines of the Cavalry Field Ambulance, and admitted two of them for treatment.	
25th hrs		

Forms/C. 2118/10.

Army Form C. 2118.

WAR DIARY
or
INTELLIGENCE SUMMARY.
(Erase heading not required.)

Instructions regarding War Diaries and Intelligence Summaries are contained in F. S. Regs., Part II. and the Staff Manual respectively. Title pages will be prepared in manuscript.

Hour, Date, Place	Summary of Events and Information	Remarks and references to Appendices
BLEU-TOUR 26th Nov.	Took over 2 horse lines from the 7 Brigade Hqs, a new Hqs issued by the Supply Column. two men instructed in horse management.	
27th Nov.	Riding School and drill for new men, horses in better form owing to account of no supply trip issued by the S/A & Column for two days. Dock men 1 two from the 10th Lancers. Received instructions from HQRs not to execute any more horses unless further notice / the Sick horse to be walked away by a Sergeant	
28th Nov.	Riding School and drill for new men, admitted 1 horse from Cavalry Field Ambulance, two Lancers from the Depot.	

Army Form C. 2118.

WAR DIARY
or
INTELLIGENCE SUMMARY.
(Erase heading not required.)

Instructions regarding War Diaries and Intelligence Summaries are contained in F. S. Regs., Part II. and the Staff Manual respectively. Title pages will be prepared in manuscript.

Hour, Date, Place	Summary of Events and Information	Remarks and references to Appendices
BLEN-TOER 29th Nov.	Observation & Care of 4th Echelon 3rd Car. Bde. Drill for the men, exercised horses. Received orders from O.O.R.S to take Charge of the Divisional Train until the arrival of an Officer of the Company to do so.	H.Q.
30th Nov.	Riding, extent and drill, exercised horses & Rations. A supply of stores drawn from the Ordnance Stores. Total Rank within the section is now 7. all doing well.	

WAR DIARY

of

N° 8 MOBILE VET SECTION

2ⁿᵈ CAVALRY DIVISION

DECEMBER - 1914.

121/4197

Lio S. Ludhili Vilg: Sector.

Vol V.

Army Form C. 2118.

WAR DIARY
or
INTELLIGENCE SUMMARY.
(Erase heading not required.)

Instructions regarding War Diaries and Intelligence Summaries are contained in F.S. Regs., Part II. and the Staff Manual respectively. Title pages will be prepared in manuscript.

Hour, Date, Place	Summary of Events and Information	Remarks and references to Appendices
1st December 1915 BLEUE-TOUR.	Riding school and drill for the Res men, both new and tone from II Cavalry Division.	
" " 2nd	Riding school and drill, checked six horses of "B" Echelon for wounds (slight).	
" " 3rd	Took over and took horses from "B" Echelon, handed over one of the Section Wallers to III Cavalry Field Ambulance. Received instructions from A.D.V.S. II Cavalry Division to assume Veterinary charge of the II Cavalry Division Train Am Echelons consisting of 113 horses, also "A" Echelon. The horses of the former Amd - in a very bad condition, sore backs, sore hocks, mange, rope galls, broken knees, lousy, leat.	

Army Form C. 2118.

WAR DIARY
or
INTELLIGENCE SUMMARY.
(Erase heading not required.)

Instructions regarding War Diaries and Intelligence Summaries are contained in F. S. Regs., Part II. and the Staff Manual respectively. Title pages will be prepared in manuscript.

Hour, Date, Place	Summary of Events and Information	Remarks and References to Appendices
BLEUE-TOUR. 4th December 1915	Evacuated Enema and dressed cases.	
5th " "	The "B" Echelon and the Field Ambulance are to be inspected and sick camp dressed daily from today, the men of the Section followed all cases.	
6th " "		
7th " "	Stopped one Lorry of II Cavalry Ambulance for fracture of Pelvis.	
8th " "	Evacuated Section Lorries, washed 4th Echelon and Field Ambulances and dressed 202 Cases.	
9th " "	New men of the Section received during induction in the use of a rifle.	
11th " "		
12th " "	Ambulance very hot and well, roads very muddy.	

Army Form C. 2118

WAR DIARY
or
INTELLIGENCE SUMMARY.
(Erase heading not required.)

Instructions regarding War Diaries and Intelligence Summaries are contained in F. S. Regs., Part II. and the Staff Manual respectively. Title pages will be prepared in manuscript.

Hour, Date, Place	Summary of Events and Information	Remarks and references to Appendices
RIEVE - TOUR 13th December	Took over on Lorries (2ids) from Cavalry Corps and eighteen from Royal Horse Guards, received orders from HQRS. Hain 2nd Lorries of the Lancers Juisted on following day up to 11 am.	
14th "	Took over 7 Lorries and others - 3" Jun in enable to repair.	
15th "	Took over 31 more sick Lorries from III Cavalry B repair workshop. Total sick with the Depot - 57. Indent 46 Lorries to the Brass accompanied by six men of the Dichin.	
16th "	Exermines 19 Armoured Mek Corps discharged 3 Lorries cruel to the III Cavalry Field Ambulance.	

WAR DIARY
or
INTELLIGENCE SUMMARY.
(Erase heading not required.)

Army Form C. 2118.

Hour, Date, Place	Summary of Events and Information	Remarks and references to Appendices
BLEUE-TOUR 17th December	Exercised and dressed cases, conducting party returned from Base, very wet and cold.	
18th "	Teaching Orders parade for the Section, exercised and dressed two cases of lice in "B" Echelon.	
19th "	"	
20th "	Exercised horses, dressed sick cases in Ambulance and "A & B" Echelons, drilled men of Section.	
21st "	"	
22nd "	"	
23rd "	"	
24th "	Took over and settled 7th & 8th Base 9 with lorries from the East Brigade, (ambulance on convoy suspected huange which was issued in a report sent to ABBEVILLE), sent a man of the Section	

Army Form C. 2118.

WAR DIARY
or
INTELLIGENCE SUMMARY.
(Erase heading not required.)

Hour, Date, Place	Summary of Events and Information	Remarks and references to Appendices
BEAUR-TOUR		
26th December	Examined horses and dressed cases	
26th "	Spent a happy Xmas.	
27th "	Took over 1 horse (run) from D'Divisional Vet; Qn	
28th "	Horses eases, very wet, raining all day.	
29th "	Inspection duty at H.Q' Eskdens and Field Ambulances	
30th "	Horse sick cases; chiller now of Declin	
31st "		

Instructions regarding War Diaries and Intelligence Summaries are contained in F. S. Regs., Part II. and the Staff Manual respectively. Title pages will be prepared in manuscript.

121/4668.
2c

2nd Cavalry Division.

No 8. Mobile Vety: Sec.

Vol VI

January and
February 1915.

AVD

Army Form C. 2118.

WAR DIARY
or
INTELLIGENCE SUMMARY.
(Erase heading not required.)

Instructions regarding War Diaries and Intelligence Summaries are contained in F.S. Regs., Part II. and the Staff Manual respectively. Title pages will be prepared in manuscript.

Hour, Date, Place	Summary of Events and Information	Remarks and references to Appendices
BLEVE - TOUR		
January 1st 1915	Examined section horses, drew cases [illegible] returned being school and m/B stuff for new men of section	
" 2nd "		
" 3rd "	Took over Veterinary Charge of "A" Echelon under orders of A.D.V.S. II Cav. Division, on about 7 cars of lines of "A" Echelon, some of these hurt in a very dirty condition most of them having lice.	
" 4th "	Collected and sent to the base 30 horses from II Cav. Division on "unexpected change" returned with the section for treatment.	
" 5th "	Took charge of 16" Section where there Officer was away in charge for a week. Examen and dressing etc.	

WAR DIARY or INTELLIGENCE SUMMARY

Army Form C. 2118.

Hour, Date, Place	Summary of Events and Information	Remarks and references to Appendices
BLEUE-TOUR 6th Jan 1916	Inspected "C" Squadron 16th Lancers, took over our tent & hut except one for Saturn about admitted cases.	
7th " "	Inspect "A" Squadron and Inspecting Jan orders 16th Lancers. Horses looking very well and clean.	
8th " "	Inspected "B" Squadron 16th Lancers. Horses looking well.	
9th " "	hay ant, examined and dressed Hospital cases.	
10th " "	Sergeant Knap transferred to M.G. Section. Sergeant Dale " " " to No 8. Section.	
11th " "	Orders received for Sergeant Senn to proceed to 1st O.S. Station Abbeville, Compn. turned out.	

Army Form C. 2118.

WAR DIARY
or
INTELLIGENCE SUMMARY.
(Erase heading not required.)

Instructions regarding War Diaries and Intelligence Summaries are contained in F. S. Regs., Part II. and the Staff Manual respectively. Title pages will be prepared in manuscript.

Hour, Date, Place	Summary of Events and Information	Remarks and references to Appendices
BLAVE-TOUR Jan 12th 1915	Boys went collected one horse from O'Bathory, removed the	
13°	Collected 33 horses from 3rd Cavalry Brigade. Total 4 Coys in readiness to proceed. Total intent 30 6/the rest at NEUFCHATEL incorrectly imported.	
	From STEENWERCK in charge of one NCO and three men of our Section.	
14th "	Proceeded from BLEVETOUR to AIRE, halted for the night under "B" Echelon, no note made with section.	
15th "	Proceeded to DOHEM and halted Section with Fres. Cav. Am. Park. =	
16th "	Two hut men joined Section from two sergeants.	

Army Form C. 2118.

WAR DIARY
or
INTELLIGENCE SUMMARY.
(Erase heading not required.)

Instructions regarding War Diaries and Intelligence Summaries are contained in F. S. Regs., Part II. and the Staff Manual respectively. Title pages will be prepared in manuscript.

Hour, Date, Place	Summary of Events and Information	Remarks and references to Appendices
DOHEN 17th 1915	Inspected to Capt. Dutt Ambulance & Lorus. General Cave regarding N.C. men of Sudan dulled daily. The two men just arrived knowing next work about anything at.	
18th		
19th		
20th	No men arrived 7 days C.B. for absence from stables.	
21st	Under orders for move received charge of Royal Hotel, 16th January, a Station in Esbekier to all these horses. Very killed at THEODIENNE 6 miles away, important. The route taken (Dewe who are in charge about Grade 6 - England).	
22nd	Received orders for move to form a very hospital, for badness of suspected about cases. This has carried out.	

Army Form C. 2118.

WAR DIARY
or
INTELLIGENCE SUMMARY.
(Erase heading not required.)

Instructions regarding War Diaries and Intelligence Summaries are contained in F. S. Regs., Part II. and the Staff Manual respectively. Title pages will be prepared in manuscript.

Hour, Date, Place	Summary of Events and Information	Remarks and references to Appendices
R.O.H.P.M. 23rd Jan 1915	Admitted 2 suspected cases 8th Jan evs, 7 cases from "C" Coy, Durr On Kelner, have been immediately and clipped	
24" 25" 26"	4 - Suspected cases derived today, king of them cases are much all of hair work "C" Coy of them. had to been derived with Care Royal Engrs. Dalmatur there are other than those now in T. Tents	
27" 28"	Derived cases ex-mined and divided men of Sektin, my est.	
29"	Cleaned out disinfected to the tent of 4 tows cost of the Reports Officer a.M.o.v.s. in charge of M.C.S. and Davin men of the Sektor.	

Army Form C. 2118.

WAR DIARY
or
INTELLIGENCE SUMMARY.
(Erase heading not required.)

Hour, Date, Place	Summary of Events and Information	Remarks and references to Appendices
DOHEM 30th Jan 1915	Examined them unofficially. Told Zen next To 6 Mon made for inspection. Cold feeling air on 31st. Brigade orders at 11 p.m. to march next morning to SEC BOIS	
31st "	Marched to See Bois arriving 4.30 p.m. Got billets for our Section at Lambles improvised beds. Had feeling air Level. inspent and cold.	

Army Form C. 2118.

WAR DIARY
or
INTELLIGENCE SUMMARY.
(Erase heading not required.)

Instructions regarding War Diaries and Intelligence Summaries are contained in F.S. Regs., Part II. and the Staff Manual respectively. Title pages will be prepared in manuscript.

Hour, Date, Place	Summary of Events and Information	Remarks and references to Appendices
SEC BOIS Feb 1st 1915	Built Shelters for Cook House to protect them from the River	
1st	gutter (see there had been very heavy storms)	
2nd	Drew new of Packies and Jersey Regiment	
3rd	Entrained Pack'in Horse and pack Harness to "B" + "C".	
4th	Extra duty to other Officers having leave enough for this duty.	
	Orders received for Sergeant Graham to proceed to Boulogne	
5th	to join a new Mobile Section	
	Collected and despatched to the Base 59 Hd Car Horses	
	in charge of an N.C.O. and 3 men	
6th		
7th	Examined and cleared harness neglected [by?] units of the Brigade	

Army Form C. 2118.

WAR DIARY
or
INTELLIGENCE SUMMARY.
(Erase heading not required.)

Instructions regarding War Diaries and Intelligence Summaries are contained in F. S. Regs., Part II. and the Staff Manual respectively. Title pages will be prepared in manuscript.

Hour, Date, Place	Summary of Events and Information	Remarks and references to Appendices
SEC BOIS 8th Oct 1915		
9 am	Two new men joined Section, these returned and others sent men went on leave for 7 days. Men came along very well, their there are about [?] The Coy are in fair condition and are getting on too fast.	
10 am	Requisitioned a Motor Car. The Head Qr Division and proceeded to from Authority was in the THIEQUVNNE district to make sure there was nothing of any value. These 2 toms in wagons [?] guns and collected 3 which were registered [?] free from the THIEQUVNNE in charge of an N.C.O. Inspected lines of Brigades etc.	
11 am		

Army Form C. 2118.

WAR DIARY
or
INTELLIGENCE SUMMARY.
(Erase heading not required.)

Instructions regarding War Diaries and Intelligence Summaries are contained in F. S. Regs., Part II. and the Staff Manual respectively. Title pages will be prepared in manuscript.

Hour, Date, Place	Summary of Events and Information	Remarks and references to Appendices
SEC. BOIS 2nd Dec. 1915	Collected and despatched to the Base 25 horses of 3rd Can. Regt in charge of one N.C.O. and three men.	
13"	A.D.V.S. inspected the Sick Cases in Hospital and said they were however very well and were quite clean and would soon be fit. Kevin & their unit.	
14"	Admitted 2 horses of Canning Corps Inc. Leamington. Cases clipped and dressed. Both officers men of Line.	
16"	Received three drawn horses from one Jno W. Berg.	
16"	Four horses the property of an Officer proceeding to England.	

Army Form C. 2118.

WAR DIARY
or
INTELLIGENCE SUMMARY.
(Erase heading not required.)

Instructions regarding War Diaries and Intelligence Summaries are contained in F. S. Regs., Part II. and the Staff Manual respectively. Title pages will be prepared in manuscript.

Hour, Date, Place	Summary of Events and Information	Remarks and references to Appendices
See B.O.S.		
17th January 1915	Ambulance shifted out attempt 4 cars affected upon tire	
18th "	They were not fully affected and were sent back to the lines. He visited their Ambulance sick cars over been employed. D.D.M.S. and A.D.M.S. inspected hospital cars, and they are looking well.	
19th "	Shifted 3 tons for the chinese and cleared them infected units of Brigade.	
20th "	General Officer Commanding Corps inspected the section. A.D.M.S. informed us that it was well placed together Le Cour	

Form/C. 2118/10.

Army Form C. 2118.

WAR DIARY
or
INTELLIGENCE SUMMARY.
(Erase heading not required.)

Instructions regarding War Diaries and Intelligence Summaries are contained in F. S. Regs., Part II. and the Staff Manual respectively. Title pages will be prepared in manuscript.

Hour, Date, Place	Summary of Events and Information	Remarks and references to Appendices
See 130/5	Inspected Units of Brigade & received last draft from	
21st Feb 1915	and 2nd Lt. Ashwell as R.T.O. Men were seen knocked up after journey well.	
22nd	Received orders for Sergeant Hall to proceed to No 10 Vety Section north Base, kindgun carried out.	
23rd	Inspection of Col. Jones Ambulance, everything in order	
24th	One of the Ambulance sent back to No 1 Cav. Field Ambulance at Dammanny 3 h.ts wounded	
25th	Footn Farris escorted from the Brigade and despatched to RoP Base from STRAZEELE in charge of an NCO and four men	

Forms/C. 2118/10.

Army Form C. 2118.

WAR DIARY
or
INTELLIGENCE SUMMARY.
(Erase heading not required.)

Instructions regarding War Diaries and Intelligence Summaries are contained in F.S. Regs., Part II. and the Staff Manual respectively. Title pages will be prepared in manuscript.

Hour, Date, Place	Summary of Events and Information	Remarks and references to Appendices
S.E.C - 12015		
26th Dec. 1915	Sergeant and Lce Corporal Jones, the Section from hd 10 Base Crops Hospital.	
27th Dec. 1915	As Lieut. Mc entered and sent the Sec. in charge of an N.C.O. J. Anton	
28th "	Received Orders to proceed back to the old Billeting area at C.2 ETY. on the morning of 1st all preparation were made.	

Forms/C. 2118/10

121/5266

2nd Cavalry Division

Co. S. Mohd. Vly: Sector

Vol VII 1.3—30.6

March 1915

Army Form C. 2118.

WAR DIARY
or
INTELLIGENCE SUMMARY.
(Erase heading not required.)

Instructions regarding War Diaries and Intelligence Summaries are contained in F. S. Regs., Part II. and the Staff Manual respectively. Title pages will be prepared in manuscript.

Hour, Date, Place	Summary of Events and Information	Remarks and references to Appendices
March 1st 1915 CLETY	Horse of O' Battery R.H.A admitted dressed two cases with slight wounds	
2nd	Finished train kits at INGHEM and trained at Bayeux the G.S. hotels not good	
3rd	Conducting parties returned from Base at transferred two E. Coy Sermon admitted with debility Trainers. Sick escorts for WIZERNES Station arrange My last, make my mirror and have to travel on	

Forms/C. 2118/10.

Army Form C. 2118.

WAR DIARY
or
INTELLIGENCE SUMMARY.
(Erase heading not required.)

Instructions regarding War Diaries and Intelligence Summaries are contained in F. S. Regs., Part II. and the Staff Manual respectively. Title pages will be prepared in manuscript.

Hour, Date, Place	Summary of Events and Information	Remarks and references to Appendices
March 4th 1915 INGHEM	One horse of "A" Echelon admitted with wound in Chest. Loss of "A" + "B" Echelons inspected and all seen fuelled.	
5.	Horse of Pte 114/45 R.H.A. Left Kennel in Fields nr CAUCHIE-D-EOQUES destroyed for incurable injuries. arrangements made to cover some horse left behind by Regiments in case latter	
6.	advance. One horse left behind motored to VIEUX BERQUIN. One horse was ill. Base, on discharge from hospital for awhile infirm, fun horses started for larger their Regiments, viz not out and duly	
7.	Inspected F Canny Duke Ambulance at DOHEM and E. & R. Echelons at INGHEM.	

Forms/C. 2118/10.

WAR DIARY
or
INTELLIGENCE SUMMARY.
(Erase heading not required.)

Army Form C. 2118.

Hour, Date, Place	Summary of Events and Information	Remarks and references to Appendices
INGHAM 8th March 1915	Received orders to be in readiness to move	
9 a.m.	Four tons of Ammunition Column ammunition	
	Sixteen horses collected and entrained. Base for	
	WIZERNES in charge of 1 N.C.O. and two men.	
10	On train collected from 6th Divn. two trucks and rations.	J. Bean
	for WIZERNES	
11	Seven trucks from INGHAM 6 Sec. Bois	
	Sergeant Dale in charge. Hospital to transfer A.I.R.E.	
	Returning from Iny Coord.	

Army Form C. 2118.

WAR DIARY
or
INTELLIGENCE SUMMARY.
(Erase heading not required.)

Instructions regarding War Diaries and Intelligence Summaries are contained in F. S. Regs., Part II. and the Staff Manual respectively. Title pages will be prepared in manuscript.

Hour, Date, Place	Summary of Events and Information	Remarks and references to Appendices
March 12th 1915 S. & C. BOIS	Finished HNEXF-18FXRV1N and Sent to eastry making for ordnance survey. Orders received to hold in for the night.	
13th	Rested and made others copies of map for HAZEBROUCK. Pattern number used S&C-B913	
14th	Inspected R.A.S.C. Stations and T. & A.S. Am. Column. all the Forces were in a great improvement in the condition of horses. g.A.T. Echelon marched to new Billets	
15th	Few cases of wastage reported for evacuation	
16th	[illegible] Date Released for Hospital	

Army Form C. 2118.

WAR DIARY
or
INTELLIGENCE SUMMARY.
(Erase heading not required.)

Hour, Date, Place	Summary of Events and Information	Remarks and references to Appendices
SEC-BOIS 17th March 1916	Pte Jones admitted to hospital. Divnl Off Tries admitted and evacuated to Field Hosp Jm. HAZEBROUCK in charge of Oc NCO and Ugt Ness. issued orders for S.E. mm officers duty for morning and night duties.	
18th	Eight gun tents forwarded to RTO STRAZEELE in complance with a Routine Order ration returns to the Stores.	
19th	Section moved into new billets, on loose ground and to Ammunition Column. Fire Control cuts and coal to Ammunition Column. Our new furnaces arrived from Base Field Hospital. Pte Bourgeo...	

Army Form C. 2118.

WAR DIARY
or
INTELLIGENCE SUMMARY.
(Erase heading not required.)

Instructions regarding War Diaries and Intelligence
Summaries are contained in F. S. Regs., Part II.
and the Staff Manual respectively. Title pages
will be prepared in manuscript.

Hour, Date, Place	Summary of Events and Information	Remarks and references to Appendices
March 20th 1915	Lt 314 Pte Harley R.A.M.C. joined Corps at Sevenoaks	
21st	On arrival Sevenoaks detailed for usual fatigues	
22nd	Usual routine, weather very fine	
23rd	Corporal Boyd Jameson to W9 Hospital Dieppe for duty	
24th	Usual routine	
25th	One Squadron of Cavalry Corps admitted for evacuation	
	One Squadron of 7th Cav. Division Ambulance also admitted for evacuation	

Army Form C. 2118.

WAR DIARY
or
INTELLIGENCE SUMMARY.
(Erase heading not required.)

Instructions regarding War Diaries and Intelligence Summaries are contained in F. S. Regs., Part II. and the Staff Manual respectively. Title pages will be prepared in manuscript.

Hour, Date, Place	Summary of Events and Information	Remarks and references to Appendices
March 25th 1916 Seet-18018	Few bunks arrived at MAZE BROVER. Moved onwards, but confusion of Section.	
27th "	One N.C.O. and eight men sent to Base were 67 horses from MAZEBROVER.	
28th "	Later help Latin horses came onwards weather fine	
29th "	Continuing party schools - few horses	
30th "	D.D.M.S. and A.D.M.S. made and inspected Section	
31st "	Indian Officer inspected Lebris and complained he is sick &c &c &c. Pte Clayton admitted to Hospital	

WAR DIARY or **INTELLIGENCE SUMMARY**

Army Form C. 2118.

7/08 MVS 2nd Cav Div

Hour, Date, Place	Summary of Events and Information	Remarks and references to Appendices
April 13th 1915	On turn of 6th Empty Ambulance admitted vehicle arrived at 6 a.m.	
	Rest and feed ad lib. inspected sundry and horses at 2 p.m.	
2 p.m.	Lt. Lane R.E. admitted for treatment	
3 p.m.	Mr Voules from the Veterinary Hospital paid Surprise Inspn	
4 p.m.	Fourteen horses despatched to Base from HAZEBROUCK in charge of Dv A.C.O. and Cont Room	
5 p.m.	Inspected stables in marching order at 2 P.M. by Detachment Orderly tasting.	

Army Form C. 2118.

WAR DIARY
or
INTELLIGENCE SUMMARY.
(Erase heading not required.)

Instructions regarding War Diaries and Intelligence Summaries are contained in F. S. Regs., Part II. and the Staff Manual respectively. Title pages will be prepared in manuscript.

Hour, Date, Place	Summary of Events and Information	Remarks and references to Appendices
April 6th 1915		
7 am	Rec. inspiration reffers from starting period of Defences	
8 am	Issued instructions now to Div. Coms officer	
9 am	Quiet. There are three companions	
10 am	Went route and route march from 1 to 2 to held out to form	
	2 Pm to 3 Pm	
11 am	Physical exercises from 6.6 - 7.30 am darky (Command)	
	Received men too old & heavy and the reserve throught	
	War & recruit Section	

Army Form C. 2118.

WAR DIARY
or
INTELLIGENCE SUMMARY.
(Erase heading not required.)

Hour, Date, Place	Summary of Events and Information	Remarks and references to Appendices
April 12th 1915	D.O. & S. inspect Section in Marching Order	
13"	by present train inspection and complement met in the turn out. On arrival at ... from Brigade for instruction	
	at Kiver ... for trainees, makes his ... to ... under instructor	
14"	a K.C.O and man (member of Stanwecks Coy) sent on way to ... S.S. I ate complete ... interview of Command.	
15"	The R.C. 3rd Coy Btn ... reported for ... The Inv K.O.S and ... ... to Brigade in 4 column. He now paraded in marching order at 7.30 am and reported to the B.G.	

Army Form C. 2118.

WAR DIARY
or
INTELLIGENCE SUMMARY.
(Erase heading not required.)

Hour, Date, Place	Summary of Events and Information	Remarks and references to Appendices
August 15th (continued)	Despatch rider sent from patrol to Chief of the R.E.	
16th	out from river for HEER RIVER	
17th	horse watering, waterings and inspection	
18th		
19th		
20th	Own force in contact returned to delay enemy	
	at Evans' Drift slipped, and taking up well.	
21st	Col. Com. & M. Eckler 5th Cavalry Brigade Katsuyal	
	to corrobor	
22nd		
23rd	Own forces attacked Townsenden	
	M.O.'s arrive Durban	

Army Form C. 2118.

WAR DIARY
or
INTELLIGENCE SUMMARY.
(Erase heading not required.)

Instructions regarding War Diaries and Intelligence Summaries are contained in F. S. Regs., Part II. and the Staff Manual respectively. Title pages will be prepared in manuscript.

Hour, Date, Place	Summary of Events and Information	Remarks and References to Appendices
April 26th 1916	Pte Lewis & D. Bailey RAMC discharged to duties.	
26th	Pte A.R.O. and Wm. Dunn sent to Field Base from Hosp. & Rest.	
	Admit 28 Sick Tirus	
	Camp routine maintained Fini	
27th	Day temperature around 90 Dunn BRC to S.E. H.Q.	
28th	2669 Pte Owens and No. 418 Pte W. Parker officially left New Zealand.	
	La Colonne	
29th	Eleven Tirus sent to Base in charge Orderly C.O. and Cor Orderly	
30th	Camp routine.	

Army Form C. 2118.

WAR DIARY
or
INTELLIGENCE SUMMARY.
(Erase heading not required.)

Hour, Date, Place	Summary of Events and Information	Remarks and references to Appendices
Aug 1st 1915	Sec-Bon: Sergt Hale and 11 men to Hannescamps for collecting wounded horses	
" 2nd "	15 horses brought back to Sec Bois	
" 3rd "	11 horses despatched to Base.	
" 4th "	Sect-in Snatched to latter form of Brigade had moved, billeted at Hautkerque. Sent N.C.O. to find whereabouts of Brigade	
" 5th "	Section marched to Hondhoeft. (Ordnance party returned from Base with stores)	
" 6th "	return our stores distributed to units	
" 7th "	Paid Section. Section marched to old billets at Sec Bois	

WAR DIARY
or
INTELLIGENCE SUMMARY.

Army Form C. 2118.

Hour, Date, Place	Summary of Events and Information	Remarks and references to Appendices
May 8th 1915	Lee-Bro O'Willis sent to units to inspect numbers of horses for evacuation.	
" 9th	So 4543 Pte Snashen 14th Hussars transferred to Veterinary Hospital, Neufchatel So 10418 Lance Cpl Wurden and S. 469 " " transferred to No 7 Veterinary Hospital 37 horses sent to Base. Pte Biddles admitted to hospital	
" 10th	1 horse 5th Lancers admitted	
" 11th	Pte Springett and did 7 days F. P. No. 2 " Kass " 14 " " " " " 14 " " " S.S. adams arrived from No 12 Section	

Army Form C. 2118.

WAR DIARY
or
INTELLIGENCE SUMMARY.
(Erase heading not required.)

Hour, Date, Place	Summary of Events and Information	Remarks and references to Appendices
12th May 1915	Sgt Bird David Krisick A.S.C. 4 defects 4 days duty. 2 horses harnshein artillery admitted 1 horse D Battery R.H.A "	
13th "	Brought horses left behind by units & billets at 8 am	
14th "	1 horse Hamrick artillery failed to trace from Reserve Depot Raining continuously, Usual routine	
15th "		
16th "	Raided 19 horses to Base Lieut Dale and 2 other horses to Mammoth to collect sick horses	
17th "	1 horse 16th Lancers A Labelling Knr. admitted	

Army Form C. 2118.

WAR DIARY
or
INTELLIGENCE SUMMARY.
(Erase heading not required.)

Instructions regarding War Diaries and Intelligence Summaries are contained in F. S. Regs., Part II. and the Staff Manual respectively. Title pages will be prepared in manuscript.

Hour, Date, Place	Summary of Events and Information	Remarks and references to Appendices
18th Aug 1915	Sea Bois.	
	The three signals O.C. admitted	
19th "	Two horses " " "	
20th "	Two reinforcements (men) arrived	
21st "	Four horses sent to base.	
	Two " " removed arrived	
22nd "	Tried the horses (new) in draught went very well	
	Instruction & rifle drill for section.	
23rd "	I am with Ford at post admitted him to Hospital	
24th "	Riding & school specially enlisted men.	
25th "	Three horses sent to Base	
26th "		
27th "	Riding & school & usually R/C drill Pack section	
28th "	I am with Ford at post. Sent to Base.	
29th "	Issued quinine	

Army Form C. 2118.

WAR DIARY
or
INTELLIGENCE SUMMARY.
(Erase heading not required.)

Instructions regarding War Diaries and Intelligence Summaries are contained in F.S. Regs., Part II and the Staff Manual respectively. Title pages will be prepared in manuscript.

Hour, Date, Place	Summary of Events and Information	Remarks and references to Appendices
30th May 1915.	Lee Boir. Two reinforcement men arrived from Rouen. Work routine.	
31st "	Section moved into Res. billets at Hondeghem. Eight horses sent to Buise.	

19/5874

2nd Cavalry Division

No 8. Lille Vity Sector

Vol VIII. 1.6 — 30.6.15

WAR DIARY
or
INTELLIGENCE SUMMARY.

(Erase heading not required.)

Army Form C. 2118.

Hour, Date, Place	Summary of Events and Information	Remarks and references to Appendices
June 1st 1915	Hondeghem	
	Pte Dove admitted to hospital	
	Riding school and drill inspected saddlery	
2nd	Our Horse B echelon admitted	
3rd		
4th	Went to Base	
5th	Inspected kits, found satisfactory	
6th	Horses continue	
7th	Riding school. Another horse for Sergeants	
8th	Section inspected by Brigadier General Vaughan very satisfactory	
9th	One horse B echelon admitted	
10th	" " "	
	Horses continue. Inspection of our section	
11th	admitted one horse H.Q. 3rd Cav. Brig	
12th	20 horses for evacuation admitted	

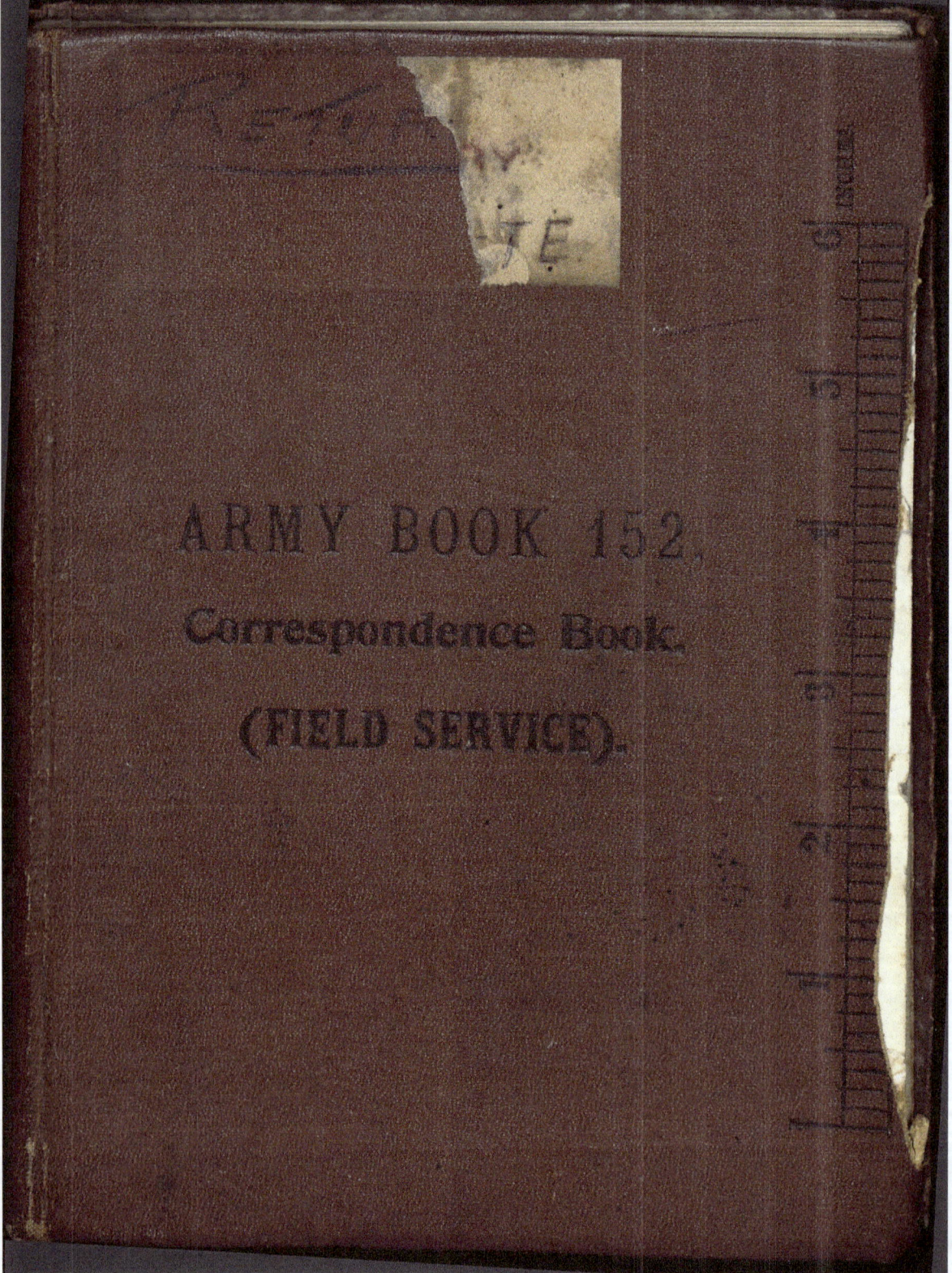

Opened on July 8. 1915

Closed on July 31 - 1916

The Squares in this book are ¼ inch.

Thursday July 8. 1915 Hondeghem

Lieut T.J. Faithfull AVC (SR) arrived + took over command of section from Lieut J.S. Young AVC (Temp).

Admitted 2 horses + 1 mule from Leicestershire Yeomanry ~~Cavalry Corps Headquarters~~ T.J.F. for evacuation.

Driver J. West ASC transferred to section from 4th Dragoon Guards.

Friday July 9 1915

S.S. Greene O.C. joined the section for duty from No 1 M.V.S. (without rifle or bandolier)

Inspected personal kit. Condition fair
Inspected horses. Condition V.G.

Saturday July 10. 1915

Eight horses evacuated to No 10 Veterinary Hospital.
Two Isolation cases returned to D. Battery.
Private Springett granted leave from 11th – 16th July.

Sunday July 11. 1915

Riding School was held the own horses on the whole jumping well.

Monday July 12. 1915

Saddlery Inspection   Good.

Tuesday July 13. 1915

Riding school
6 horses collected from II Hussars & 4 Hor. & 16 Lancers.

Wednesday July 14. 1915

Staff Serg 293 Dale R.E. left the section to join staff of No 19 Veterinary Hospital at Woolwich.

No 537 Private Cook G. left the section for a short Vety course at No 5 Vety Hospital. Twenty five horses evacuated to No 10 Vety Hospital.

Thursday July 15. 1915

Section moved billets from Houdeghem to Volkerinckhove. Lieut T.G. Faithfull left to take

over temporary charge of No 27
M.V.S.
Lieut Going A.V.C. took over
temporary command of section.

Friday July 16
    Usual Routine

Saturday July 17
Pte Springett returned from leave

Sunday July 18th
1 Horse admitted from D Battery
1 Horse 16th Lancers fetched from No 7 section left behind at St Marie Capel on July 14". (See page 13)
Church Parade at D Battery

Monday July 19th
A.D.V.S. visited section.
1 Horse returned cured to B. Echelon

Tuesday July 20th
1 Horse No 2 Cavalry Ambulance B. Echelon returned for duty
Lieut Faithfull returned to Section from temporary employment with No 27 M.V.S.

Wednesday 21st
6 horses 4th Lancers 2 16th Lancers
admitted.
Lieut Going handed over section to
Lieut Faithfull. Pte Batman awarded 3 days
F.P. No 2.
Thursday 22nd
Eight horses evacuated to Base Vety Hos.

Friday 23rd
1 horse (Remount) from 4th Lancers

Sunday 18th Cont. Pte 4608 Springett
14th Hussars & Pte 5405 Willis 6th D.G.
transferred to Cav Reinforcements Rouen

Saturday 24th
General Routine
4 horses 3 from D Battery 1 A Echelon
admitted. 8 men dismissed took duty

Sunday 25th
Admitted 1 Charger H.Q.
5 Horses evacuated by road under
Sergt Fyffe to Gournehem Remount
Depot.

Monday July 26th

1 horse admitted for treatment H.Q. 3rd Cav Bde
Sergt Fyffe & party returned from
Gonnehem Remount Depot.

Br/Gen Vaughan's charger received
for No 3. Vety Hospital.

Col Martin D.D.V.S. Cav Corps visited
the section.

Tuesday July 27th

Corpl Gold returned from Base with
stores.

O i/c attended demonstration
by Lieut Hobday on palpebral
innoculation of mallein.

Wednesday July 28th

23 Horses cast by A.D.V.R admitted
for evacuation.
1. 4th Lancer horse cast by G.O.C.
1. Charger G.O.C. 3rd Cav Bde Treatment
1. L.D. No 2 Cav Field Amb

Thursday 29th 1915

23 Cast. 8 Sick Horses evacuated to No 10 Base Vet Hospital.
Brig Gen Vaughn visited the section

Friday 30th 1915

432 L. Copl Gold J.W. promoted Corp on approval of D.D.V.S. Dates 28.7.15
Instruction given to N.C.Os + men as to the method of chloroforming a horse standing.
Rifle drill.

Sat July 31st 1915

Usual Routine
Pte Woodruff 2665 awarded 3 days F.P. No 2 for absence from parade on 30th.

16

<u>August 1st Sunday</u>
Private Vass returned from leave
Church parade 11.20 P'
~~Monday August~~
Corp Hardy returned from base and
reported Pte Batten absent from
8pm the preceeding day.
<u>Monday August 2nd 1915</u>
S²Pte 3670 Lucas. W. & S². 3160 Osborn
A.1 joined section from No9 M.V.S.
S². 165 Pt Matthews ? from No 6
Veterinary Hospital
Pte Batten returned at noon was
charged & remanded.
Corp Hardy 31.4. admitted hospital
Section received riding drill (i.e
Troop training)
<u>Tuesday August 3rd 1915</u>
Usual Routine   Batten remanded for C.M.
<u>Wednesday August 4th 1915</u>
19 horses admitted
1 horse destroyed for ~~XII~~ Lancers

17

Thursday August 5th

Pte 346 Cathem awarded 28 days
F.P. No 1 by F.G.C.M.
11 sick & cast horse evacuated.

Friday August 6th

Section moved off at 7.30 & trecked
via Nieppe, Lynde Witter to new
billets at St Quintin.

Saturday August 7th

Sergt 234 Compton promoted
Staff Sergeant (temp) from 26.7.15.
Corp Hardy returned to duty from No 20
Clearing hospital & O men.
Two horses A & B Echelon admitted for
treatment.

Sunday August 8th 1915

Church Parade. Usual routine.

Monday Aug 9th 1915

1 Horse Bro Amm Col admitted
Serg Bradley reported for duty
from No 9 M.V.S.

Tuesday Aug 10th

1 Horse admitted M.M.P.
Riding school for section
1 horse admitted from 3rd dy troop
SSerg Compton left for duty with No 10 B.V. Hos

18

Wednesday Aug 11th 1915

1 horse returned B. Echelon

Pte Fairhead left on leave

DDVS. Col Martin visited section
Condition of horses etc satisfactory.

Thursday Aug 12th 1915

Pte 3704 Allen O.T. reported for duty from
No 6 V.H.

14 horses admitted 16 evacuated to
No 10 Base Vety Hospital.

Friday Aug 13. 1915

Riding School for Section.
2 horses admitted. 1 Cav Corps. 1. 2nd Cav Div
1 horse destroyed for A. Echelon 3rd Cav Bgy
DDVS. DADR Cav Corps visited section
also DADR 1st Army.
Promotion of L.C. Gold J.W. to Corpl ratified
by Local Corps Order 25.

Saturday Aug 14. 1915

Three horses transferred to Field
Remount Depot Gournehem.
Usual routine.

Sunday Aug 15. 1915

Usual Routine

Monday Aug 16. 1915

2 horses discharged to Signal Troop 3rd Bgd
1 horse admitted 17 Lancers

Tuesday Aug 17. 1915

Riding School. 1 horse admitted J Battery
7897 Pte Wards joined section from No 6 C.H.

Wednesday Aug 18 1915

Usual Routine
Pte Fairhead returned from leave

Thursday 19 Aug 1915

19 horses admitted
16 sick + 1 cast evacuated to Base
Pte Kinnock proceeded on leave to England

Friday 20 Aug 1915

Riding School + Troop Drill.
3 Horses from 7th Hussars 1 from 17 Lancers
1. Cav Corps Headquarters

Saturday 21 Aug 1916

Usual Routine.

Sunday Aug 22 1915

1 horse admitted IV Hussars
Corp Gold returned reporting 1 horse
injured by shunting Calais 9:30/20/8/15.

Monday Aug 23 1915

Lieut General Fanshawe C.B & Brig Gen Taggart
visited the section with Col Martin
& was apparently satisfied with everything.
2 Horses discharged to IV Hussars
1 to Brig Headquarters (dog)
1 Horse admitted from Cav Corps H.Q.
S.S Greene left on leave.

Tuesday Aug 24. 1915

usual routine

Wednesday Aug 25 1915

1 Horse handed to the Sec P on instructions
from D A & R Cav Corps.
1 Horse 7th Lancers 1 Horse Cav Corps Sig
admitted
A A & Q M G 2nd Cav Div (Col Chance)
visited the section. O.K.
D Kinnoch returned from leave.

Thursday Aug 26th

Evacuated 1 Off Charger fat
2 Cast + 12 sick horses
Admitted 1 horse Vth Lancers
Destroyed 1 horse for IX Hussars.

Friday Aug 27th 1915

2 Horses evacuated to Field R.D. Gouneken
1 Horse admitted D. Battery.
1 Mule (Remount) for Gouneken.

Saturday Aug 28th 1915

1 Mule evacuated to Gouneken
Usual Routine.

Sunday Aug 29th 1915

Usual routine
2 horses returned IX Hussars

Monday Aug 30th

1 Horse admitted Vth Lancers.
Corp Vero returned from Base
Pte Chapman admitted Hospital

22

Tuesday Aug 31st
1 Horse discharged to C Sqd No 2 C.7.cl
1 " " " " V th Lancers.
1 Charger Major Musgrave H.Q. 1st Army
admitted
Pte Batten returned after expiration
of 28 days F.P.

Wednesday Sept 1st 1915
Pte Bowes left on 6 days leave.
Admittances 1 Horse D.Sec 2 C.7.A.
1 Charger H.Q. 2nd Cav Div.
3 from 5th Lancers. 4 from IV th Hussars
1 Horse for conveyance to F.R. Section.

Thursday Sept 2nd 1915
1 Horse admitted H.Q. 2nd Cav Div
2 " suspected mange IV th Hussars
14 Horses evacuated to V.H. Neufchatel.

Friday Sept 3rd 1915
Admittances 1 Horse X Battery, 2 Horses
Lahore Div Machine Gun School.
1 Horse 1st Army H.Q.
Plans for winter Horse standings forward d to
A.D.V.S. 2nd Cav Div. & Staff Capt 3rd Cav Bde.

23

Saturday Sept 4 1915
1 Horse sent to 7 R.D. Gonnehem
2 Horses returned to V th Lancers
Usual Routine

Sunday Sept 5th 1915
1 Horse admitted Vth Lancers
Usual Routine

Monday Sept 6th
1 Pony for 7 R.S Gonnehem from
No 1 M.V.S.
Riding Drill for Section
A.V.S unfavoured Temp Unpaid appoint of
Tuesday Sept 7 the Pte Vansart Corp.

3 Horses admitted H.Q. 2nd Cav Div
1 pony to Gonnehem
Wednesday Sept 8th 1915

1 Horse to 6th Lancers 1 to IV Hussars
1 Horse admitted H.Q. 2nd Cav Div
1 Horse   H.Q. Cav Corps
1   19th field Ambulance
Pte 899 Chaplin transferred to No 10
Mobile Vety Section T.T.
S.S. Green admitted Hospital Sidney

24

Thursday Sept 9 1915
11 Horses admitted from 5th Lancers
2 from 19 Hussars
2 " H.Q Cav Corps
Evacuated 23 horses
Transferred to S.A.R 1st Army 1 horse
Issued to Reg officer on authority of
G.O.C 3rd Bde   1
Returned to H.Q. Cav Corps   1

Friday Sept 10, 1915
Pte Batten transferred to No 10 MVS
1st Cav Div.
1 Horse admitted A Echelon 3rd Cav Bde

Saturday Sept 11 1915
1 Horse H.Q. 3 Cav Bde gun V. charge
admitted
5 horses admitted 1st B Train R.E.

Sunday Sept 12 1915
Pte Compton returned from leave
1 horse H.Q Cav Corps
2 " 106 Brigade R.F.A.
Inspected section paraded ready
to move. Time taken for preparation
1 hour 10 minutes.
1 horse to H.Q Cav Corps on instruction
from Det D.R Cav Corps.

Monday Sept 13th 1915

At I.V.S Cav Corps Col Martin & A.D.V.S 2nd?
inspected section & went into subject
of loading transport & as to form
A & B Echelon.
1 horse returned to duty from Col 3rd Dgns
S.S. Tuplest joined section temp from No 7 M.V.S.

Tuesday Sept 14th 1915

15 horses evacuated to base (No 10)
including Brig Gen & 4 officers chargers
admitted 8th? Lancers 4. 11th Hussars 2

Wednesday Sept 15th 1915

No 71— Pte Carter sent to No 5 Vet Hos
for course of training as shoeing Smith
SS 2335 Pte Fairhead awarded 14 days
F.P. No 2 for "not complying with an order".

Thursday Sept 16th 1915

1 Charger Capt Jukk Ross Lahore D.
Machine Gun School admitted.

Friday Sept 17 1915

admitted 2 horse 76 Bde R.F.A
3 Collected for 1st Army 1 from
Acm & 2 from Sillenhecque

26

Saturday Sept 18 1915

2 Horses collected from Fr 36eme
Corps Armée Francais. AIRE
2 admitted from 5th Lancers
1 from A Echelon

Sunday Sept 19 1915

Usual Routine

Monday Sept 20th 1915

Admittances 5 Cav Corps H.Q.
5 from 4th Lancers. 3 XVI Lancers
5 from IX Hussars 1 3rd Cav Bde H.Q.
1 horse returned to IV Hussars

Tuesday Sept 21 1915   MAMETZ
by Noq Mil Archives
Evacuated 25 sick horses, 1 cast.
Admitted 1 to Battery horse left at
M Noyelles Farm 8A Querrieu
1 horse from A Echelon 3rd Cav Bde
Section left billets at 2.30 with 28 horses
Rocquetoire & went from there
to new billets at Mametz. Forage
cart with 2 horses being left
with 3rd Cav Bde as B' Echelon
Section now came under ADRVS
2nd Cav Div forming part of Divisional
Troops. Horse issued to 3rd Cav Bde

27

Wednesday Sept 22nd 1915

7 horses admitted. 8 evacuated to
No 7 M.V.S.
A.D.V.S visited the section & gave
instructions that no horses were to
be evacuated until further notice
which were capable of doing a
ten mile journey.

Thursday Sept 23 1915.

4 horses admitted.
1 issued to 2nd Field Squadron R.E.

Friday Sept 24 1915.

Admitted 4 horses
1 Issued to Padre B Section 2nd Field
ambulance.
Section moved out of billet at 5.45
for rendezvous & trekked via Istree
BLANCHE HEUCHIN & MONCHY
arriving at 3.30 a.m.
Major Leyland ## Hussars was
detailed to take charge of A echelon
& joined the section at MAMETZ.
No 8 Section has been chosen to be
the advanced section & to travel
with A Echelon it being considered
impossible for the section to remain
5 horses collected by No 9 M.V.S.

with their Brigades should the proposed
scheme for an advance be successful.
Should an advance be made the
three sections will wield work
in line the last section supplying
the train conducting porters.

Saturday 25th

Section moved from MONCHY to
LOCINGHAM at 3 pm arriving at
midnight.
Admitted 3 horses
Issued 1 P. H.Q R.H.A.

Sunday 26th Section stood to
to move at 40 minutes notice.
Detachments of No 7 & No 9 M.V.S arrived
after distributing remounts to Brigades
No 7 detachment returned to
B Echelon evacuated 11 horses
Admitted 11 horses

Monday 27th Orders received
at 3.15 am to stand by for move
at 5am order cancelled at 4.45
the section to again stand to at 40
minutes notice.
Evacuated by No 9 M.V.S at 11.30 am 12 horses
1 Horse issued to 1th Lancers.

Monday 27th Sept Continued   29
Admitted 9 (?) horses
Tuesday 28th Sept 1915

Order received to be ready to move
at 5.30 cancelled at 5.35 Stood
to to move at an hours notice.
Admitted 3 horses 1 inspected shoes
Evacuated 3 " by No 9 M.V.S.
Wednesday 29th Sept FERFAY
Ordered at 9am to move at 10 am to
FERFÂY one horse left at
farm near church at LOZINGHEM.
T. Corp Vass detailed to remain
at Marles le Mines in charge of an
injured horse belonging to General
Chetwode.
Admittances nil
Thursday Sept 30th 1915

O.C. visited Gen Chetwodes charger
at Marles les Mines & destroyed
the horse left behind yesterday
at LOZINGHAM.

Sept 30th Cont

arranging with the adjutant of the Bedfordshire Yeomanry for the burial of the carcase.

Pte S Coggill (32450) R.H. joined the section from No 3 Hospital.
Admittances 11
2 horses issued 1 or IXth 1 & XII
15 " evacuated to No 7 H.V.S. who collected at MAZINGHAM on St HILAIRE - AIRE road.

Sept 3 →

31

October 1st 1915
Col. Martin ADVS Cav Corps visited the section with Major Hunt, & made enquiry as to the efficiency of the transport.
Admitted 11.

October 2nd 1915 Saturday
Admitted 2. OC No 9 MVS arrived at 3.30 pm with remounts.

Sunday Oct 3rd 1915
12 horses evacuated by No 9 MVS.
Admitted 1.
Order received at 12.45 pm to move billets to Ham en Artois destination altered en route to NORRENT-FONTES arrived at new billets at 4.30 pm.

Monday Oct 4th 1915 NORRENT.
Admitted 5. Issued 63rd Bry H.Q.

Tuesday Oct 5th 1915
OC visited HARLES LES MINES to attend a horse for Brig Gen Vaughan.
Col Martin ADVS Cav Corps visited the section
Admitted 5.
~~Col Hannon DDVS Army visited the section~~

Wednesday Oct 6. 1915

Evacuated 14 to No 7 M.V.S
Admitted 4.
O.C. Visited at horse at Sellens for
No 7 Clearing Station not strong

Thursday Oct 7. 1915

Admitted 3 horses + 1 Mule

Friday Oct 8. 1915

Admitted 5 Horses & 8th Lancers
Col Martin & Major Hunt visited the
section the Wednesday worked ½ day 7P. No 2

Saturday Oct 9 1915

1 Horse of mm Col. 2nd Cav Bde
Destroyed
1 Mule collected for strafiring from
GOARBECQUE
7 horses 2 mules evacuated to No 7 M.V.S
2 horses admitted

Sunday Oct 10 1915

1 horse Major Gen Chetwode Mange
sent to No 9 M.V.S for treatment

Monday Oct 11th 1915

42 Sergt Fyffe charged for "Conduct to the prejudice of good order & military discipline" & (2) neglect of duty.
Case adjourned for inquiry & to be dealt with by O.C. Hospital.

2 Horses admitted
1 horse returned to A.D.M.S. 2nd Cav Div
1 issued to 2 Field Signal Co
1 Mule collected for 1st Army.

Tuesday Oct 12 1915

1 horse collected from farm at BERBOETTE.
6 horses admitted including 1 shoe case & 2 in contact from III Hussars.
Summary of evidence against Sergt Fyffe taken & forwarded to A.A. & Q.M.G. 2nd Cav Div.

Wednesday Oct 13 1915

Second summary of evidence in case of Sergt Fyffe taken by Major Seyfred.
7th Hussars O.R. at Lotelen 2nd Cav Div
Evacuated to No 7 V.S.

8 Sick, 1 Shoe, 2 in contact —
admitted 8 Sick
Received 4 from No 9 M.V.S. for issue
(1 Mule G.V. Sys)

Thursday Oct 14. 1915

Admitted 6 including Coy. Sgt Vaughn
charger attached from MARLES LES
MINES

1 Horse from No 9 issued to 3rd Hussars
2 issued to Armd Cd 2nd Cav Div.
9 H.v. mule evacuated to No 7 MVS.

Friday Oct 15. 1915

1 IIᵗʰ Hussar moved
1 Coy Sgt Vaughts charger to No 7 MVS
Received 3 horses

Saturday Oct 16 1915

Admitted 6
Evacuated by +to No 7 M. V.S . 6.

Sunday Oct 17. 1915

Section moved billets at 12.15 to
ROMBLY
Admitted 3.   1 mule to A.D.M.H.
Monday Oct 18. 1915   to No 7 MVS.

L.G.C.M in the case of Sergt. Fyffe R
at BELLERY.
Admitted 3
Issued 1 to IIᵗʰ Hussar

Tuesday Oct 19. 1915

Section shifted to billets at northern end of village.

1 horse collected on float from billet of No 7 M V S at COYECQ

1 stray admitted

Wednesday Oct 20 1915

10 Horses evacuated to No 10 B V H
1 Collected from St Andre farm
1 left by No 7 MVS from 80 AEM

Thursday Oct 21st

1 horse R H A Guards Div collected from FONTAINE LES HERMANS
1 Horse E Battery R H A from HEDON
1 Horse J Battery R H A WITTERNESSE
3 abandoned horses collected by gendarmerie from H.Q. 1st Army.

Dr Kinock awarded 7 days FP No 2 for absence from stable.

Sgt Lyth reduced to the ranks by sentence of F G C M dated Oct 18th

Friday Oct 22nd 1915

Usual Routine.

Saturday Oct 23 1915

4. B.E.F. horses & 8 Lancers admitted
A.D.V.S. visited the section

Sunday Oct 24 1915   St QUENTIN

S. Sec. moved billet at 1 p.m. to
St Rosella farm at St Quentin.
Sick horses were put under cover.

Monday Oct 25 1915

The section spent day preparing a barn
for reception of section & accomplishing
the work put up for a bath

Tuesday Oct 26 1915

Continuation of arrangements of
winter quarters

Wednesday Oct 27 1915

7 horses admitted
Issued 1st Reserve Book & IV horses
on application from 11th H^y Brig Coy

Thursday 28th 1915
Usual Routine Pte 730 Sumner } Awarded 4 days
              2665 Woodroff   } F.P. No 1 for absence
                                 from morning stables
Friday 29th 1915 Pte Allen & Tyff admonished
1 horse No 1 Reserve Park A.S.C. admitted
17 horses evacuated including
2 suspicious skin cases.
1 horse returned to "J" Battery R.H.A.
494 L.Corp Jukes R. promoted Corporal
dated 27.10.15.

Saturday 30th Oct 1915
Usual routine

Sunday 31st 1915
Church Parade 2.30
8 Horses sent to Ammn Col & 1 "B"
Batt horse transferred to No 7 MVS.
by orderly from No 7.

November 1st 1915   ST QUENTIN.

Corp. Hardy returned from base with Capt Leith Ross charger & Major Musgrave's charger. The former returned to owner and his present charger brought to the section.

1 horse returned to XVI th Lancers cured.

1 horse admitted from No 1 Reserve Park.

C.O. attended remount casting parade & arranged for collection of cast horses.

Pte Chesman left on 7 days leave to England.

November 2nd 1915

One horses admitted from 22n Cas C. Staton

One mule collected by French. Auth.

28 Cast & 6 Remounts collected from regiments.

28 Cast evacuated to No 10 Base V.H.

November 3rd

1 Charger & 6 remounts sent to Field Remount depot Gonnehem.

9 horses 16th Lancers 4 from IV th Hussars collected.

Progress made with preparation of stables for the winter.

Thurs November 4th 1915

1 horse admitted to No 1 Canadian Casualty Station
1 from 5th Lancers (charger) for treatment.
15 evacuated.
A.D.V.S. visited section & examined horses for evacuation.

Friday Nov 5th 1915

2 horses returned to 16th Lancers
1 horse 16 Lancers admitted for treatment

Saturday Nov 6th 1915

1 charger admitted for treatment

Sunday Nov 7th 1915

1 charger admitted for treatment
12 horses collected from Remount train also 1 mule. 5th Bry + Amun Col.

Monday Nov 8th 1915

12 horses + 1 Mule (Remounts) sent on to No 9 M.V.S.
9 horses admitted from 1st Bridging Train R.E.
S/Sgt #433 Bradley went sick & sent to Clearing hospital

Tuesday Nov 9th 1915

1 horse admitted. D Battery.
Baird's charger destroyed.
Preparations for winter continued
forage barn made roofed with
petrol tins, sides of thatch made
with willow poles & reeds from the
road. NCOs & men paid.
Lt Chewman returned from leave.

Wednesday Nov 10th 1915

1 charger returned to Capt Nutting H.Q.
3rd Cav Division.
1 horse collected from 34 Sikh pioneers
1. — admitted from XV Hussars.
Order received to cease making horse
standing & the Div will probably change
billets.
Order received from DDVS Cav Corps
to assist DDVS 1st Army with evacuation
of horses etc on request.

Thursday Nov 11th 1915

Admitted 1 XVI Lancer 2 V Lancers
2. IX Hussars.
16 horses evacuated to the base.

Friday Nov 12th 1915

Two horses collected from MERRUT M.V.S. MORBECQUE.

1 admitted for treatment from "D" Battery.

Sergt Bradley returned from clearing hospital AIRE.

Saturday Nov 13th 1915

2 horses + 3 mules received from 1st Army

4 horses + 3 mules 1st Army evacuated to the base No 10 Vety Hos.

1 Horse received from "Depôt de chevaux malades d'Aire sur la Lys. This horse had been left by the farmer since 28 Oct/14.

2 horses collected from 6th Lancers.

Sunday Nov 14 1915

1 horse admitted 2nd Cav Field Amb.
1 abandoned horse collected from WESTREHEM
1 mule from ROBECQ.
1 mule from CANTRAINE.

Monday Nov 15 1915

Admitted 1 H.a 3rd Cav Brg. 2 6th Hussars
6th Lancers 7. 32 Horses + mules 1st Army.
1 Charger H.Q. 1st Army.
Evacuated to base 29 horses 9 mules

Tuesday Nov 16. 1915   42

Lieut T.J. Faithfull AVC proceeded to England on nine days leave. Capt J. S. Young AVC assumed temp command of the section. Six horses evacuated to Gonneham of the 40th Pathans. 1 horse admitted from B echelon 3rd Cav: Bde

Wednesday Nov: 17 1915
Section moved to new billets at Campagnette.

Thursday Nov: 18 1915.

Section settled into new billets & made horse standings. Usual routine.

Friday Nov: 19 1915.
L. Cpl. Vass. left to collect horse abandoned by 16th L. at Liettres.

Saturday Nov: 20 1915.
Return of L. Cpl. Vass with horse. A.D.V.S. visited section. Evacuated 2 mules 1st Army. 3 horses 3rd Cav: Bde
1 horse 18th Hussars abandoned by that unit.
1 horse B echelon 3rd Cav: Bde discharged cured.
1 " 5th L. horse discharged cured to unit
L. Cpl. Jukes promoted Cpl. from 27=10=15 LCO 39
Cpl. Codd   "   Sergt. " 13=11=15 LCO 40

Sunday. 21 = Nov: 1915.
Section moved billets to Grand Manillet.
1 horse 5 L destroyed - open elbow joint.
1 horse 5 L sent for evacuation kept back
for treatment developed gangrenous pneumonia
in dying condition destroyed.

Monday. 22 = Nov: 1915.

Arrangement of billets. Usual Routine.
Two sound mules sent to No 9 M.V.S.
by order of D.A.D.R.T.

Tuesday 23 = Nov: 1915.

Usual Routine.

Wednesday 24 = Nov: 1915.

Usual routine.
Pte Fyffe awarded 14 days No 1 F.P.
Pte 498 Turner transferred from No 13
Vety Hospital.

Thursday 25 Nov 1915
Lieut T.J. Faithfull returned from leave
+ took over command of section
There were transferred to No 10
Base Vety Hospital on authority
A.C. Records
Cont over

Thurs Nov 25th Cont 44

Serg 432 Gold. 314. Corp Hardy,
Pts. 429 Vass. SE3804 Walker. 954 Chessman
891 Chaplin. 730. Sumner 2335 Fairhead
To No 13 Vety Hospital ats C according
4.26 Pte Fyffe in charge of Corp Major
M.M.P.
The following arrived from No 10
Vety Hospital
693 Serg Houston W. SE3865 Corp Waterton
Pts. S2. 6671 Adler. 324 Fryer
SE 4110 Gordon. 551 Lacey 2004 Lloyd
3621 Refoy.
Admitted 1 Suspect Strn. V'th Lancer

Friday Nov 26th 1915

Admitted 1 Susp. Strn H.Q. 3rd Cav Brg
1 Mule from Supply Horse transport.

Saturday Nov 27th 1915

Corp Waterton placed und instruction
in office.

Sunday Nov 28th 1915

Pte 3670 Lucas. 3160 Osborne
appointed acting unpaid L.Corp on
authority of A.D.V.S.

45

Sunday Nov 28th 1915 Couff

Admitted 1 Remount, 1 Susp. Strain from Amm Col 2nd Cav Div.
2 horses from C Battery.
Church Parade.

Monday Nov 29th 1915

Admitted 1 horse D Battery 1. 11th Bde RHA
1 Horse 83rd Battery. 1. 84th Bat. 1 horse 85 Bat.
H.Q. & S. 2nd Cav Div. verbal section

Tuesday Nov 30th 1915

Admitted 6 horses V th Lancers
1. 2nd Cav F. Amb. 1 Hd. 3rd Cav Bde
6. No 3 Res Park, 1Th Hussar (both) B.R.E. Station
Evacuated. 22 including 4 skin cases,
Transferred 1 horse to 2nd Cav F. Amb.
Reinforcements attended a demonstration by gas expert at Bde H.Q.

Wednesday Dec 1st 1915 — 46

Admitted 8 horses 84 Bat. R.F.A.
1. Horse 18th Hussars.
1. Std. Car Corps (Sig).
Kit Inspection condition very
fair.

Thursday Dec 2nd 1915

Sergt Bradley. G. went on leave
to England.
1 Horse transferred to No 3
Reserve Park at ESQUERDES.
Rifle instruction for reinforcements

Friday Dec 3rd 1915

Usual Routine

Saturday Dec 4th 1915

Usual Routine.
O.C. & four men attended at
Rail Head to meet Remount train

Sunday Dec 5th 1915

1 horse collected at that from WIZERNE
Bat R.F.A.

47

Monday Dec 6th 1915

Adm. Horses 3 horse 1 Nette stomach
2nd Cdn Div 2 mules Reserve Park
2nd Cav Div
1 horse returned to XII Lancers.
Rifle instruction for reinforcements

Tuesday Dec 7th 1915

Admitted 4 XII Lancers.
3 V th Lancers 7. IV Hussars
1. H.Q. A&C 2nd Cav Div
Evacuated to No 13. V.H. Horses 20
Mules 2.

Wednesday Dec 8th
1 Mule returned to Supply Transport.
Foot Drill.

Thursday Dec 9th
Sgt Bradley returned from leave
Rifle drill for reinforcements.

Friday Dec 10th
Usual Routine

Monday Dec 13th 1915
498 Pte Turner went on leave to England
O.C. visited NEUFCHATEL to see
demonstration of mallein test.
Foot Drill

Tuesday Dec 14y. 1915

Admitted 1 horse H.Q. 2nd Cav Div
1 horse 2" Cav F Amb.
2 mules (cart) Army Horse Transport.
Rifle instruction. Section paid.

Wednesday Dec 15- 1915

Admitted 4 horse No 7 M.V.S. for evacuation
1. horse Signals Cav Corps for treatment,

Thursday Dec 16 1915

Admitted 16 Lancers 4. XII L. 1
Army horse transport 3. H.Q 2nd Cav Brig 1
H.Q 2nd Cav Div 2. IX Hussar 1
Evacuated to No.16. 18 horses + 4
mules sick + 2 Mules cast.

Friday Dec 17. 1915
1 horse returned 16th Lancers.

Saturday Dec 18th 1915

324 Pte Fryer left on leave to England.

Sunday Dec 19th

1 Horse issued to S.C. H.Q. 2nd Cavalry on authority of D.A.D.R. Cav Corps

Monday Dec 20th

Party attended at H.Q. IV Hussars to assist with malleining the regiment. 609 horses + mules malleined.
Pte 3670 Lucas left on 7 days special leave to Paris on authority of G.O. Commanding 3rd Cav Bgde
Pte Turner returned from leave.

Tuesday Dec 21st 1915

67 horses of H.Q. 3rd Cav Bgde + Signal troop malleined.

Wednesday Dec 22 1915

Admitted 1 horse No 3 Reserve Park 4 IV Hussars.

Thursday Dec 23

A.D.V.S. inspected horses of the section + approved of their condition.

Friday Dec 24th 1915

4 horses returned to the
18th Hussars. 1 Horse 18th Hussars
received
Pte Fryer returned from leave.
Pte Woodruff & Driver Kwak
awarded 8 days F.P No 2 for absence
from roll call 7.45.
Pte Facey admonished.

Saturday Dec 25th

1 horse remount 1th D.G admitted
for treatment.

Sunday Dec 26th

Usual Routine
Pte Lucas returned from leave
2016 Pte Lloyd left on leave
to England.

Monday Dec 27th

Admitted 2 horses 16 Lancers
1 horse sent to 18th Hussars
4110 Pte Gordon went sick
Foot drill for section.

Tuesday Dec 28th 1915

1 Horse returned to Divn Col.
Admitted 1 horse Divn Col.
1 Mule Aux Horse Transport
2 horses 9th Lancers Shiv?
Shivering Helmet, parade Divn Col
1 horse for listing from H 2nd Cav Div

Wednesday Dec 29th

491 S.S. Lambert dispatched to base
No 12 V.H. 6891 S.S. Benstead arrived
from No 12 V.H.
Admitted 2 mules Aux Horse Transport
2 horses IV Hussars.
Evacuated 8 horses & 3 mules to
No 13. V.H. Including 1 Proroptic mange.

Thursday Dec 30th

Friday Dec 31st

Rifle Instruction
Major Gen Vaughan C.O. 3rd Cav Div
visited the section.

Sat Jan 1st 1916   GD. MANILLET

Mallening party to WILLIAMETZ
110 horses Field Squadron R.E. nallen
Party to meet remount train
6 Scots Greys taken to section for the
night.

Sun Jan 2nd 1916

6 horses Scot Greys collected by
regiment.
5 9th Lancers 4 16th 1 Amm Col
2nd Cav Div Admitted.
Pte. Lucas & Refoy sent to WIZERNES
to take charge of horses of 2nd & 3rd
Bde West Indies R.F.A.

Monday Jan 3rd 1916

1 horse issued to Field Squadron R.E.
on authority of DADR Cav Corps.
1 horse returned to 9th Lancers.
Admittances, 1 horse & 1 mule Amm Col
2nd Cav Div. 1 horse Field Sy R.E.

Jan 4th Tuesday 1916

2 OR & 1 Mule evacuated to the
base. (1 of West Lanc Bde R fct.)

Wednesday Jan 5th 1916

2 horses (Shiv) admitted to "Army
Riding School for reinforcements

Thursday
Foot Drill

Friday Jan 7th

Admitted 2 horses No 3 Reserve Park
(Suspected Shiv)
1 horse (remount) sent to VII D.Gs.

Saturday Jan 8th

13 horses evacuated to the base
6 horses 3rd Reserve Park received at
station
Party built remount tram &
distributed 3 Brigade horses to units.
Authority received for transfer of
Pte South 14th Hussars to AVC No 1056

Sunday Jan 9th 1916
Usual routine
Monday Jan 10th

2 horses suspected Broughé mange
admitted from III Hussars.
Tuesday Jan 11th 1916
Smoke Helmet parade.
Wednesday Jan 12th 1916
1 horse from XII Lancers 2 Anna Col
Thursday. Jan 13th
Pte 714 Compton dispatched for duty
with dismounted division
Friday Jan 14th

2 horses Prov. Mange III Hussars
1 Skin case XII Lancers
Usual Routine
Saturday Jan 15th

1 horse returned B. echelon 3rd C.Fd
1 horse received 3rd Reserve Park
ASC

Jan 19th 1916

Admitted 10 horses 4th Lancers
1 from 21st Lancers
2 No 3 Reserve Park
Evacuated to Base Veterinary 18 horses

Jan 20th 1916 Thursday

Pte 1165 Woodruff & 2474 Beecham granted
5 days leave of absence to Dysford
1 horse admitted for treatment B Echelon

Jan 21st 1916

Pte 1156 Smith granted 4 weeks
leave on reengaging until end
of war. Gen Hughs pony destroyed.
1 horse admitted from No 3 Reserve
Park ASC

Jan 22 1916 Saturday

1 horse H.Q 3rd Cav Bde admitted.

Jan 23. 1916

1 horse admitted 7th Hussars

25 Jan 1916

1 horse returned I Lancers
1 " XVI Lancers
1 rider admitted from 2nd Cav't [Bde]
& 1 K.D. sent home.
1 Charger H.Q. 3rd Cav Bde destroyed
fractured pastern

Wed Jan 26th 1916

Pte Woodruff returned from leave

Thurs Jan 27 1916

Pte Beecham returned returned
from leave giving reason –
sickness for reason of delay. Medical
report confirmed this.

Friday Jan 28th 1916

1 horse suspicious taken from Drum
Col 2nd Cav Div. 2.50 PM stoggat proceedr
on leave to England
1 horse returned B Schelon
3rd Cav Bde

Saturday Jan 29th

Party attended at rail head to
meet remount train.

57

Sunday Jan 30th
 Usual Routine.

Monday Jan 31st

324 Pt Fryer dispatched to Dismounted
Base to relieve Pte Compton
detached for cook of No 2 base Hos.
2 horses admitted from 2nd Siegus Squadron

February 1916 Tuesday
Pte 41/6 Beckham transferred to
Nzg MVS. Admitted 1 horse to Tancred (Cast)

Wednesday Feb 2nd 1916
Pte Compton rejoined from dismounted
Brigade

Thursday Feb 3rd 1916
Pte 714 Compton despatched
for course of instruction in shoeing
at No 2 Hospital.
Pte Slegget returned from Base
6 sick & lame horses evacuated
to base.
2 horses returned to 2nd Sig Squadron.

Friday 4th 1916
3484 Pte Crocker left on leave to England.
4 horses of Bde HQ collected
for the 1st Army
1 horse admitted from XIII Hussars
(shin)

Saturday Feb 6th
1 horse admitted from Etchelon
3rd Cav Bde

Sunday Feb 7th
1 horse (Prophtic?) from 2nd
Reserve Park

Thursday Feb 11th
Admitted 5 horses XII Lancers 1 Kings
& IV Hussars
Evacuated to the Base 14 horses
S.S. 2450 Pte Leggett E H awarded extra
guards + cost of new cap for destroying
same.
Pte SS 470 Turner T awarded fine of 3/- +
value of a cap for losing the same
by neglect

Friday Feb 12th
Pte Crocker returned from leave

Saturday Feb 13th
Admitted 1 horse (skin) IV Hussars
SS7311 Pte West proceeded on leave
to England, Accompanied Sgt Oakley to
WIZERNES to meet Remount train.

60

Sunday 13th Feb 1915
Usual Routine
Admitted ~~II Lancers 6 XVI Lancers 4~~
~~IV Hussars 4~~
~~Evacuated 15~~
~~Tuesday~~ Monday 15th
4 sick cases evacuated to base
Wednesday 16th
B2 & H4 Troops returned with Secunderabad
Brigade
Thursday 17   1 horse II "Hussars"
1 XVI Lancers admitted
Saturday Feb 20
6/3 Sergt Horton granted leave of absence
Monday Feb 21st   to Ireland (5 days)
Horses — change — signed to Major
Genl Vaughn 3rd Cav Div.
Tuesday Feb 23rd
Admitted II Lancers 6. XVI Lan
4   IV Hussars 4. Evacuated 15
to No 13 Base Vety Hospital.

61

Wednesday Feb 23rd
Usual Routine &
Foot Drill

Thursday Feb 24th
1 L.D. horse sent to No 1 Reserve
on p. Screws on authority of
A.D.V.S. Cav Corps
2 horses (24th Snow) evacuated
to base by No 9 M.V.S.
admitted 1 horse from 4th Fd Cav Bat & IV Army
Bug

Friday Feb 25th
Usual routine
Admitted 1 horse from Col 20th Indiv.

Saturday Feb 26th
1 horse H.Q. ... Cav Bde admitted

Monday Feb 28th
Admitted 7 Cart & 2 sick H.A. Car Cops
& L" Battery

Tuesday Feb 29th
Admitted 1 horse evac'd jaundice & Ill Sherwood

1st March 1916 — Wednesday

435 Sergt Bradley W.G. despatched to Headquarters 2nd Scots Regiment 4th Division for one months attachment before proceeding to Cadet School

Authority A.G. Staff A/11124
Cav Corps 4007. 2nd Cav Div Q.Z. 6552

Admitted 4 horses 2nd Field Sqn R.E.
9. 12th Lancers. 5 XVI Lancers.
1 mule struck off & sent Cav Brd. 2 Horses
& Cattle.

Evacuated to base 27 horses.
1 mule sick 43 horses Cast.
1 horse transferred to H.Q. 2nd Cav Div

2nd March 1916

Admitted 2 ponies (sick) from 16th Lancers under instruction
& A.D.R.
H.Q. 2nd Cav Bde 1 horse sick
4th Hussars Cat   1 horse Smyth
                    evacuated to No 22
1 Pony from No 7 M.V.S. Cas Clearing
                          Station

Monday March 6
Admitted   II Pitrooss 3
H Qr 3rd Cav bde 1 (Cast)
Ams Col   6 cast, 1 pony remount
2 sick (soldier)
7th Jancers 5. H Q Cav Corps
1 Charger Gen Bingham
Evacuated 6 cast   11 Sick, 1
cast

Tuesday March 7th
Usual Routine

Wednesday March 8th
3 ponies & Machine Gun Squadron
on instructions from * AVS

Thursday March 9th
Admitted 1 horse (mare) to Colkay
& 1 H Q 3rd Cav Bde

Friday March 10th
Admitted 2nd Machine Gun Squadron
1 from 9th Labour Battalion

64

Saturday March 11th

Admitted 1 pony H.A. 3rd Cav Bde

Monday March 13th

Admitted 1 horse 2nd Mach Squad
for treatment
1 " from 9th Cav Bde "

Tuesday March 14th

Admitted 1 mule chars H.T. 1 horse
American Col. 3rd Cav Div for treatment
1 X Section 2 H.A. R.H.A. 3rd Cav Div.
3 3rd R.H. Pack, 4 Cav Corps Signals
Evacuated 13 horses & 1 mule to
No 18 Vety Hospital

Wednesday March 15th

Usual Routine

Thursday 16th   Admitted
1 horse H.A. 3rd Cav Bde

Friday 17th
1 horse H.A. Cav Corps Sig.

Wednesday March 22

Admitted 1 horse to Battery for treatment. 1 horse H.Q. 3rd Cavld (Brig Genl Bell Smyther charger)

Thursday March 23

494 Corp Jukes R proceeded on 6 days leave to England.

Pte 760 Dudley, 755 Latham, SS 8081 Whitehead joined section from No 13 Vety Hospital.

Tuesday March 28th

Admitted 1 horse 3 Mach Gun Squadron
Capt Touthfull returned to duty.

Wednesday March 29th

Admitted 1 horse H.Q. 3rd Cavlde treatment. 1 horse ditto.
1 Tkt H. (Skin) 2 O Battery. 2 Aust Horse Trans mules.

2450 Pte Skoggit returned to duty on expiration 42 F.P. No 1.
12 5 Pte Matthen to be acting unpaid L.C.

April 1st 1916

Corp Waterton proceeded to England
on 6 days leave. Invalided out doll

Sunday April 2nd

Usual Routine.

Monday April 3rd

Admitted 1 horse XII Lancers
Foot Drill.

Tuesday 4th

Admitted 1 horse 3rd Mac Gun Squadron

Wednesday April 5th

Admitted 1 mule Aux H.T.
3 horses Amm Col 2nd Cav Div.
2nd Field Sq R.E. 2. 3rd Reserve Park 3
Cav Corps Signals 1 nch x 1 Cart.
1 2nd Cav Field Ambulance
Evacuated 10 nch x 1 cart
to No 3 V.H.

Thursday April 6th

Riding School with jumping.
Admitted 6 V" Lancers 2 XVI Lancers

Friday April 7. 1916

T/q Pte Compton returned from course of instruction in shoeing at No 2 2 V.H.
Evacuated 9 horses (shing) to base

Saturday April 8th 1916

1 horse from Cyclist Squadron
2nd Army
4 from 3rd Mach Gun Squadron.
Pte Reford left on 6 days leave
Riding school. 1 horse admitted H.Q. 3rd Cav Bde

Sunday April 9th

Usual Routine

Monday April 10th

Admitted 1 them 3rd Mac Gun Sq
1 from B Echelon (shing).
Mounted Drill + Riding school

Tuesday April 11th

4 horses admitted 3rd Mac Gun Squadron
1 horse returned H.Q. 3rd Cav Bde,

Wednesday April 12th

Admitted 2 horses to Battery.
4 V th Lancers 3 XII Lancers 1 3rd Hussars
Evacuated to base 18 horses
Admitted Pack ponies 3rd Hussars 3, 12th L. 1, XX Hrs 2

Thursday April 13

000011 Pte Whitehead left on 6 days
leave to England.
1 horse ignus H.Q. 3rd Cav Bde
1 Prooptic case from Col Goddard
for destruction.
News received that all leave cancelled
& men to return by the 18th
Pack ponies V th Lancers 2, XII 1.
T3/E30341 Knungh R.W. evacuated to No 20. C.C.S.

Friday April 14

8 ponies evacuated by Road to
Boulogne under Corp Lucas.

Saturday April 15

5 horses skin admitted from Col.
Smith Helmet drill

Sunday April 16

Admitted 1 horse H.Q. 3rd Cav Bde
T/33640 Driver McCabe P joined the section
from H.Q. 3rd Cav Bde

Monday April 17th Riding School
Admitted 1 horse IV Hussars
1 F. Battery. 2 Amm Col. 1 Mac Gun Sect
1 17th Lancer 2 Mules Aux H Transport
Tuesday April 18th
12 horses & 3 mules evacuated to base
No 13 Hospital.
Two Remount trains met at WIZERNES.

Wednesday April 19th
Usual Routine . Mounted Drill

Thursday April 20th

Friday April 21st
Usual Routine.

Saturday April 22nd
Admitted 2 horses IV Hussars
1 Sent to M.M.P. on authority of Staff Capt
3rd Cav Bde.

Sunday April 23rd

Monday April 24th
Admitted 1 Charger Remount

Tuesday April 25th
Admitted IV Hussars 5. V Lancers 2
XVI Lancers 3. 2nd C.F.A. 1

Wednesday April 26th
14 horses evacuated to No 13 Base V.H.

Thursday April 27th
Admitted 2 cases Shoe to Battery
Smoke Helmet Drill.

Friday April 28th
Admitted 2 Mules Aux Horse Transport
Drill Mounted.
175 bdle R.T.A ett 3½ Div 3.

May 1916

Monday May 1st

Admitted 5 Amm Col 2nd Cav Div including 1 shin. 1 160 Bde R.F.A
1 4th Hussars (shin) 1 "E" Battery R.H.A.
1. 175 Bde R.F.A.
42.1 Sergt Harries A.B. taken on strength from No 12 Vety Hos.
693 Serg Houston W dispatched to No 12 Hospital
2665 Pt Woodruff P.C. dispatched to No 2 Vety Hospital Havre.

Tuesday May 2nd

Party to meet Remount train
Received 1 L.D. from Remounts
Major Parks visited the station.
Admitted. Glasgow Yeomanry 1
17th Lancers 3. 3rd Machine Gun Squad 1
K Battery R.H.A.1. Scots Greys 1.

74

Wednesday May 3rd

Admitted 160 Bde R.F.A 3
B. Echelon 1.
Evacuated to No 13 Vety Hos 24 horses 1 Mule
to No 22 Hospital 16 horses cast
of 2nd Machine Gun Squadron.
& 1 Stray with section.

Thursday May 4th

Admitted 160 Bde R.F.A. 3
Discharged. 2 to 16th Lancers.

Friday May 5th

Admitted C Battery 175 Bde R.F.A 1 horse
No 5 Cavalry Field Ambulance 1
Smoke helmet parade

Saturday May 6th

Admitted Cast horse drawn col
2nd Cavn Div 9.
Rich HQ 3rd Cav Bde Signals 2.
16 Lancers 1 skin. 175 Bde R.F.A
1 horse collected from BAYENGHEM.
Returned 1 horse to 2 3rd Cav Bde.

75

Sunday May 7th
Usual Routine.

Monday May 8th   6671 Pte Adley
                  granted 6 days leave.
2 Cast horses issued to Aux H.T
1st Cav Divn Authority L of A.D.R.
admitted 1 Cast horse to Battery

Tuesday May 9th
Admitted   4th Hussars 8. 16 Lancers 3
3rd Mac Gun Squd .1. Northants Yeo .1.
L Battery R.H.A.1. H.A. 3rd Bde R.H.A. 1

Wednesday May 10th
                                    to Neufchatel
Evacuated 22 Sick & Cast
3 Cast to Abbeville
Admitted 1 Case (skin) 16th Reserve Park
1 16th Lancers.

Friday May 12th
Drill mounted
Admitted 1 Mule Aux H.T.

Saturday May 13
Smoke helmet drill.

76

Monday May 15th 1916

Collected 1 horse Madame LARDOUR of
SETQUES left by 152 Bde R.F.A. 34 Div.
Admitted 1 Glasgow Yeomanry.
2 (Cart) Amm Col 2nd Can Div

Tuesday May 16th

Admitted 4th Hussars 2. Amm Col 2
5th Lancers 7. 16th Lancers 4
Army Vet.7. 3 Mules HQ 3rd Cav Bde 1.
Transferred 1 HD to No 10 Reserve
Park authority DADR Wire Y724.

Wednesday May 17th

Evacuated 18 horses & 2 mules to No 13
V.H. Admitted IX Hussars 1.
Returned XVI Lancers 1. Amm Col 1
D. Battery 2.

Thursday May 18th

Admitted 1 Sum Cav 16th Lancers
Transferred to No 7 M.V.S. 2 Cart & 1
from 5th Cav Field Amb.

77

Friday May 19th
Capt Faithfull left on leave to England.
1 skin case HQ 3rd Cav Bde admitted

Saturday May 20th
Admitted 1 Mule collected from
SENNINGHEM 34th D.A.C.

Sunday May 21st
Section moved to RECQUEBREDCQ

Monday May 22
Admitted 1 Mule collected COLQUHEY
34 D A C.
2 horses from Col 2nd Cav Bde skin

Tuesday May 23
Admitted 1 Charger (Cast) 3rd M.G. Sqn
Transferred to Base 2 skin cases
68955 Bursfield went on 6 days leave.
Rifle Inspection Smoke Helmet Drill.

Wednesday May 24
Admitted 1 Charger HQ 3rd Cav Bde Signals

Thursday May 25
Admitted 1 IV Hussars

78

Friday May 26
Usual Routine

Saturday May 27
Usual Routine

Sunday May 28th
Party attended Remount Farm
LUMBRES.

Monday May 29th
Capt Faithfull assumed command
on return from leave.

Tuesday May 30th
Admitted XVI Lancers 3. IX Hussars 3
V Lancers 3. 10th Res Park 7.
Kit Inspection.

Wednesday May 31st
Evacuated 17 horses & 1 mule to
No 13 Vety Hos.

RECQUEBREUCK 79

1st June Thursday 1916

1 Mule destroyed 34 Div Amm Col.

2nd June Friday

Admitted 16 Lancers 1 skin case

3rd June Saturday

Admitted 2 Case skin 16th Lancers
Collected 1 horse (10th Reserve Park)
Compayne les Bois on M+13.
Destroyed 1 Mule   Rifle Drill

4th June Sunday

Evacuated to base 5 skin cases.

5th June Monday

Usual Routine

6th June Tuesday

Admitted Yorkshire Dragoons 2.
Amm Col 6. 3rd M.G. Sqd 3.
Wilts Yeomanry 3. R.A.A H.Q 1.
16th Lancers 2. 10th Lancers 3.
18th Hussars 1. 2nd L.F.R.S. 3.
3rd F. Ambd. H.Q A.S.C. 2

Wednesday June 7th
Evacuated to base 28 horses
Admitted 2 suspicious cases. Shu
& Glanders.

Friday June 9th
Admitted 1 t.b. Yorkshire Dragoon

Saturday June 10th
1 Charger & saddle from APM ret Corkw.
Yorkshire Dragoons 3 Cast. Rifle Drill

Sunday June 11th
Returned 2 mules to Aux H.T. retaking
Admitted 1 horse collected from 34th
Div. Mob de.
Photo with Remount train.

Monday June 12th
Admitted 2 Yorkshire Dragoons.
1 4th Hussar for remount.

Tuesday June 13th
Admitted XXL Hussars 8 Cast.
IX 13 4th Hussars 8 2nd Nor Yeo 9.

Wednesday June 14th

Admitted 1 Cart (filly) 2nd Can Div Rl Ind
XVI Lancers 1 Shire.
Evacuate 43 Cart to Abbeville.

Thursday June 15th

1 Charger returned to Wilts Yeomanry
1 ditto admitted.
Evacuate 5 to No 23 Hos St OMER.

Friday June 16th 1916

755 Pte Jotham left on 6 days leave

Saturday June 17th 1916

1 bay taken on strength of section
on authority of DADR.

Sunday June 18th 1916

1 horse returned to Q.O. Yorkshire Drag
a ditto to Ammn Col.
Admitted to battery 1 Q.O. Yorkshire
Dragoons 2. 1 Charger (Capt Rattray) from
HQ 3rd Cav Bde.
Pte Whitehead admitted to No 10 Stationary Hospital.

Monday June 19

Admitted from Col 4 2?3 R?1 D Bath
RHA 1. 4th Hussars 1.
Transferred 2 ?? to dism Cav Div
toa on authority of ADMS wire.
Evacuated to No4 CH?TEL 3
St OMER 10.

Section moved at 7.30pm via
HAZEBROUCK to STRAZEELE
arriving at new billets at 3.30am.

Tuesday June 20   STRAZEELE

Admitted HQ 3rd Cav Bde 1 charger

Wednesday June 21

Admitted 1 Pack Pony HQ 3rd Cav Bde
1 6th ? 4th Hussars 9.

Thursday June 22
11th Lancers 4. V th Lancers 5.
evacuated to ST OMER by road. 19

Friday June 23
1 6 H.G. ~~evacuated~~ transferred to
No 7 M.V.S.

84

Saturday June 24
Admitted 1 6th Hussars 1 16th Lancers

Sunday June 25
Admitted 9th Lancers Sp. XII 1. 3rd H.S.S. 2
H.Q. 2nd Cav Bde 1.
Evacuated by road to No 23 C.H. 8

Monday June 26th
Amn Col 2nd Cav Div 3.
1 Charger 3rd Cav Bde H.Q. returned bttry

Tuesday June 27th
Admitted J Battery 1. Amm Col 1
3rd Cav Bde Sig 1.
1 Remount joined section.
Boy met remount train
Evacuated to No 23 C.H. 10

~~Thursday~~ Friday June 30th
Admitted Amm Col 2. XVI Lancers 2.
4th Hussars 1.
8653 Pte Pratt joined section from No 4 C.H.
~~Saturday~~

July 1916

Saturday July 1 1916
Admitted 2nd C.E. Sig 1.
881 Pte Whitehead returned to duty from
St Omer Hospital. Foot & Rifle Drill.

Sunday July 2 1916
Admitted from Col 1. 4th Hussars 1
to duty sent to No 2 V.H. HAVRE

Monday July 3 1916
Admitted 1 52 Bat of Pole Artl
from Col ambulance 2. 1 S R.E. 1

Tuesday July 4th
Admitted 18th Hus. cas 1
Evacuated to No 2 3 V.H. ROUEN 2 1.

Wednesday July 5th
Admitted 1 charger 5th Lanciers 1 R.
Rifle Drill
Thursday July 6th
Admitted + to hosp # Sick + 1 Cas.

Friday July 7th
Admitted J Battery 2
2nd F.S.R 2. 1

Saturday July 8th
Section moved to WALLON CAPEL

Monday July 10th
Admitted 5th S Ra 1. Div Sig (Cab)
M.M.P 3rd Cav Bde 1. 8th M.G. Squad 1
Armn Col 1. 6th Lancers 1. J Battery 1.
3rd Cav Bde Sig 1. Sent F.G.T Clarkes
charger.

Tuesday July 11th
Evacuated to No 23 VH. 19.
Admitted 1 Mange Case 1st Auxy Bn Details

Wednesday July 12th
Admitted 6th Lancers 1. HQ 3rd Ca Bde 1
gnok H dm at Work
Thursday July 13
Admitted 1 F Sig B?

87

Friday July 14th
Admitted 39th Batt RFA 1 Cas't
1 Can + Aust Cas't.   RFA Sanger 1
2nd Can Bde Hd qr 1

Saturday July 15th
Evacuated to base 6 Sick 3 Cas't
to No 23 VH
Section moved billets at 9.15 am
to MERRIS.

Sunday July 16
Party visited St Marie Capel + collected two
horses left by No 2th MVS LES CISEAUX
Par BLARINGHAM + collected 6 left by No 5 AMB
BLARINGHAM + collected 3 left to 5th Austr
Evacuated to base 11 horses.
Admitted god M G Sy 1.

Monday July 17
Admitted 1st Anzac Corps Cav 4.
+ Aus Sec 2nd Army 3.

88

Tuesday July 18
Admitted 1 horse 4th Hussars Collected from
SEE Bonn.
Admitted 4th Hussars 1.

Wednesday July 19 Collect 2 2.D. from THETRE
Admitted 4th Hussars 5   5th Lancers 1.
Collected 2 H.A. from ROUGE CROIX.
4 horses & one Anm Col
1 horse 1 Col. R.F.A. from St SYLVESTRE CAPEL.

Thursday July 20
Admitted XLI Lancers 1.
Evacuated 15 horses & one mule.

Saturday July 22
Admitted XLI Lancers 1. 3rd Mn Gn Sq. 1

X ? Lancers 3.

Sunday July 23
Evacuated 1 Pte to Field Pce due Surg Bony.
Admitted 1 from F. R sect. Stn.
Party meet Remount train.

Monday July 24 Admitted 1 Lancers 2 skn,
1/3 Ods 4 th. Evacuated 15. to No 2 3 V.H. including
Lieut Mosley charger

Tuesday July 25th
Small Return

Wednesday July 26th
Collected shoes 1 DEBOUT St SYLVESTRE CAPPE
                 2 M GROSON
                 1 A [?]   HONDEGHEM
Admitted 1 6" [?] 3rd Car Bde
          1 XII " Lancers

Thursday July 27th
Admitted X " Lancers 3

Friday July 28th
Admitted 3rd Hy Troop 1
          XVI Lancers   2   evacuated 1.

Saturday July 29th
Transferred to [?] 3 [?] A Dr
Admitted [?] [?] 6.
XVI 2 [?]

Sunday July 30
Coll [?] shoes   M MARTEN   CAESTRE
                 [?]   CAESTRE
Admitted 3 for [?] section.

Monday, July 31

Computed [?] Book 19 hrs 11.23 V.H
Astro. Ther 4th Hours 4. 0

2nd Cavalry Division

121/6760

No 8. War Diary: Lectures

Vol IX 1 — 31/20.7.15

ans

Army Form C. 2118.

WAR DIARY
or
INTELLIGENCE SUMMARY.
(Erase heading not required.)

Instructions regarding War Diaries and Intelligence Summaries are contained in F. S. Regs., Part II. and the Staff Manual respectively. Title pages will be prepared in manuscript.

No. 8 Mobile Veterinary Section
3rd Cavalry Brigade,
2nd Cavalry Division.

Hour, Date, Place	Summary of Events and Information	Remarks and references to Appendices

Army Form C. 2118.

WAR DIARY
or
INTELLIGENCE SUMMARY.
(Erase heading not required.)

Instructions regarding War Diaries and Intelligence Summaries are contained in F.S. Regs., Part II. and the Staff Manual respectively. Title pages will be prepared in manuscript.

Hour, Date, Place	Summary of Events and Information	Remarks and references to Appendices
1st July 1915 Hautinghen	1 horse admitted for knock discharged from hospital	
2nd	12 horses to Base	Usual routine
3rd	1 horse to Bathing returned to unit	
	2 intestinal cases admitted	
4th	Usual Routine	
5th	Riding school	
6th	Usual Routine	
7th	1 Horse admitted at Echelon	

Army Form C. 2118.

WAR DIARY
or
INTELLIGENCE SUMMARY.
(Erase heading not required.)

Instructions regarding War Diaries and Intelligence Summaries are contained in F.S. Regs., Part II. and the Staff Manual respectively. Title pages will be prepared in manuscript.

Hour, Date, Place	Summary of Events and Information	Remarks and references to Appendices
8th July 1915 Fridingham	Lieut T.J. Trethfull AVC (SR) took over command of section from Lieut J.S. Young AVC (TMP)	
9th July 1915	2 horses & 1 mule admitted for examination for influx strongles. Drew 1 Wolf & 4SC transferred 6 sectors from VA D.Gp. S.S. Graves OC. paid a return to duty from V.H. Shan OC. paid personal to Inspected personal kit Cavalier far horses execution N.C.	
10th July 1915	Bright horse evacuated to No 10 BVHair. One cobber came returned to S Bryon Private Youngett granted leave from 11. a.m. to 1 p.m.	
Sun 11th July	Riding School Men & horses on the whole improving well	
12th July	Saddlery Inspection. Condition good.	
13th July	10 horses admitted. Riding school.	

Army Form C. 2118.

WAR DIARY
or
INTELLIGENCE SUMMARY.
(Erase heading not required.)

Instructions regarding War Diaries and Intelligence Summaries are contained in F.S. Regs., Part II and the Staff Manual respectively. Title pages will be prepared in manuscript.

Hour, Date, Place	Summary of Events and Information	Remarks and references to Appendices
14th July 1915	Staff Sarg 29.3 Dale R.S. left to join Staff of No 19 V.H's at Woolwich.	
	No 637 Pte Cook. G left section for short duty course at No 2 V.H.	
	25 Horses evacuated to No 10 Vety Hos.	
15th July 1915 Volkerinckhove	Sixteen mules filled in from Hondeghem to Volkerinckhove	
	Lieut T.G. Faithfull left to take temp charge of No 27 M.V.S.	
	I am now taking temp command of section	
16th July 1915	Usual Routine	
17th July	Ditto	
Sun 18th July	1 horse evacuated from F Battery, 1 from 18th Lancers left behind at St Marie Capel on July 14th fetched from No 7. M.V.S.	
	Church Parade at D. Battery. Pte 460 J Spring RHA absence H.S 405: Willis 6 FG transferred to Pte 511 JH Thomas. I have returned to B Echelon	
19th July	HDVS wanted nothing	

Army Form C. 2118.

WAR DIARY
or
INTELLIGENCE SUMMARY.
(Erase heading not required.)

Instructions regarding War Diaries and Intelligence Summaries are contained in F.S. Regs., Part II. and the Staff Manual respectively. Title pages will be prepared in manuscript.

Hour, Date, Place	Summary of Events and Information	Remarks and references to Appendices
20th July 1915 Witternesse	1 horse No 2 Cav Field Ambulance returned to duty. Sent to 2 Iveltsh returned to the command of section	
21st July	2 Horses admitted	
22nd	8 Horses evacuated to Base Vety Hos	
23rd	1 horse (Recovered) admitted. Great confined	
24th	4 horses admitted	
25th	5 horses (Recovered) evacuated by road to Gonnechen Remount depot.	
26th	1 horse admitted Trivial routine By Gen Vaughn's charger received from No 10 Vety Hos Col Martin ADVS Cav Corps inspected section	
27th	Vety Stores received from base. O.C. attended demonstration by Prof Holiday of prophetical innoculation of mallein	

(73989) W41141—463. 400,000. 9/14. H.&J.Ltd. Forms/C. 2118/10.

Army Form C. 2118.

WAR DIARY
or
INTELLIGENCE SUMMARY.
(Erase heading not required.)

Instructions regarding War Diaries and Intelligence Summaries are contained in F.S. Regs., Part II and the Staff Manual respectively. Title pages will be prepared in manuscript.

Hour, Date, Place	Summary of Events and Information	Remarks and references to Appendices
28th July 1915 Lotherambon	2 & 3 Horses cast by D.A.D.V.S. admitted for evacuation. 1 hr. V.A. Jones cast 6685 B.O.R. 2 horses admitted for treatment.	
29th July 1915	2 & 3 Cast & sick horses evacuated to Base. Brig Gen Vaughn visited the section.	
30th July	L/Cpl Gold 432 promoted Temp Cpl dated 26/7/15. Instruction given to N.C.O's & men as to the method of chloroforming a horse standing. Rifle drill.	
31st July 1915	Usual Routine.	

T.T. Tuthill
Lieut. R.A.V.C.
O.C. 8th MOBILE VETERINARY SECTION

121/6743

2nd Cavalry Division

to S. Lichfield Vety Section

1st X

August 15.

WAR DIARY
or
INTELLIGENCE SUMMARY.
(Erase heading not required.)

Army Form C. 2118.

Hour, Date, Place	Summary of Events and Information	Remarks and references to Appendices
St Quentin Sunday Aug 8. 1915	Usual Routine.	
Monday Aug 9	1 Horse admitted from Am Col 2nd Car Bn. Sergt Bradley reported for duty from No 9 M.V.S.	
Tuesday Aug 10th	1 Horse admitted M.M.P. 1 from 3rd Sig Troop. Rejoining school for section. Sgt Compton reff for duty with No 10 Base Vety Hospital	
Wednesday Aug 11th	1 Horse admitted & 1 echelon. 1 ½ s. Fatched eff on leave Lt Martin A.D.V.S. visited section. Condition of horses etc satisfactory	
Thursday Aug 12th	Pte 5704 Allen O.T. reported for duty from No 6 Vety Hos. 14 horses admitted. 16 evacuated to No 11 Vety Hos.	
Friday Aug 13th	Riding school of section. 2 horses admitted 1 Can Corp 1 HA 2 nd Car Div. 1 Horse destroyed for it ichelon. SBVS, DADT, Can Corps also 2 BR rationing mules return. Promotion of cpls gold to corp ratified by Lead Corps Order 25.	

WAR DIARY
or
INTELLIGENCE SUMMARY.
(Erase heading not required.)

Army Form C. 2118.

Hour, Date, Place	Summary of Events and Information	Remarks and references to Appendices

Villers Bretonneux
Sun August 1st 1915 — Pte Vans returned from leave. Church parade. Cpl Hardy returned from Base & reported Pte Bolton absent from 8.30 pm Saturday 31.

Mon Aug 2 — S.E. Mk 3670 Lican W, + S2 3160 Pte O-Horrn at 7 pm not eaten from Maj M.V.S.
S.E. 165 Pte Matthews E joined from No 6 Veterinary Hospital
Pte Bolton returned at noon was charged & remanded
Cpl Hardy 314 admitted hospital. Section received
Riding drill.

Tues Aug 3rd 1915 — Usual Routine. Pte Bolton remanded for C.M.

Wed Aug 4th 1915 — 19 horses admitted 1 horse destroyed for XII th Lancers

Thurs Aug 5th — Mk 346 Bolton acquitted 28 days F.P. No 1 by 7.9 C M
11 inoc + 1 cart horse evacuated.

Friday Aug 6th — Section moved off at 7.30 & trekked via Heilly Lynch Walter to new billets at St Quentin

Saturday Aug 7th — Sergt 234 Compton remitted Staff Sergy (actg) 2.8.07.15
Cpl Hardy returned to duty from No 20 C. Hospital
St a new Two horses admitted for treatment.

Army Form C. 2118.

WAR DIARY
or
INTELLIGENCE SUMMARY.
(Erase heading not required.)

Instructions regarding War Diaries and Intelligence Summaries are contained in F.S. Regs., Part II and the Staff Manual respectively. Title pages will be prepared in manuscript.

Hour, Date, Place	Summary of Events and Information	Remarks and references to Appendices
St Omer France		
Sat Aug 2 & 14. 17/15	Usual Routine. 3 horses transferred to Field Remount Depot Gonnehem.	
Sunday Aug 15th	Usual Routine.	
Monday Aug 16th	2 horses discharged to Sig Troop 3rd Bde. 1 horse admitted v/ hernia.	
Tuesday Aug 17	Riding School. 1 horse admitted from S Battery 7841 Pte Woods joined section from No 6 V.H.	
Wednesday Aug 18	Usual Routine.	
Thursday Aug 19	19 horses admitted 16 sick 1 cast enucleated to Base. Pte Kersch proceeded on leave to England. 1 horse admitted. 1 horse IX Hernia 1 Influenza.	
Friday Aug 20	Riding School + Troop Drill 1 Car Corps H.Q.	
Saturday Aug 21	Usual Routine.	

Army Form C. 2118.

WAR DIARY
or
INTELLIGENCE SUMMARY.
(Erase heading not required.)

Instructions regarding War Diaries and Intelligence Summaries are contained in F.S. Regs., Part II. and the Staff Manual respectively. Title pages will be prepared in manuscript.

Hour, Date, Place	Summary of Events and Information	Remarks and references to Appendices
St Quentin Sunday Aug 22 1915	1 Horse admitted II Hussars Corps 9/th returned reporting 1 horse injured by shoeing Calais 9.30 20.8.15	
Monday Aug 23rd	Lieut Gen Fanshawe C.B. & Brig Gen Tagart visited the section with Col. Martin DDVS + were apparently satisfied with everything. Two horses discharged to II Hussars + 6 Brig H.Q. 1 Horse admitted from Cav Corps H.Q. SS Greene left on leave.	
Tuesday Aug 24th	Usual Routine	
Wednesday Aug 25th	1 Horse handed to M.M.P. on instruction from SVO Cav Corps. Horse II Fancies 1 Horse Cav Corps (sig) admitted. Col Chenu. A.ct. + D.M.S. 2nd Cav Div visited & action O.K. Lt Kernot returned from leave.	
Thursday Aug 26th	Evacuated 1 Off Charger pit 2 Cart + 13 sick horses. Admitted 1 horse D "Lancers" destroyed 1 horse II Hussars	
Friday Aug 27th	2 Horses evacuated to F.K. Dpt'L Gonnehem 1 Horse admitted F Battery 1 mule removed to Gonnehem Usual Routine	

No. 8 MOBILE
No. [illegible] SECTION

Army Form C. 2118.

WAR DIARY
or
INTELLIGENCE SUMMARY.
(Erase heading not required.)

Instructions regarding War Diaries and Intelligence Summaries are contained in F.S. Regs., Part II. and the Staff Manual respectively. Title pages will be prepared in manuscript.

Hour, Date, Place	Summary of Events and Information	Remarks and references to Appendices
Bordon		
Saturday Aug 28th/15	1 Mule to Gomshen. Usual Routine.	
Sunday Aug 29th	Usual Routine. 2 horses returned to II'k Hussars.	
Monday 30th Aug.	1 Horse admitted to II Hussars. 1 H. Chessman admitted hospital	
Tuesday Aug 31st	1 Horse discharged to B. Echelon No 2 C.T. club 1 horse to II Hussars. 1 Charger Major Hurgrove H.Q. 1 strong admitted. 1 H. Button returned to section after operation. ¶ 28 days F.C.	

J.V. Faulkful
Lieut / a/Vet
O.C. No 8. M.V.S.

2ⁿᵈ Cavalry Division

121/6983

No 8. mobile Vety: Section

Vol XL

Sept. 15

End

WAR DIARY
or
INTELLIGENCE SUMMARY.
(Erase heading not required.)

Army Form C. 2118.

Hour, Date, Place	Summary of Events and Information	Remarks and references to Appendices
ST QUENTIN Wed Sept 1st 1915 Thurs. Sept 2nd.	Pte Bowes left on 6 day leave 11 Admittances & 1 Remount for conveyance to Z Remount depot. 1 Horse admitted H.Q 2nd Can Bn. 2 hospital sick cases I Horse. 14 Horses evacuated to V.H Neuchapel.	
Friday Sept 3rd	Admittances 1 horse T battery 2 horses taken two Machine gun sect[ion]. 1 Horse 1st Battery H.A. Pam for winter horse standings forwarded to A.D.V.S. 2nd Can Div.	
Saturday Sept 4. 1915	1 horse sent to T.R.S Gonnehem Staff Capt 3rd Can Bgy to Z trenches. 2 horses returned.	
Sunday Sept 5th	1 horse admitted Z trenches.	
Monday Sept 6th.	1 pony for T.R.S Gonnehem from M.01 H.V.S. Riding drill for section. A.D.V.S authorised the temp unpaid appointment of Pte. W.Vian as Lance Corporal.	

WAR DIARY or INTELLIGENCE SUMMARY.

Army Form C. 2118.

(Erase heading not required.)

NO. 8 MOBILE VETERINARY SECTION

Hour, Date, Place	Summary of Events and Information	Remarks and references to Appendices
ST QUENTIN Tuesday Sept 7th	3 horses admitted H.Q. 2nd Cav Div. 1 horse sent to F.R.S. 90 N W & E M.	
Wednesday Sept 8th	1 horse returned to 2nd D Lancers. 1 & 2nd Hussars. 1 horse admitted H.Q. 2nd Cav Div. 1 H.Q. Cav Corps. 1 19th Hunb. S.S. Greene admitted to Clearing Hospital St Omer	
Thursday Sept 9th	1 horse admitted 2nd Lancers. 2 from 2nd Hussars. 2 H.Q. Cav Corps. 23 horses evacuated. 1 horse transferred to M.S.R. 1st Army. 1 arived to Reg Offr 2nd Cav Bde on authority of G.O.C 3rd Bde 1 horse returned to H.Q. Cav Corps.	
Friday Sept 10 1915	Pte Bratton transferred to No 10 M.V.S. 1st Cav Div 1 horse admitted at Whatou 3rd Cav Brig.	
Saturday Sept 11	1 horse admitted H.Q. 3rd Cav Brg (Gen Josephus charger) 5 horses admitted 1st B Frain R.E.	

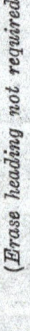

Army Form C. 2118.

WAR DIARY
or
INTELLIGENCE SUMMARY.
(Erase heading not required.)

Instructions regarding War Diaries and Intelligence Summaries are contained in F.S. Regs., Part II. and the Staff Manual respectively. Title pages will be prepared in manuscript.

Hour, Date, Place	Summary of Events and Information	Remarks and references to Appendices
ST QUENTIN		
Sunday Sept 12, 1915	Lt Compton returned from leave. 1 horse admitted H.Q. Cav. Corps. 2 from 106 Bde. R.F.A. O.C. inspected section & parallel ready to move. Time taken for preparation 1 hour 10 minutes. 1 horse sent to H.Q. Cav. Corps on instruction from D.D.V.S. Cav. Corps.	
Monday Sept 13th 1915	Col. Martin D.D.V.S. Cav. Corps & the A.D.V.S. 2nd Cav Div. inspected section & went into subject of loading transport so as to form A & B Sections. This had been done a fortnight previously. 1 horse returned to 2nd Div Ammunition Column. S.S. Conduct gained section temp from No 9 M.V.S.	
Tuesday Sept 14, 1915	15 horses evacuated to H.Q. 10 Base Vety Hos., including Bay Gn. Gn. Vaughan charger. Admittances 4 from XII Lancers 2 from II Hussars	

WAR DIARY or INTELLIGENCE SUMMARY.

Army Form C. 2118.

(Erase heading not required.)

Hour, Date, Place	Summary of Events and Information	Remarks and references to Appendices
ST QUENTIN		
Wed Sept 15, 1915	No 711 Pt Carter sent to No 5 Vet Hospital for course of training as shoesmith. S.S. 2335 Pt tried awarded 14 days F.P. No 2 for not complying with an order.	
Thursday Sept 16, 1915	1 Charger left Cavalry Hors below Divn Head Qrs & Sept admitted	
Friday Sept 17, 1915	2 horses admitted 76 Bde R.F.A. 3 horses (1 destroyed) collected 1 from CHRE & 2 from STEINDFECQUE.	
Saturday Sept 18	2 horses collected from tc 36 em Corps strains trainean AIRE 2 admitted from H.Q Lindsen 1 from cholera nebish	
Sunday Sept 19	Usual Routine	
Monday Sept 20th	Admissions, 5 from Cav Corps H.A. 5 from F Wheelers, 6 from W Hussen. 1 from 5th Cav Bde H.A. Horse returned to W Hussars.	

WAR DIARY or INTELLIGENCE SUMMARY

Army Form C. 2118.

Hour, Date, Place	Summary of Events and Information	Remarks and references to Appendices
MAMETZ Tuesday Sept 21st	Evacuated 25 sick horses, 1 Cont. by No 9 M.V.S. One of CCWE, than to Batty, admitted & left M.H hopeless form ST QUENTIN, 1 than from A. Echelon. Section left billets at ST QUENTIN at 11.30, with 28 horses for ROCQUETOIRE & went from there to new billets at MAMETZ, baggage cart with last horses being left with 3rd Cav Bde B. Echelon. Section now came under the A.A. of A.M.G 2nd Cav Bde forming part of Divisional Troops	
MAMETZ Wednesday Sept 22	A.D.V.S. visited the section & gave instructions that 7 horses admitted & evacuated to No7 M.V.S. no horses were to be evacuated until further notice which were capable of going on an early journey	

WAR DIARY or INTELLIGENCE SUMMARY.

Army Form C. 2118.

NO. 8 MOBILE VETERINARY SECTION

Hour, Date, Place	Summary of Events and Information	Remarks and references to Appendices
MAMETZ Thursday Sept 23rd	5 hours admitted 1 mule to 2nd Field Squadron R.E.	
MONCHY Friday Sept 24th	4 hours admitted 1 mule to Chaplain with 8 section 2nd Div Tin Trili Ambulance. Section moved out of billets at 5.45 & proceeded via ESTREE BLANCHE & HEUCHIN to MONCHY arriving at 2.30 a.m. Major Teyland VII Hussars was detailed to take charge of ct. echelon & passed section at MAMETZ. No. 8 M.V.S. has been chosen to be the advanced section of the Div. & to travel with ct. echelon. If being considered impossible for the section to remain with their Brigades should the proposed scheme for an advance prove successful. Should an advance be made the three sections will instead work in line the last section amplifying the train conducting patients by No. 9 M.V.S. 5 hours collects of MAMETZ by No 9 M.V.S.	

WAR DIARY or INTELLIGENCE SUMMARY.

Army Form C. 2118.

Hour, Date, Place	Summary of Events and Information	Remarks and references to Appendices
LOZINGHAM Saturday Sept 25th 1915	Section moved from MONCHY to LOZINGHAM at 3pm arriving at midnight. 3 horses admitted & issued to H.Q. R.H.A.	
Sunday Sept 26th	Section stood to Enmore at 40 minutes notice. Detachments of No.7 & No.9 M.V.S. arrived after distributing remounts to Brigades. No.7 detachment returned to B Echelon remounting 11 horses. Admittances 11.	
Monday Sept 27th	Orders received at 3.15 am to be ready for a move at 5 am. Orders cancelled at 4.45 am return to again stand to at 10 min after. Succeeded by No.9 M.V.S. at 11.30 am 12 hours I have issued to IV th Division. Admittances 14.	

WAR DIARY or INTELLIGENCE SUMMARY.

Army Form C. 2118.

(Erase heading not required.)

Hour, Date, Place	Summary of Events and Information	Remarks and references to Appendices
LOZINGHAM Tuesday Sept 28th	Orders received at 1 am 6th ready to move at 5.30 called at 5.25. Stood to & move at 3 hour notice	
FERFAY Wed Sept 29th	Advances 3. 1 suspected skin case. Ordered at 9am to move at 10 am to FERFAY Van horse left at farm near church at LOZINGHAM No. I Corp Van detailed to remain at MARIES for MINES in charge of an injured horse belonging to General Chetwood. Advances 4.	
Thursday Sept 30th	O.C. visited for Chetwodes charger at Marles Les MINES & destroyed the horse left behind yesterday at LOZINGHAM. arranging with adjutant of the Bedfordshire yeomanry for the burial of the carcass. Pte SS 2450 Suggett RH joined the section from No 3 Hospital advances 11. 2 horses missed 1 to XX McKennas 15 III tumour 15 evacuated to No 7 M.V.S. who collected at MAZINGHAM on St Hilare AIRE road	T J Foulkes Capt. A.V.C. O.C. 8TH MOBILE VETERINARY SECTION Oct 1st 1915

2nd J. Cavalry Kurain

8th M.V.S.

Dec. 15

Vol XII

131/7449

WAR DIARY or INTELLIGENCE SUMMARY

Army Form C. 2118.

Hour, Date, Place	Summary of Events and Information	Remarks and references to Appendices
Oct 1st 1915 FERFAY	Lt Martin ADVS Cav Corps visited with ADVS 2nd Cav Bde. made enquiry as to the efficiency of the transport. Admitted 11 horses	
Sat Oct 2nd 1915	Admitted 2. OC No 7 M.V.S. arrived with remount.	
Sun Oct 3rd 1915 NORRENT-FONTES	12 horses evacuated by No 9 M.V.S. I admitted order received at 12.45 pm 6 more billets to NORRENT on ARTOIS destination altered on route to NORRENT -FONTES, arrived at new billets 4.30 pm.	
Mon Oct 4. 1915	Admitted 5. I resumed to 2nd Brig H.Q.	
Tues Oct 5 1915	OC visited MARIES & S. MINES to attend horses for Brig Gen Vaughan. CO Master ADVS Cav Corps visited the section. Admitted 5.	
Wed Oct 6 1915	Evacuated 14 horses by No 7 M.V.S. Admitted 4. OC visited horse & billets to No 7 Clearing Station 1st Army.	

Army Form C. 2118.

WAR DIARY
or
INTELLIGENCE SUMMARY.
(Erase heading not required.)

Instructions regarding War Diaries and Intelligence Summaries are contained in F. S. Regs., Part II. and the Staff Manual respectively. Title pages will be prepared in manuscript.

Hour, Date, Place	Summary of Events and Information	Remarks and references to Appendices
Thurs Oct 7. 1915 NO KENT FONTES	Admitted 3 horses & 1 Mule.	
Friday Oct 8.	Admitted 5. Issued 1 to 17th Lancers 7944 Col Martin & Major Hunt vieiled the section. Pte Woods awarded 14 days F.P. No 2.	
Saturday Oct 9. 1915	1 horse from Col 2nd Div Arm destroyed 1 Mule collected for 1st Army from GOARBECQUE 7 horses & 2 mules evacuated to No 7 M.V.S. 2 horses admitted.	
Sunday Oct 10. 1915	1 horse Major Gen Chetwodes charger sent to No 9 M.V.S. for treatment.	
Monday Oct 11. 9. 15	4 & 6 Script Pyffe charged for Conduct to the prejudice of good order & military discipline + (2) night of duty Can adjourned for enquiry + to be dealt with by 5 F.C.M. 2 horses admitted. 1 horse returned to ADHS 2nd Cav Div 1 came to 2nd Field Squad C. 1 Mule collected for platoon.	

(73589) W.4141—463. 400,000. 9/14. H.&J.Ltd. Forms/C. 2118/10.

Army Form C. 2118.

WAR DIARY
or
INTELLIGENCE SUMMARY.
(Erase heading not required.)

Instructions regarding War Diaries and Intelligence Summaries are contained in F.S. Regs., Part II and the Staff Manual respectively. Title pages will be prepared in manuscript.

NO. 8 MOBILE VETERINARY SECTION
No. ....
Date ....

Hour, Date, Place	Summary of Events and Information	Remarks and references to Appendices
Tues Oct 12. 1915 NOEUX-FONTES	1 horse collected from farm at BERGUETTE. 6 horses admitted including 1 skin cases & 2 incontacts from 4th Hussars. Summary of evidence against Sergt Fyffe taken and forwarded to A+Q H.Q. 2nd Cav Div.	
Wednesday Oct 13 1915	Second summary of evidence taken in case of Sergt Fyffe taken by Major Leyland 7th Hussars O.C. "H" Echelon 2nd Cav Div. 6 to No.7 M.V.S. 8 sick. 1 skin 2 incontact evacuated to No.7 M.V.S. Admitted back. Received 4 from No.9 M.V.S. for care. 1 mule to D.D.V.S.	
Thursday Oct 14 1915	Admitted 4 including Brig Gen Vaughans charger collected from MARLES LES MINES. 1 horse from No.9 issued to 2nd Hussars. 2 issued to struck off 2nd Cav Div. 9 horses + 1 mule evacuated to No.7 M.V.S.	

Army Form C. 2118.

WAR DIARY
or
INTELLIGENCE SUMMARY.
(Erase heading not required.)

Instructions regarding War Diaries and Intelligence Summaries are contained in F.S. Regs., Part II and the Staff Manual respectively. Title pages will be prepared in manuscript.

Hour, Date, Place	Summary of Events and Information	Remarks and references to Appendices
Fri Oct 15. 1915 NORRENT-FONTES	1 IV Hussar from No 9 MVS invec. 1 horse by Gen Vaughn charger, ind to No 7 MVS. Received 3 horses.	
Sat Oct 16. 1915	Admitted 6. Evacuated by No 9 MVS 6.	
Sun Oct 17. 1915 ROMBLY	Section moved to billets at 12.15 pm to ROMBLY. Admitted 3. 1 from No 9 MVS. issued to QOO Hussars.	
Mon Oct 18 1915	7 S.C.R. in in care of Sergt Tyfft R. at BELLERY Admitted 3. Issued 1 to IVth Hussars.	
Tuesday Oct 19. 1915	Section shifted to billets at northern end of village. 1 horse collected in Float from billet of No7 MVS at OHEY. 1 other admitted.	
Wednesday Oct 20. 1915	10 horses evacuated to No 10 Base Vet Hosp. 1 collected from ST ANDRE Farm. 1 left by No7 MVS from COHEM.	

Army Form C. 2118.

WAR DIARY
or
INTELLIGENCE SUMMARY.
(Erase heading not required.)

Instructions regarding War Diaries and Intelligence Summaries are contained in F.S. Regs., Part II and the Staff Manual respectively. Title pages will be prepared in manuscript.

NO. 8 MOBILE VETERINARY SECTION

Hour, Date, Place	Summary of Events and Information	Remarks and references to Appendices
Thursday Oct 21st 1915 ROMBLY	1 Horse R.F.A. Guards Div collected from FONTAINE LES HERMIN. 1 Horse "E" Battery R.H.A. from NEDON. 1 Horse "J" Battery R.H.A. from WITTERNESSE. 3 Abandoned horses (collected by Gendarmerie) from H.Q. 1st Army. T Kernick A & S.C. awarded 7 days F.P. No 2 for absence from Stables. Sergt Fyffe reduced to the ranks by sentence of F.G.C.M. dated Oct 18th.	
Friday Oct 22nd 1915	Usual Routine.	
Saturday Oct 23rd 1915	4 XIII Hussars + 1 Lancer admitted. ADVS visited the section.	
Sunday Oct 24 1915 ST QUENTIN.	Section moved billets at 1pm to M Bayelle farm at ST QUENTIN. Sick horses put under cover.	
Monday Oct 25. 1915	The section worked preparing a barn for reception of section horses, completing the work just before dark.	
Tuesday Oct 26 1915	Continuation of arrangements for winter quarters.	

Army Form C. 2118.

WAR DIARY
or
INTELLIGENCE SUMMARY.
(Erase heading not required.)

Instructions regarding War Diaries and Intelligence Summaries are contained in F.S. Regs., Part II and the Staff Manual respectively. Title pages will be prepared in manuscript.

Hour, Date, Place	Summary of Events and Information	Remarks and references to Appendices
Wed. Oct 27. 1915 ST QUENTIN.	7 horses admitted. I moved to post Reserve Park, 1st Thomas as instructions from 1st D.R. Car Corps.	
Thursday Oct 28th 1915	Usual Routine. Pte 730 Furney + 2665 Woodruff awarded 4 days F.P. No 1 for absence from morning stables. McCellan + Syffe admonished.	
Friday Oct 29th 1915	1 horse No 1 Reserve Park H.S.C. admitted. 17 horses evacuated including 2 suspicious skin cases. 1 horse returned to J Anthony R.H.A. No 1 2 Corp John R promoted corporal dated 27.10.13	
Saturday Oct 30th 1915	Usual routine	
Sunday Oct 31st 1915	Church Parade 2.30. 1 horse [struck off] sent to from C.O. + 1.8. Battery horse transferred to No 7 M.V.S by orderly from NOT M.V.S.	T.I. taubful of WE O.C hospital M.V.S O.C Mob. M.V.S

2nd Cavalry Division

No. 8. Mob. Vet. Sec.
Nov. 1915.
Vol XIII

121/764

Army Form C. 2118.

WAR DIARY
or
INTELLIGENCE SUMMARY.
(Erase heading not required.)

Instructions regarding War Diaries and Intelligence
Summaries are contained in F. S. Regs., Part II
and the Staff Manual respectively. Title pages
will be prepared in manuscript.

Hour, Date, Place	Summary of Events and Information	Remarks and references to Appendices
ST QUENTIN Mon Nov 1st	Capt Hardy returned from Base with Capt Fitzherbert's charger & 2nd groom. Hungerous charger. The former returned to owner & hispenn charger brought to the section. 1 horse returned to XII Corps reserved. 1 horse admitted from No1 Reserve Park. 60 attended remount auction parade + arranged for collection of cast horses. Pte Chisman left on 7days leave to England.	
Tues Nov 2nd 1915	One horse admitted from 22nd Cav Clearing Station. One mule collected from French authorities. 28 Cast & 6 remounts collected from regiments. 28 Cast evacuated to No10 Base V.H.	
Wed Nov 3rd 1915	1 charger abandoned sent to field Remount Depot GONNEHEM. 9 hoses IX Wagoners + 4 from IX Wagoners collected. Progress made with preparation of stables for the winter.	
Thursday Nov 4th 1915	1 horse admitted from No. Cav. Clearing Station. 1 from 2nd Cavalry 3 mules for treatment (charges) 15. evacuated. 9 Cav mules action 2 returned to 2nd Division. 1 horse admitted from 2nd Division for evacuation.	
Friday Nov 5th 1915 Saturday Nov 6th 1915	1 charger admitted for treatment 12 horses collected from remount train also. 1 mule (2nd K. Shop & Amm Col.)	

Army Form C. 2118.

WAR DIARY
or
INTELLIGENCE SUMMARY.
(Erase heading not required.)

Instructions regarding War Diaries and Intelligence Summaries are contained in F.S. Regs., Part II. and the Staff Manual respectively. Title pages will be prepared in manuscript.

NO. 8 MOBILE VETERINARY SECTION
No. .... Date ....

Hour, Date, Place	Summary of Events and Information	Remarks and references to Appendices
Mon Nov 8 1915 ST QUENTIN	12 horses (remounts) sent to No 9 M.V.S, 9 horses admitted from 1st Bridging train R.E. Sergt. 433 Brodie went mob. & sent to Clearing hospital AIRE via 2nd Dep.	
Tues Nov 9 19/15	1 horse admitted S. Battery. Brush charges destroyed. Preparations for winter continued forage barn made, roofed with patrol tins. Sides of sheds made with willow poles & reeds from moat. Kits & new pack Pte Chessman returned from leave.	
Wed Nov 10 1915	1 charger returned to Capt Mulkern H.Q. 3rd Can Div. 1 horse collected from 34 Sikh Pioneers 1 admitted from VI Hussars. Orders received to cease making [up] stabling & the Div. will probably change billets Orders received from A.D.V.S Can Corps to meet A.D.V.S 1st Army with evacuation of horses on request Admitted 1 XII Lancers 2 II & Lancers 2 II Hussars 16 horses evacuated to the Base.	
Friday Nov 12th	Two horses collected from HERUT MRS. MORBECQUE. 1 admitted for treatment from B Battery Serg Brodie returned from Clearing hospital to IRE.	

Army Form C. 2118.

WAR DIARY
or
INTELLIGENCE SUMMARY.
(Erase heading not required.)

Instructions regarding War Diaries and Intelligence Summaries are contained in F.S. Regs., Part II and the Staff Manual respectively. Title pages will be prepared in manuscript.

Hour, Date, Place	Summary of Events and Information	Remarks and references to Appendices
ST QUENTIN. Saturday Nov 13. 1915	2 horses + 3 mules received from 1st Army. 4 horses + 3 mules 1st Army evacuated to base No 10 Vety Hos. 1 horse received from Depôt de chevaux malades d'Aire kur. to dep. This horse had been kept by the former men. 28 Oct 1914. 2 horses collected from II Division.	
Sunday Nov 14. 1915	1 horse admitted 2nd Cav Field Ambulance. 1 abandoned horse collected from WESTREHEM. 1 mule from ROBECQ. 1 mule from CANTRAINE.	
Monday Nov 15. 1915	Admitted 1 from H.Q. 2nd Cav Brig. 2. III Hussars. 7 I Hussars. 32 horses + mules 1st Army. 1 charger H.Q. Mesying. Evacuated to base 27 horses + 9 mules.	
Tuesday Nov 16. 1915	Lieut T.J. Faithfull AVC proceeded on leave to England on nine days leave. Capty J. Young AVC assumed temp command of the section. Six horses 40th Pathans evacuated to GONNEHEM. 1 horse admitted from B. Echelon 2nd Cav Brg.	

Army Form C. 2118.

WAR DIARY
or
INTELLIGENCE SUMMARY.
(Erase heading not required.)

No. 8 MOBILE VETERINARY SECTION

Hour, Date, Place	Summary of Events and Information	Remarks and references to Appendices
CAMPAIGNETTE		
Wed. Nov 17th 1915	Section moved to new billets at CAMPAIGNETTE.	
Thurs Nov 18.19.15	Section settled into new billets & made horse standings. Usual routine.	
Friday Nov 19. 9.15	L. Corp. Van left to collect horse abandoned by XVI Lancers at LIETTRES.	
Saturday Nov 20.1915	Return of L. Corp Van with horse. A. D.V.S. visited section. Evacuated 2 mules 1st army, 3 horses 3rd Cav Bde. 1 horse 19th Hussars abandoned by that unit. 1 horse 6. Echelon 2nd Car. Bde discharged cured. Sergt. L. Cpl. Jukes promoted Cpl. from 27.10.15 ZCA 39 Cpl. Gold promoted Sergt from 12.11.15; ZC.0.40.	
GRAND. MANILLET.		
Sunday 21 Nov 1915	Section moved billets to Grand Manillet. 1 horse II Lancers destroyed open elbow joint. 1 horse I.Horse sent for evacuation kept back for treatment developed gangrenous pneumonia in dying condition destroyed.	

Army Form C. 2118.

WAR DIARY
or
INTELLIGENCE SUMMARY.
(Erase heading not required.)

Instructions regarding War Diaries and Intelligence Summaries are contained in F.S. Regs., Part II. and the Staff Manual respectively. Title pages will be prepared in manuscript.

NO. 8 MOBILE VETERINARY SECTION

Hour, Date, Place	Summary of Events and Information	Remarks and references to Appendices
SAANR MANILET		
Monday Nov 22. 1915	Arrangement of Exhibit. Usual Routine. 2 wound mules sent to No 9 MVS by order of DA DRVS	
Tuesday Nov 23. 1915	Usual Routine.	
Wednesday Nov 24. 1915	Usual Routine. Pte Tytte awarded 1X days No1 F.P. Pte 498 Turner transferred from No.13 Vety Hospital.	
Thursday Nov 25. 1915	Lieut T.J. Faithfull returned from leave & took over command of section. Three men were transferred to No 10 Base Vety Hos on authority of AVS Records :- Sergt 432 Gold 314 Cpl Hardy, Pte 429 Vann S2 3804 Walker 954 Chanmeur 891 Chaplin 730 Bunsen 2335 Fairhead. To No13 Vety Hospital AVS Records 426 Pte Tytte in charge of Cpl Major M.M.P. The following arrived from No.10 Vety Hos 693 Bmy Hontor W. S2 3665 Corp Wickerton Pte S2.6671 Stiller 324 Fryer S2.4110 Gordon 551 Facey 2004 Floyd 362 Rufus. Admitted 1 suspected strain in la Fancoun	

Army Form C. 2118.

WAR DIARY
or
INTELLIGENCE SUMMARY.
(Erase heading not required.)

Instructions regarding War Diaries and Intelligence Summaries are contained in F.S. Regs., Part II and the Staff Manual respectively. Title pages will be prepared in manuscript.

Hour, Date, Place	Summary of Events and Information	Remarks and references to Appendices
GRAND HAMLET.		
Friday Nov 26 '15	Admitted 1 inspected skin H.A. 2nd Cav Bgn. 1 mule from supply store Transport.	
Saturday Nov 27	Corp Watson placed under instruction in office.	
Sunday Nov 28th '15	Pte 3670 Lucas. 3160 Osborne appointed acting corporal L. Corp on authority of A.D.V.S. Admitted 1 Remount. 1 Inspected skin from chum Col 2nd Car Bgn - 2 horses from D Battery. Church Parade.	
Monday Nov 29 '15	Admitted 1 horse D Battery, 1 11th Bde R.F.A. 1 horse 83rd Battery, 1 87th Battery, 1 horse 85th Battery. A.D.V.S and Cav Bgn visited section.	
Tuesday Nov 30 '15	Admitted 3 horses 7th Lancers, 1 2nd Car F. Amb. 1 HQ 2nd Cav Bgn, 6 No 3 Res Park, 1 IV Hunn. Evacuated 22 including 4 skin cases LUMBRES station. Transferred 1 horse to 2nd Car F Amb. Reinforcements attended a demonstration by Gas expert at Bde HQ.	T.J. Fairleigh R O. M.R.C.V.S.

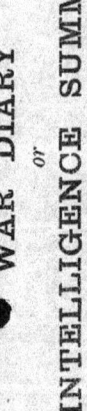

2 Cav

8. Mob. Vet. Sec.
Dec 1915.
vol. XIV

Army Form C. 2118.

WAR DIARY
or
INTELLIGENCE SUMMARY.
(Erase heading not required.)

Instructions regarding War Diaries and Intelligence Summaries are contained in F. S. Regs., Part II. and the Staff Manual respectively. Title pages will be prepared in manuscript.

Hour, Date, Place	Summary of Events and Information	Remarks and references to Appendices
General MANILLET		
Wednesday Dec 1st 1915	Admitted 84th Batt R.F.A. 2 horses. II Hussars 1. 40 Div Cyc Cps 1. Kit inspection. Sanitation inspection.	
Thursday Dec 2nd	Sergt Bradley & Liff on leave to England. 1 Horse transferred to No 3 Remount Park ESQUERDES. Rifle instruction for reinforcements	
Friday Dec 3rd	Usual Routine	
Saturday Dec 4th	Ditto. O.C. + four men attended at rail head to meet Remount train.	
Sunday Dec 5th	1 Horse R.F.A. attacked in float from WIZERNES.	
Monday Dec 6th	Admittances 3 horses + 1 Mule from QE 2nd Can Div 1 horse returned to XIII Division. Rifle Instruction.	
Tuesday Dec 7th	Admitted 4 XIII Tancers 3 II Lancers 7 R. Hussars 1 H.A. + S.C. 2nd Can Div. Inoculated to No 13 Hors Hcses. 20 Mules 2.	
Wednesday Dec 8th	1 Mule returned to Army Horse Transport 2nd Can Div. Foot Drill	

Army Form C. 2118.

WAR DIARY
or
INTELLIGENCE SUMMARY.
(Erase heading not required.)

Instructions regarding War Diaries and Intelligence Summaries are contained in F.S. Regs., Part II. and the Staff Manual respectively. Title pages will be prepared in manuscript.

Hour, Date, Place	Summary of Events and Information	Remarks and references to Appendices
GRAND MANILLET		
Thursday Dec 9th	Serg Bradley. S. returned from leave Rifle drill for reinforcements.	
Friday Dec 10th	Usual Routine	
Sat + Sun 11th & 12th	ditto	
Monday Dec 13th	4.98 Pte Turner went on leave to England. O.C. visited NEUFCHATEL to see demonstration of Mallein testing for Drill.	
Tuesday Dec 14th	Admitted 1 horse HQ 2nd Cav Bri "2", 1 2nd Cav Field Amb 2 mules (Cart) stray from transport Rifle Instruction Action pack Corps for treatment.	
Wednesday Dec 15th	Admitted 4 horses No 7 M.V.S. for evacuation. 1 horse Fig Can	
Thursday Dec 16th	Admitted I Lancers & XIII Lancers 1 Aus H. T. 3 HQ 2nd Cav Bde 1. HQ 2nd Cav Bre 2. III Hussar 1. Evacuated to No 13 V. Hos. 18 horses + 4 mules nick + 2 mules cast	
Friday Dec 17th	1 horse returned to 10th Lancers	

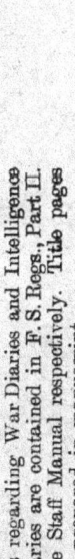

Army Form C. 2118.

WAR DIARY
or
INTELLIGENCE SUMMARY.
(Erase heading not required.)

Hour, Date, Place	Summary of Events and Information	Remarks and references to Appendices
Grand MANILLET Sat Dec 18/915 Sun Dec 19th	S/Sgt. Ph. Tryon left on leave to England. 1 horse issued to O.V.C. HQ 2nd Car from on authority of DADV Cav Corps.	
Mon Dec 20th	Party attended at HQ II Hussars transit with mallenveuz the regiment. 609 horses + mules mallenveuz. Pt. 3670 Freneay left on 7 days special leave to Paris on authority of S.O. commanding 3rd Car Bde. Ph. Turnschurhed from leave.	
Tuesday Dec 21st	67 horses of HQ 3rd Cav Bde & Sig Troops mallenveuz.	
Wednesday Dec 22	Admitted 1 horse. No 3 Reserve Park 4th II Hussars for resting.	
Thursday Dec 23	OTSVS 2nd Car Bde inspected horses of the section & approved of their condition.	
Friday Dec 24th	4 horses returned to II Hussars. 1 horse II Hussars received. Ph Tryon returned from leave. Ph. Wyckmoff & Driver Knisack staff awarded 8 days FP No 2 for absence from roll call 7:45 am. Ph. Tracy admonished.	

WAR DIARY or INTELLIGENCE SUMMARY

Army Form C. 2118.

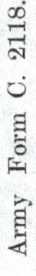

Hour, Date, Place	Summary of Events and Information	Remarks and references to Appendices
GRAND MANILLES	1 horse (sprained) IZ & Zz admitted to treatment	
Sat Dec 25th	Annual Routine. Mr. Evans returned from leave	
Sun Dec 26th	2.00 p.m. Capt Hegh left on leave to England.	
Mon Dec 27th	Admitted 2 horses 1 Ct. Zouaves 1 horse mule 6 IZ Hussars Foot drill for section	
Tuesday Dec 28th	1 horse returned to Amm. Col. Admitted 1 horse Amm. Col. 1 mule Sup horse Trans 2 horses Zouaves (skin?) Smythe helmet parade 1 horse returning from Amm Col. saddle step.	
Wednesday Dec 29th	491 SS Boudet despatched to No 12 V.H. 6891 SS Bouchard arrived from No 12. Admitted 2 mules sup horse transport 2 horses Zouaves Evacuated 3 horses 13 mules to No 13 V.H. including 1 prophic mange.	
Friday Dec 31st	Rifle Instruction. G.O.C. 2nd Corps Major Gen. L. Vaughan visited the section.	T. Mulliford L O.C. 8th Mobile Veterinary Section

Officer Commanding,

8 M.V.S

      As War Diaries furnished by Army Veterinary Corps Officers are frequently passed to this Office from D.A.G., 3rd Echelon, for insertion of the Unit to which they refer, it is notified for general information that War Diaries are the Diaries of the Unit and not their own personal Diaries, and should always be marked with the designation of the Unit.

      Original War Diaries should be sent to D.A.G., G.H.Q., 3rd Echelon.

      Duplicate War Diaries should be sent to Officer i/c A.V.C. Records, WOOLWICH.

                            (Sgd) J. FISHER.
                                   Lieut. & Qr.Mr., A.V.C.
                        Officer i/c A.V.C. Base Records.

G.H.Q.
3rd Echelon.
16th October, 1915.

8 Modèle Nuly Lee 2C
Jan 1916
Vol XV

Army Form C. 2118.

WAR DIARY
or
INTELLIGENCE SUMMARY.
(Erase heading not required.)

Instructions regarding War Diaries and Intelligence Summaries are contained in F.S. Regs., Part II. and the Staff Manual respectively. Title pages will be prepared in manuscript.

Hour, Date, Place	Summary of Events and Information	Remarks and references to Appendices
G.D. MANIHETZ		
Sat Jan 1st 1916	Wallowing party to WILLIAMETZ to unload 100 lorries 2nd Field Squadron R.E. Party to meet remount train at rail head. 6 Scots Greys taken to rations for the night	
Sun Jan 2nd	6 horses Scots Greys collected by regiment. Admitted 5 II Lancers & XVI Lancers. 1 drum Col 2nd Car Bde & R.Q. Fraser & M. Retrop sent to VIZERNES to take charge of horses of 2nd & 3rd Bde except horses R.F.A.	
Monday Jan 3rd	1 horse issued to Field Squadron R.E. on authority of DDVR Car Corps. 1 horse returned to II Lancers. Admitted 1 horse & 1 mule Staff Car Col 2nd Car Bde. 1 horse to Field Squadron R.E.	
Tuesday Jan 4th	2 horses & 1 mule (1 S of W off Fan Car Bde R & H) evacuated to the base	
Wednesday Jan 5th	2 horses mm admitted I Lancers. Riding School for reinforcements	
Thursday Jan 6th	Foot drill	
Friday Jan 7th	Admitted 2 horses No 3 Reserve Park horse (remount) sent G.H.D.G.	

Army Form C. 2118.

WAR DIARY
or
INTELLIGENCE SUMMARY.
(Erase heading not required.)

Instructions regarding War Diaries and Intelligence Summaries are contained in F.S. Regs., Part II. and the Staff Manual respectively. Title pages will be prepared in manuscript.

Hour, Date, Place	Summary of Events and Information	Remarks and references to Appendices
G.D. MAMILLET. Saturday Jan 9th 1916	13 horses evacuated to the base. 6 horses 2nd Reserve Park received at station. Party met remount train & distributed 3rd Brigade horses & units. Authority received for transfer of Pte Smith 14th Hussars to H.Q. new number 1056.	
Sunday Jan 9th	Usual routine	
Monday Jan 10th	horses inspected range (musketry) obtained from IV Hussars	
Tuesday Jan 11th	Shade helmet parade	
Wednesday Jan 12th	Admitted 1 horse XII Hussars 2 strain cl 2nd Cav Bde	
Thursday Jan 13th	719 Pte Crafton despatched for duty with dismounted division.	
Friday Jan 14th	Admitted 2 horse Prospere range IV Hussars 1 skin car XII Hussars.	
Saturday Jan 15th	1 horse returned & Schola 2nd Cav Bde 1 horse received 2nd Reserve Park H.S.C.	
Sunday 16th Mon 17th Tuesday 18	Usual Routine	
Wednesday Jan 19th	admitted 16 horses II Hussars 1 horse XII Hussars 2 No 3 Reserve Park evacuated base V.H. (Storm.)	

Army Form C. 2118.

WAR DIARY
or
INTELLIGENCE SUMMARY.
(Erase heading not required.)

Instructions regarding War Diaries and Intelligence Summaries are contained in F.S. Regs., Part II. and the Staff Manual respectively. Title pages will be prepared in manuscript.

Hour, Date, Place	Summary of Events and Information	Remarks and references to Appendices
G.P. MAILLET		
Thursday Jan 20th 1916	2665 Pte Woodruff & 2474 Pte Beecham days leave of absence to England. 1 horse for treatment admitted "B" Echelon 2nd Cav Bde.	
Friday Jan 21st	1156 Pte Smith granted 7 days leave on urgent private affairs. Few nights pony destroyed admitted horse from No 3 Kavan, Park H.S.C.	
Saturday Jan 22nd	Admitted 1 horse H.Q. 3rd Cav Bde.	
Sunday Jan 23rd		
Tuesday Jan 25th	More III Horses. 1 horse returned to France. 1 horse to XVI Lancers. Admitted 1 horse 2nd Cav & Amb. 1 horse small France 1 charger H.Q. 3rd Cav Bde destroyed fractured pastern.	
Wed Jan 26th	Pte Woodruff returned from leave.	
Thursday Jan 27th	Pte Beecham returned from leave going sickness appear too delay. Medical report enforced this.	
Friday Jan 28th	Admitted 1 horse suffering skin from 2450 Pte Floggitt proceeded on leave to England 1 horse returned to Echelon "B" 2nd Cav Bde	

WAR DIARY
or
INTELLIGENCE SUMMARY.
(Erase heading not required.)

Army Form C. 2118.

Instructions regarding War Diaries and Intelligence Summaries are contained in F.S. Regs., Part II. and the Staff Manual respectively. Title pages will be prepared in manuscript.

Hour, Date, Place	Summary of Events and Information	Remarks and references to Appendices
Camp MAUREPAS		
Saturday Jan 29th	Party attended at rail head to meet remount train.	
Sunday Jan 30th	Usual routine.	
Monday Jan 31st	3 2nd Lieutenants dispatched to demounted Bde to relieve 2nd Lt Crompton detailed for course at No 22 Base V.H. Admitted 2 horses from 2nd Signal Squadron	

T.P. Faulkhul Capt & Adjt

Army Form C. 2118.

WAR DIARY
or
INTELLIGENCE SUMMARY.
(Erase heading not required.)

Instructions regarding War Diaries and Intelligence Summaries are contained in F.S. Regs., Part II. and the Staff Manual respectively. Title pages will be prepared in manuscript.

Hour, Date, Place	Summary of Events and Information	Remarks and references to Appendices
GRAND MANIELET January Feb 1. 1916	Pte 2474 Buchan transferred to 1/1/09 M.V.S. Admitted 1 horse 2nd Lancers.	
Wednesday Feb 2	Pte Crompton reported from Dismounted Brigade	
Thursday Feb 3rd	714 Pte Crofton dispatched for course of instruction in shoeing at No 22 Hospital. Pte Claggett returned from leave. 6 sick + 1 cast horse evacuated to Base. 2 horses returned to 2nd Life Squadron.	
Friday Feb 4th	3484 Pte Crocker left on leave England. 1 horse 34 Bde R.F.A. attached for the 1st Army 1 horse admitted from 17th Lancers (skin)	
Saturday Feb 5th	Admitted 1 horse B' Echelon 2nd Cav Bde.	
Sunday Feb 6th	1 horse admitted from 3rd Recon Regt (Prophit charge)	
Thursday Feb 10th	Admitted 5 horses XII Lancers 1st Lancers 2 IV Horse Evacuated to Base 14 horses. Sgt 2450 Pte Claggett R.H. awarded extra guard + cost of new cap for destroying same. 3E & 9B Turning + awarded pm of 2nd value for exp + leaving room by neglect.	

WAR DIARY
or
INTELLIGENCE SUMMARY.
(Erase heading not required.)

Army Form C. 2118.

Hour, Date, Place	Summary of Events and Information	Remarks and references to Appendices
Grand MANILLET		
Friday Feb 13th	At Crocker returned from leave	
Saturday Feb 14th	Admitted 1 horse (shein) IV Hussars	
	33 I/S 313 Pte West proceeded on leave to England	
	Parts under Sergt Bradley to WIZERNES to meet	
	Remount train	
Sunday Feb 15th	Usual Routine	
Tuesday Feb 15th	4 Skin cases evacuated to Base	
Wednesday Feb 18th	324 Pte Tryer returned with dismounted Brigade	
Thursday Feb 19th	admitted 1 horse IV 9 Lancers. 1 XII Lancers	
Friday Feb 20th	693 Sergt Houston granted leave of absence to	
	Ireland (5 days)	
Monday Feb 22nd	1 horse (Strangles) returned to Major Gen Vaughan	
	3rd Cav Div	

Army Form C. 2118.

WAR DIARY
or
INTELLIGENCE SUMMARY.
(Erase heading not required.)

Instructions regarding War Diaries and Intelligence Summaries are contained in F.S. Regs., Part II. and the Staff Manual respectively. Title pages will be prepared in manuscript.

Hour, Date, Place	Summary of Events and Information	Remarks and references to Appendices
GRAND MANNIL		
Tuesday Feb 22	Admitted II"K"Lancers 6. XII Lancers & III Hussars & evacuated 15 to No 13 Gen Vety Hospital.	
Wednesday Feb 23rd	Football & usual Routine	
Thursday Feb 24th	1. TB horse sent to No1 Reserve Park DESIRES on authority STSR Cav Corps. 2 horses II Lancers evacuated France by No 9 M/S. Admitty 1 horse 9th Feb Bat + 1 III Hussars (Skin). Usual Routine	
Friday Feb 25th	Admitted 1 horse attan E2 and another. Admitted 1 horse HQ 2nd Cav Bde	
Saturday Feb 26th		
Monday Feb 28th	Admitted 7 cart + 2 rid horses HQ Cav Corps 1 "D" Battery.	
Tuesday Feb 29th	Admitted 1 horse 2nd Cav Field Ambulance III Hussars	

T.P. Faulkner
Capt & VO
i/c No 8 M.V.S.

WAR DIARY or INTELLIGENCE SUMMARY.

(Erase heading not required.)

Army Form C. 2118.

Hour, Date, Place	Summary of Events and Information	Remarks and references to Appendices
9 AM D MANILLET Wed March 1st 1916	433 Sergt Bradley W.G. dispatched to Headquarters 2nd Army Regiment 4th Division for one months attachment before proceeding to Cadets School. Authority A.G. Staff #/11124 Can Corps 4007 2nd Can Div. R.L. 655-2. Admitted 4 horses 2nd 7 Squadron R.E. 9 5th Hussars 5 18th Hussars 1 mule Div #1 2nd Canadian 2 horses D Battery. Evacuated to Base 27 horses 1 mule & 43 horses each 1 horse transferred to 2nd Canadian.	
Thursday March 2nd	Admitted 2 ponies (fit) from 4th Fusiliers under instruction S.A.R. H.B. 3rd Cav Bde. 1 horse. Pt Smith evacuated to No 22 Casualty Clearing Station.	
Saturday March 4th	Admitted 1 pony from No 7 M.V.S.	
Sunday March 5th	Admitted 4th Hussars 3. #62 3rd Cav Bde 1 (East) Anvum Col 2nd Can Div 6 cast 1 pony movement 2 sick (riding) 5th Lancers 5 Hd. Car Brig. 1 Chargen Gen Bingham. Evacuated to Base 1 mule & 7 cast	
Wednesday March 8th	Admitted 1 horse (chain) D Battery, 1 H.B. 3rd Cav Bde.	
Friday March 10th	Admitted 2 30th Machine Gun Squadron. 1 9th February Batt.	
Saturday March 11th	Admitted 1 pony H.Q. 3rd Cav Bde.	

Army Form C. 2118.

WAR DIARY
or
INTELLIGENCE SUMMARY.
(Erase heading not required.)

Instructions regarding War Diaries and Intelligence Summaries are contained in F.S. Regs., Part II. and the Staff Manual respectively. Title pages will be prepared in manuscript.

Hour, Date, Place	Summary of Events and Information	Remarks and references to Appendices
GRAND MANLET	Admitted 1 horse 3rd Mach. Gun Squadron for treatment. 1 9 A.Fd. Bde. M.	
Monday March 12th		
Tuesday March 14th	Admitted 1 mule stray H.T. 1 horse Amm Col. 2nd Car Bde for treatment. 1 staff mare. 2 H.Q. R.A.F. 2nd Bde. 3 2nd Reserve Regt. 1 cow left hynds. Evacuated 13 horses + 1 mule to No. 13 Vety. Hospital.	
Wednesday March 15th	Usual Routine	
Thursday March 16th	Admitted 1 horse H.Q. 2nd Car Bde.	
Friday 17th	Admitted 1 horse H.Q. Car Corps Signals.	
Wednesday March 22"	Admitted 1 horse D Battery RHA for treatment. 1 horse H.Q. 2nd Car Bde (By Gen Bell Smythes Charger)	
Thursday March 23	494 Cpl John R proceeded on 6 days leave to England. Pte B.60 Bradley 755 Fulham Rd. B.091 Whitehead joined the action from No. 13 Vety. Hospital.	
Tuesday March 28th	Admitted 1 horse 3 Mach Gun Squadron.	
Wednesday March 29th	Admitted 2 horses H.Q. 2nd Car Bde. 1 & N Hunter. 2 & Anthony. 1 mule stray H.T. 2450 Pte Stoogart returned Gstrictly at reprimention of 4 2 days S.P.No.1 115th Matthews appointed Wapp acting unpaid Lance Corporal.	7) 7mh Nahfellphitefe
Friday March 31	Usual Routine	

Army Form C. 2118.

WAR DIARY
or
INTELLIGENCE SUMMARY.
(Erase heading not required.)

Hour, Date, Place	Summary of Events and Information	Remarks and references to Appendices
GRAND MANILLET.		
Saturday April 1st 1916	Corp. Waterton proceeded England on 6 day leave.	
Sunday April 2nd	Smoke Helmet drill. Usual Routine.	
Monday April 3rd	Attended 1 horse 10th Lancers. Foot drill.	
Tuesday April 4th	— 1 horse 2nd Mac Gun Squadron.	
Wednesday April 5th	Admitted 1 mule, stores H.Q., 3 horses Amm. Col. 2nd Cavstri 2 & 2nd Field Squadron R.E., 3 3rd Reserve Park, 2 Can Corps Signals (1 sick & 1 cast) 1 & 2nd Car Field Ambulance. Evacuated 10 mules & 1 cavell to No. 13 V.H.	
Thursday April 6th	Riding School with jumping. Admitted 8 Standards 2 10th Lancers.	
Friday April 7th	7.19 Pte Crompton returned from Course of instruction in shoeing at No 22 V.H. Evacuated 9 horses (skin) to base.	
Saturday April 8th	Admitted 1 horse from Cyclist Squadron 2nd Army 1 2nd Mac Gun Squadron. 1 H.Q. 2nd Cav Bde. Pte Retor left on 6 days leave. Riding School.	

WAR DIARY or INTELLIGENCE SUMMARY.

Army Form C. 2118.

(Erase heading not required.)

Instructions regarding War Diaries and Intelligence Summaries are contained in F.S. Regs., Part II. and the Staff Manual respectively. Title pages will be prepared in manuscript.

NO. 8 MOBILE VETERINARY SECTION

Hour, Date, Place	Summary of Events and Information	Remarks and references to Appendices
GRAND MANILLET Sunday April 9th 1916	Usual Routine.	
Monday April 10th 1916	Admitted 1 horse (skin) 2nd Trench Gun Squadron. 1 Robuller 3rd Cavcbde. Mounted Drill + Riding School.	
Tuesday April 11th 1916	Admitted 4 horses 3rd Mac Gun Squad. 1 horse returned HQ 3rd Cavbde.	
Wednesday April 12th 1916	Admitted 2 horses D Battery. 4 Lancers 3. 16th Lancers 1. 2nd Mac G. Squad. Evacuated three 18 horses. Admitted Nash ponies 2nd Hussars 3. 12 Lancers 1. XX Hussars 2.	
Thursday April 13th 1916	3009 Pte Whitehead left on 6 days leave England. Admitted 1 horse Sig HQ. 3rd Cav Bde. 1 Prophylic case Anum of 2nd Cav for destruction. News received that all leave is cancelled & men to return by the 18th. Admitted 2 Pack ponies 5th Lancers. 1 16 Lancers. 73/1030341 Kimach R.W. evacuated to the base. No 2.2. Cav Cl. Hosp.	
Friday April 14th	8 Pack horses evacuated by road to Boulogne under Corp Pires.	

Army Form C. 2118.

WAR DIARY
or
INTELLIGENCE SUMMARY.
(Erase heading not required.)

Instructions regarding War Diaries and Intelligence Summaries are contained in F.S. Regs., Part II. and the Staff Manual respectively. Title pages will be prepared in manuscript.

Hour, Date, Place	Summary of Events and Information	Remarks and references to Appendices
GRAND MANILLET.		
Saturday April 15 1916	5 horses (mares) admitted Army Col 2nd Cav Bre. Shoeing behind drill.	
Sunday April 16 1916	Admitted 1 horse H.Q. 3rd Cav Bde 7/33,640 Archer McCabe. I perused the sections from H.Q. 3rd Cav Bde	
Monday April 17	Riding School. Admitted 1 horse 4th Hussars 1.S. Anthony, 2 Arm Col, 1 Rue Green Sqnd. 1st Fusiliers 2 men horses # 7.	
Tuesday April 18	Evacuated 12 horses + 2 mules to Base No 13 1/4. Two remount trains were met by a party at WIZERNES.	
Wednesday April 19th	Usual Routine. Mounted drill.	
Thursday April 20th	------	
Saturday April 22nd	Admitted 2 horses 4th Hussars. I went to A.V.M.P on authority. 77/11 Capt got cast bil.	
Monday April 24th	Admitted 1 charger remount HQ 3rd Cav Bde.	
Thursday April 27th	Admitted 4th Hussars 5, 5th Fusiliers 2, 1st Fusiliers 3, 2nd Cav Field Amb 1.	

WAR DIARY or INTELLIGENCE SUMMARY.

Army Form C. 2118.

(Erase heading not required.)

Instructions regarding War Diaries and Intelligence Summaries are contained in F.S. Regs., Part II and the Staff Manual respectively. Title pages will be prepared in manuscript.

Hour, Date, Place	Summary of Events and Information	Remarks and references to Appendices
GRAND MANILLET 1916.		
Wednesday April 26th	14 horses evacuated to No. 9 Base V.H.	
Thursday April 27th	Admitted 2 cases shoein. D Battery R.H.A. Smoke helmet drill.	
Friday April 28th	Admitted 2 mules were H.T. Shows 175 Bde R.F.A. Still mounted.	

N Faithfull Capt RAVC

WAR DIARY or INTELLIGENCE SUMMARY

Army Form C. 2118.

8 Mot. Vety Sec

Vol 20

Hour, Date, Place	Summary of Events and Information	Remarks and references to Appendices
RECQUEBREQ SUIRE WIRQUIN		
Thursday June 1st 1916	1 Mule destroyed. 34 Div stvun Col.	
Friday June 2nd 1916	Admitted 16th Lancers 1 case (farcy).	
Saturday June 3rd 1916	Admitted 1st Lancers 2. Collected Horse (16th Lancer Park) CAMPAGNE LES BOULOGNAS. Destroyed 1 mule. Rifle Drill.	
Sunday June 4th 1916	Evacuated to base 5 skin cases.	
Monday June 5th 1916	Usual Routine.	
Tuesday June 6th 1916	Admitted Yorkshire Dragoons 2. Struma Col 6. 3 h. G Sq 3. Wilts Yeomanry 3. R.H.A. H.Q. 1. 5th Lancers 2. 16th Lancers 3. 4th Hussars 1. 2nd F.S. R.F. 3. 2nd Cav Fotmnd 1. HO+SC 2.	
Wednesday June 7th 1916	Evacuated to base 28 horses. Admitted 5th Lancers 2 suspicious skin case.	

Army Form C. 2118.

WAR DIARY
or
INTELLIGENCE SUMMARY.
(Erase heading not required.)

Instructions regarding War Diaries and Intelligence Summaries are contained in F. S. Regs., Part II. and the Staff Manual respectively. Title pages will be prepared in manuscript.

Hour, Date, Place	Summary of Events and Information	Remarks and references to Appendices

RECQUE BREUCQ

Thursday June 8. '16 — Usual Routine.

Friday June 9 '16 — Admitted Yorkshire Dragoon 1 H.A.

Saturday June 10 1916 — Admitted 1 horse & saddle from 4 P.M. 2nd Can Div Yorkshire Dragoons 3 Cast. Rifle work

Sunday June 11 1916 — Returned to duty H.T. 2 Mules. Admitted 1 horse collected from 3 4th Div. 160 Bde. "Party not removed team".

Monday June 12.1916 — Admitted Yorkshire Dragoons 2. 4th Hussars 1 for resmol [?]

Tuesday June 13. 1916 — Admitted 16th Lancers 8 Cast. 5th Lancers 13. 4th Hussars 8. 3 M.G. Sqdn 9 all cast.

Wednesday Thursday June 14 1916 — Admitted 1 Cast (Filly) 2nd Cav Div Reserve Park. 16th Lancers 1 (Sham) Evacuated 43 Cast to Abbeville

Army Form C. 2118.

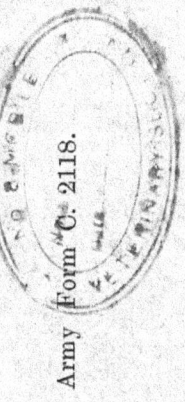

WAR DIARY
or
INTELLIGENCE SUMMARY.
(Erase heading not required.)

Instructions regarding War Diaries and Intelligence Summaries are contained in F.S. Regs., Part II. and the Staff Manual respectively. Title pages will be prepared in manuscript.

Hour, Date, Place	Summary of Events and Information	Remarks and references to Appendices
ROQUEBRECQ		
Thursday June 15.1916	Returned to Wilts Yeomanry 1 horse. Admitted ... 1 ... 1 ... Evacuated 5 men by road to No 23 KH ST OMER.	
Friday June 16.1916	755 Pte Latham left on 6 days leave.	
Saturday June 17.1916	1 boy taken on strength on section on authority of AA #R	
Sunday June 18.1916	1 horse returned to Q.O. Yorkshire Dragoons. 1 ... to Amm Col. 2nd Cav Div. Admitted "D" Battery RHA 1. Q.O. Yorkshire Drag 2. HQ. 2nd Cav Bde 1 charger (#B Nutting) Pte hitched sent to No 10 Stationary Hospital.	
Monday June 19.1916	Admitted Amm Col 4. 2nd F.S.R.E. 1. D Battery 1. 4th Hussars 1. Transferred 2 F.D. to Amm Col 2nd Cav Div without DADR wire. Evacuated to NEUFCHATEL 2. ST OMER beyond 10. Section moved billets at 7.30 pm taking position in column of Sqns	

Army Form C. 2118.

WAR DIARY
or
INTELLIGENCE SUMMARY.
(Erase heading not required.)

Instructions regarding War Diaries and Intelligence Summaries are contained in F.S. Regs., Part II. and the Staff Manual respectively. Title pages will be prepared in manuscript.

Hour, Date, Place	Summary of Events and Information	Remarks and references to Appendices
STRAZEELE Tuesday June 20. 1916	Section travelling via HAZEBROUCK arrived in new billet at 3.30 am. Admitted H.Q. 3rd Cav Bde 1 charger.	
Wednesday June 21. 1916	Admitted H.Q. 2nd Cav Bde 1 Pack Pony, 6 D.G. 1 & H.Farmers 9	
Thursday June 22. 1916	Admitted 16th Lancers 4. 5th Lancers 5. Evacuated to St OMER by Road 19.	
Friday June 23. 1916	1 car 6 D.G. transferred to 209 M.V.S.	
Saturday June 24. 1916	Admitted 4th Hussars 1. 10th Hussars 1.	
Sunday June 25. 1916	Admitted 5th Lancers 4. 18th Lancers 1. 3rd M.G. Squad 2. H.Q. 2nd Cav Div 1. Evacuated by road to St OMER 8.	
Monday June 26. 1916	Admitted from Col 2nd Cav Div 3, Returned H.Q. 3rd Cav Bde 1 Charger.	

Army Form C. 2118.

WAR DIARY
or
INTELLIGENCE SUMMARY.
(Erase heading not required.)

Instructions regarding War Diaries and Intelligence Summaries are contained in F.S. Regs., Part II. and the Staff Manual respectively. Title pages will be prepared in manuscript.

Hour, Date, Place	Summary of Events and Information	Remarks and references to Appendices
STRAZEELE		
Tuesday June 27th 1916	Admitted J. Battery 1. strain Cl 1. 2nd Dig Troops 1. 1 Remount taken on strength Questn. Party met remount train Evacuated to No 23 VH. STOMER by road 10.	
Wednesday June 28 1916	Rifle drill.	
Thursday June 29 1916	Usual Routine	
Friday June 30 1916	Admitted strain Cl 2. 1 R/Lancers 2. 4th Hussars 1. S.S. 653 Pk Draft joined section from No 4 V.H.	

T. Tulloch Capt AVC

Vol 21

CONFIDENTIAL.

WAR DIARY

of

8th Mobile Veterinary Section - 2nd Cav. Div.

from 1st July.   to 31st July. 1916.

(Volume ~~XXIII~~).

Army Form C. 2118.

WAR DIARY

INTELLIGENCE SUMMARY.
(Erase heading not required.)

Instructions regarding War Diaries and Intelligence Summaries are contained in F.S. Regs., Part II. and the Staff Manual respectively. Title pages will be prepared in manuscript.

NO 8 MOBILE VETERINARY SECTION

Hour, Date, Place	Summary of Events and Information	Remarks and references to Appendices
STRAZEELE		
Saturday July 1st 1916	Admitted 2nd Sig Squadron 1. SS 881 Pte Whitehead returned to duty from ST OMER. Foot + Rifle drill.	
Sunday July 2 1916	Admitted 5th Inn Cldn Bde Div 1. 4th Hussars 1. SS 557 Pte Facey sent to No 2 Vety Hos HAVRE.	
Monday July 3 1916	Admitted 4-2 Batt 7 Bde A Amm Col 1. 2nd Cav Div 2. 2nd Sq R.E. 1.	
Tuesday July 4 1916	Admitted 16th Lancers 1. 3 A.S. Squad 1. Charger Lieut Setchell evacuated to No 23 V.H. ST OMER. 21.	
Wednesday July 5 1916	Admitted 1 Charger Major Tyrrell + 1 R. 5th Lancers. Rifle drill.	
Thursday July 6 1916	Admitted F.R. Section gorstrung Sick 2 Cont 1.	
Friday July 7 1916	Admitted J Battery 2. 2nd Sq R.E. 1. Party mounted train 11 am.	
WALLON CAPEL		
Saturday July 8 1916	Section moved to new billets at 3 pm	
Sunday July 9 1916	Usual Routine.	

WAR DIARY or INTELLIGENCE SUMMARY.

Army Form C. 2118.

Hour, Date, Place	Summary of Events and Information	Remarks and references to Appendices
WALLON CAPEL		
Monday July 10th 1916	Admitted 2nd F. Sq R.E. 3. 2nd Sig Squadron 1 Cort. R.H.Q. 3rd Cav Bde 1 3rd M.G. Squadron 1. Army Col 1. 5 Lancers 1. J Battery 1. 2nd Sig Troop 1. H.Q. 3rd Cav Bde 1 Changes (Lieut T.J.W. Clark XII Lancers).	
Tuesday July 11th	Admitted 1 Aircraft Out Details 1 (Skin). Evacuated to No 23 V.H. ST OMER 19. It was possible on this day for the evacuating party to return the same day without calling at Rest Station.	
Wednesday July 12th	Admitted 5th Lancers 1. H.Q. 3rd Cav Bde 1. Smoke Helmet Drill.	
Thursday July 13th	Admitted 2nd F. Sg R.E.1.	
Friday July 14th	Admitted 39th Bat R.F.A. 1 (Cont) 2 other cast road 4 SDR 2nd Army 16th Lancers 1. 3rd Sig Troop 1.	
Saturday July 15th	Evacuated to No 23 V.H. Et OMER. 6 inch + 3 Cast. Section moved billets at 9.15 am to MERRIS.	

WAR DIARY
or
INTELLIGENCE SUMMARY.

(Erase heading not required.)

Army Form C. 2118.

Hour, Date, Place	Summary of Events and Information	Remarks and references to Appendices
MERRIS Sunday July 16. 1916	Party collected two horses left by No 2 A.M.V.S. at St MARIE CAPEL 6 left by No 5 A.M.V.S. at LES CISEAUX par BLARINGHEM + 3 left by 5th Cavalry Division at BLARINGHEM. Four of these horses were short of one or more shoes. Dispatched horses on collected to Rest station EBBLINGHEM returned to MERRIS + dispatched shoeing smith with shoes. Total mileage for day 35. Admitted 3 rd the Guns Sq. 1.	
Monday July 17. 1916	Admitted 1st ANZAC Details 4. Field Rem Sect. 2nd Army 3. S/Sgt Compton examined by Board at HQ for appointment as S/Smith.	
Tuesday July 18. 1916	Collected from SEC BOIS one horse left by 4th Hussars. Admitted 4th Hussars 1. Dismounts still.	
Wednesday July 19. 1916	Collected 2 horses left by at Amm Col at FLETRE. Admitted 4th Hussars 5. 5th Lancers 1.	
Thursday July 20. 1916	Admitted 16th Lancers 1 Sarcocele 16 stones × 1 mule.	
Friday July 21.	Usual Routine.	

Army Form C. 2118.

WAR DIARY
or
INTELLIGENCE SUMMARY.
(Erase heading not required.)

Instructions regarding War Diaries and Intelligence Summaries are contained in F.S. Regs., Part II and the Staff Manual respectively. Title pages will be prepared in manuscript.

Hour, Date, Place	Summary of Events and Information	Remarks and references to Appendices
MERRIS Saturday July 22	Admitted 16th Lancers 1. 3rd Mac Gun Sqd 1. 5th Lancers 3. Collected 2 H.D. from ROUGE CROIX (PRADELLES) 4 horses shot shot for Army Col in billet at ST SYLVESTRE 1 horse 6 Bde R.F.A. ST SYLVESTRE. CAPEL CAPEL or ECKE	
Sunday July 23	Evacuated 1 E.D. to F.R. Sect 2nd Army. Admitted F. R. Section 1. Just received train with usual party of 6 men + 1 N.C.O. Enquiry has been raised by 2nd'vs 2nd Army whether M.V.S. can be used for their work. Am of opinion that Staff can use M.V.S. as they work as long as Vety work not interfered with.	
Monday July 24 1916	Admitted 18th Lancers 2 (1 Rein) 3rd Bde H.Q 1. Evacuated 15 to No 23 V.H. including 1 Charger	
Tuesday July 25 1916	Usual Routine. Destroyed 1. IV Hussar. Lieut Inglis v. Homer?	
Wednesday July 26. 1916	Collected 2 horses from M. DEBOUT at SYLVESTRE CAPEL 2 " from M. GROS ON ditto 1 " " MINNEQ HONDENGHEM. Admitted "B" Echelon 2nd Cav Bde 1. 16th Lancers 1.	

WAR DIARY or INTELLIGENCE SUMMARY.

(Erase heading not required.)

Army Form C. 2118.

Hour, Date, Place	Summary of Events and Information	Remarks and references to Appendices
MERRIS.		
Thursday July 27th 1916	Admitted 5th Lancers 3.	
Friday July 28th 1916	Admitted 3rd Sig Troop 1 18th Lancers 2 2nd Cav L. Amb 1.	
Saturday July 29th	Transferred to L Rem Section 3 pit I.D.s Admitted L Rem Section 6 18th Lancers 2 (Skins) Pte Tozer wounded 6 days F.P. No 2 not cropping.	
Sunday July 30th	Collected 1 horse M. MARTENS, CAESTRE. 1 ... HUGHES Admitted L.R. Section 3.	
Monday July 31st.	Evacuated to No 23 V.H. ST OMER 14 horses Admitted 4th Hussars 4.	

T.J Faulkner Captain
OC No 8 M.V.S.

CONFIDENTIAL.

WAR   DIARY   OF

8th MOBILE VETY. SECTION

for August, 1916.

VOL ~~XXIV~~

Army Form C. 2118.

WAR DIARY
or
INTELLIGENCE SUMMARY.
(Erase heading not required.)

Instructions regarding War Diaries and Intelligence Summaries are contained in F.S. Regs., Part II and the Staff Manual respectively. Title pages will be prepared in manuscript.

Hour, Date, Place	Summary of Events and Information	Remarks and references to Appendices
MERRIS		
Tuesday August 1. 1916	Admitted 5th Lancers 1.	
Wednesday August 2. 1916	2 am notice of possible arrival of gas shell precautions taken. Collected 1 horse left by 2nd Division at Andover BASSART DELAVAL; STEENJE Commune of BAILLEUL. 1 horse left by Oxford Hussars at "M. DELAREL DE LIESSCHE; DOULIED. Admitted 3rd R.G. Squadron 2. Transferred to 7. Run section II Army I.Z.D.	
Thursday August 3 1916.	Usual Routine.	
Friday August 4.	Saddlery inspection.	
Saturday August 5.	Party met removal train 11am shorn from Col tehnl to Section until collected.	
Sunday August 6.	Admitted 5th Lancers 1. & kerosene oil collected by unit. ADVS visited section. Pte Matthews admonished for absence from roll call.	
Monday August 7	10 horses evacuated to No 23 V.H. by road. 2 Cars returned to Field Remount Section II Army. A-D.g.S + T complemented section on turnout of horses sent to Station for supplies.	

Army Form C. 2118.

WAR DIARY
or
INTELLIGENCE SUMMARY.
(Erase heading not required.)

Instructions regarding War Diaries and Intelligence Summaries are contained in F. S. Regs., Part II. and the Staff Manual respectively. Title pages will be prepared in manuscript.

No. 3 MOBILE VETERINARY SECTION

Hour, Date, Place	Summary of Events and Information	Remarks and references to Appendices
MERRIS		
Tuesday August 8. 1916	Admitted 5th Lancers 2. (Skin)	
Wednesday August 9. 1916	Admitted 16th Lancers 1. 3rd M.S. Squad 1. Smoke helmet drill for all ranks.	
Thursday August 10. 1916	Smoke helmet inspection. Party collected 1 horse from the Northumberland M.V.S. 30th Div. One R.E.O. + one man left to bring in cab. cases. Admitted 8th Lancers 1.	
Friday August 11. 1916	Collected from Northumberland M.V.S. 2 horses sick, 1 horse debil. 1 mule for casting.	
Saturday August 12. 1916	Evacuated to No 23 V.H. 7 horses + 1 mule. Returned to 4th Hussars 1 horse. Kit inspection. 34283 Pte Hall Y.R. joined the section from H.Q 3rd Army	
Sunday August 13. 1916	Destroyed 1 horse 3rd Hussars. P.M revealed Boulay swing ball with cinder centre.	
Monday August 14. 1916	Admitted 5th Lancers 3. 324 Pk Coyr dispatched to No 2. V.H. RODEN.	
Tuesday August 15. 1916	Evacuated 2 horses to same via ESTAIRES.	

Army Form C. 2118.

WAR DIARY
or
INTELLIGENCE SUMMARY.
(Erase heading not required.)

Instructions regarding War Diaries and Intelligence Summaries are contained in F.S. Regs., Part II and the Staff Manual respectively. Title pages will be prepared in manuscript.

Hour, Date, Place	Summary of Events and Information	Remarks and references to Appendices
MERRIS		
Wednesday August 16. 1916	Returned to 4th Hussars 1 horse. Admitted sick 16th Lancers 2. Cast 4th Hussars 1. 5th Lancers 3.	
	16th Lancers 3. 3rd Mac Gun Squadron 7. Collected from M Hours Front FLETRE one mule left by	
Thursday August 17. 1916	Evacuated to No 23 V.H. 14 horses + 1 mule cast 4 horses + 1 mule sick. Admitted for treatment 1 horse 2nd Cav F Amb.	
Friday August 18. 1916	Admitted 5th Lancers 2.	
Saturday August 19. 1916	Rifle drill.	
Sunday August 20. 1916	S² 8891 S.S. Banstead sent to No 23 V.H. St OMER.	
Monday August 21. 1916	Admitted 5th Lancers 3. Taken on strength 1 remount.	
Tuesday August 22. 1916	Evacuated to No 23 V.H. 5 skin cases. Admitted 16th Lancers 1. 5th Lancers 4.	
Wednesday August 23. 1916	Collected 1 Mule left by 50th Divn at OUTERSTEIN.	
Thursday August 24. 1916	Admitted 5th Lancers 2.	
Friday August 25. 1916	Admitted 5th Lancers 1. Drill mounted + riding school.	

WAR DIARY
or
INTELLIGENCE SUMMARY.
(Erase heading not required.)

Army Form  2118.

Instructions regarding War Diaries and Intelligence Summaries are contained in F.S. Regs., Part II. and the Staff Manual respectively. Title pages will be prepared in manuscript.

Hour, Date, Place	Summary of Events and Information	Remarks and references to Appendices
MERRIS Saturday 26 August 1916	Evacuated 10 horses to No 23 V.H. including 3 cases on strength of Section. 1 mule sent to No 2 ¥ Remount Section. 3 horses H.Q. 3rd Can Bde taken temp on strength of section.	
Sunday August 27. 1916 SE.14283	Pte Hall G.R. sent to isolation hospital BAILLEUL.	
Monday August 28 1916	Usual Routine.	
Tuesday August 29 1916 SE 11908	Pte Lucas H. joined the section from No 23 Vety Hos.	
Wednesday August 30 1916	O.C. attended conference at Div H.Q. called to consider the best method of using M.V.S. when cavalry are being employed as cavalry. It was agreed that the only practical method when cavalry are working divisionally is to use the three M.V.S. in echelon. This opinion is to be put before a higher conference to be attended by the D.D.V.S.	
Thursday August 31. 1916	Admitted 5 officers 1 charger (Light Kettle) 16th Lancers 1. A.D.V.S. visited the section.	

T.J. Faithfull
Capt AVC
O.C. 8TH MOBILE VETERINARY SECTION

SECRET.

WAR DIARY

of

NO. 8 MOBILE VETERINARY SECTION

for September, 1916.

VOLUME ~~XXX~~

Army Form C. 2118.

WAR DIARY
INTELLIGENCE SUMMARY
(Erase heading not required.)

Instructions regarding War Diaries and Intelligence Summaries are contained in F.S. Regs., Part II and the Staff Manual respectively. Title pages will be prepared in manuscript.

Hour, Date, Place	Summary of Events and Information	Remarks and references to Appendices
MERRIS Friday Sept 1. 1916	Admitted 3rd line G. Squad 3.	
Saturday Sept 2 1916	Rifle Inspection	
Sunday Sept 3 1916	Usual Routine	
	Evacuated 6 horses from ESTAIRES 1 horse	
	Returned 1 horse to 2nd Cav. & Amb.	
	Admitted 4th Hussars 2. 5th Lancers 2ill 16 Lancers 7.	
	Including changers of Capt Hone Lieut Robertson Lieut Rooney Lieut Brooke.	
Monday Sept 4 1916	Evacuated to the 23 V.H. ST OMER. 12 horses.	
Tuesday Sept 5. 1916	Saddlery Inspection.	
	14823 Pte Hall repaired section from No7 V.H. ST OMER.	
ROBECQ Wednesday Sept 6 1916	Section moved from MERRIS at 9.30 am & moved in rear of column without incident & arrived	
	at ROBECQ arriving 1.30 pm.	
CONTEVILLE Thursday Sept 7 1916	Section marched via LOZINGHAM & CONTEVILLE	
	Admitted 5th Lancers 3. No7 M.V.S. 1.	
WAIL Friday Sept 8 1916	Evacuated 4 horses from St POL	
	Section moved at 9.30 to WAIL arriving about 2 pm	
	Admitted 4 Hussars 3.	

WAR DIARY or INTELLIGENCE SUMMARY

Army Form C. 2118.

Hour, Date, Place	Summary of Events and Information	Remarks and references to Appendices
WAIL Saturday Sept 9. 1916	Usual routine.	
OUTREBOIS Sunday Sept 10. 1916	Section moved at 9.30 am via FILLIERE & WAVAMS to OUTREBOIS. At the former place 3 horses sick were transferred to No 9 M.V.S. for evacuation. Admitted 4 horses 3 16th Lancers 1.	
WARGNIES Monday Sept 11. 1916	Section moved with Brigade from WAIL at 9 am. Collected 1 Bay I.D. Septicaemia belonging to 162 Bd R FA left with M. Derome on Sept 9th. Destroyed & buried.	
BONNAY Tuesday Sept 12. 1916	Section moved with Brigade to BONNAY. On the way received 3 mules from M.M.P. at TALMAS.	
Wednesday Sept 13. 1916	Admitted 5th Lancers 4. 16th Lancers 3. 3rd Horse Guns Squadron 1. charges front Foy of 5th Lancers. Evacuated to No 9 M.V.S. 1 st No 7 Vety Hosp. 12 horses & 3 mules.	
Thursday Sept 14. 1916 SERNANCOURT	Section moved to area occupied by Div. Troop & came under command of O.C. L.S.C. Section joined by No 9 M.V.S.	
Friday Sept 15. 1916	Section moved to area allotted us at SERNANCOURT. 1 horse admitted. O.O.O.H.	

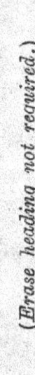

Army Form C. 2118.

WAR DIARY
or
INTELLIGENCE SUMMARY.
(Erase heading not required.)

Instructions regarding War Diaries and Intelligence Summaries are contained in F.S. Regs., Part II and the Staff Manual respectively. Title pages will be prepared in manuscript.

NO. 8 MOBILE VETERINARY SECTION

Hour, Date, Place	Summary of Events and Information	Remarks and references to Appendices
DERNANCOURT		
Saturday Sept 16, 1916	Admitted Anne Col. 2nd Cav Bde 1.	
Sunday Sept 17, 1916	Evacuated 1 horse to No 7 MVS at BONNAY	
Monday Sept 18, 1916	Usual Routine. Orders received to hand 6 at 1 hour notice	
Tuesday Sept 19, 1916	Admitted 1 own E Battery RHA. Evacuated to No 7 at GROVETOWN: without. Officers visited the action.	
Wednesday Sept 20, 1916	Admitted btty. 1. Evacuated 1 G No 7 M.V.S. Rifle + Shoots. Usual inspection.	
Thursday Sept 21, 1916	Admitted J Battery R.H.A. 1. S/2450. Pte Slaggett R.H. despatched to 7th Inf Base Depot Havre on authority S.H.G. C.R. 35240-H. 623 Sergt Brian J. taken on strength from No 9. M.V.S.	
Friday Sept 22, 1916	Admitted 1 from Mobile Supply Column.	
Saturday Sept 23, 1916	Admitted 1 E Battery R.H. 1. Transferred 1 GNo 7 MVS. Officers visited the action.	
Sunday Sept 24, 1916	Admitted Mobile Supply Column 1. Transferred 1 GNo 7 MVS.	
Monday Sept 25, 1916	Admitted "J" Battery 2. HQ 4SC 1. Transferred 3 GNo 7 MVS. Returned 1 Field Supply Col.	

Army Form C. 2118.

WAR DIARY
or
INTELLIGENCE SUMMARY.
(Erase heading not required.)

Instructions regarding War Diaries and Intelligence Summaries are contained in F.S. Regs., Part II. and the Staff Manual respectively. Title pages will be prepared in manuscript.

Hour, Date, Place	Summary of Events and Information	Remarks and references to Appendices
DERNANCOURT Tuesday Sept 26. 1916	Admitted 1, 53 Batt. R.F.A. 4575 rinked action.	
Wednesday Sept 27. 1916	Evacuated 1 to No. 22 M.V.S.	
Thursday Sept 28. 1916	Usual routine	
Friday Sept 29 1916	Admitted 1 from 109 Batt R.F.A. sick.	
Saturday Sept 30 1916	Admitted 3 Battery R.F.A. 1. Party out remount train.	

T.J. Faulkhill
Capt. AVC

O.C. 8TH MOBILE VETERINARY SECTION

SECRET.

WAR DIARY

of

8th MOBILE VETERINARY
SECTION.

OCTOBER, 1916.

VOL. ~~XXVI~~.

Army Form C. 2118.

WAR DIARY
INTELLIGENCE SUMMARY.
(Erase heading not required.)

Instructions regarding War Diaries and Intelligence Summaries are contained in F.S. Regs., Part II and the Staff Manual respectively. Title pages will be prepared in manuscript.

Hour, Date, Place	Summary of Events and Information	Remarks and references to Appendices
DERNANCOURT October 1st 1916.	Admitted 1 charger H.Q. 2nd Cav Div. Party met remount train at HERICOURT 7.65pm Matthews sent away sick.	
Monday Oct 2nd 1916	Usual Routine.	
Tuesday Oct 3rd 1916	Admitted J. Battery R.H.A. 1. ADVS visited the section.	
Wednesday Oct 4th 1916	Admitted 1 from motels Supply Col.	
Thursday Oct 5th 1916	1 charger returned to H.Q. 2nd Cav Div. Admitted 18th Lancers 1. Lt. Matthews returned to duty.	
Friday Oct 6th 1916	Admitted S Battery R.H.A. 3. (chargers) 5th Lancers 5. 18th Lancers 1, 4th Hussars 1. Evacuated 11 through No 9 M.V.S.	
Saturday Oct 7th 1916	Admitted HQ R.H.A. 1	
Sunday Oct 8th 1916	Usual Routine.	
Monday Oct 9th 1916	Admitted 18th Lancers 2, rifle inspection.	
Tuesday Oct 10th 1916	Admitted 4th Hussars 1.	
Wednesday Oct 11th 1916	Admitted B. Echelon 2nd Cav Bde. 1.	

WAR DIARY or **INTELLIGENCE SUMMARY.**
(Erase heading not required.)

Army Form C. 2118.

Instructions regarding War Diaries and Intelligence Summaries are contained in F.S. Regs., Part II and the Staff Manual respectively. Title pages will be prepared in manuscript.

Hour, Date, Place	Summary of Events and Information	Remarks and references to Appendices
DERNANCOURT		
Thursday Oct 12. 1916	Admitted 5th Lancers 2. H.Q. 2nd Cav. Bde. 1 charger (Bd. Gen. Bell-Smyth) 3rd Hussars 1. Oxford Hussars 1. Evacuated 11. to No 9 M.V.S. 9 to No 7 M.V.S. 6.	
Friday Oct 13. 1916	Usual Routine	
Saturday Oct 14. 1916	Saddling Inspection.	
Sunday Oct 15. 1916	Party returned from the base.	
Monday Oct 16. 1916	Admitted 16th Lancers 3. 2 h.S. Glamm 1. 4th Hussars 1. S. Battery R.H.A. 5. 2nd M.G. Squadron 1. 5th Lancers 2. Sick mounted.	
Tuesday Oct 17. 1916	Evacuated 13 through No 7 M.V.S.	
Wednesday Oct 18. 1916	Admitted 16th Lancers 4. 4th Hussars 3. 5th Lancers 2.	
Thursday Oct 19. 1916	Admitted 3rd Signal troop 1.	
Friday Oct 20. 1916	Usual Routine	
Saturday Oct 21. 1916	Admitted 4th Hussars 4. 5th Lancers 6.	
Sunday Oct 22. 1916	Admitted 5th Lancers 3. 4 S.O.S. worked the section.	
Monday Oct 23. 1916	Evacuated 22 through No 9 M.V.S. Admitted M. Supply Col. 1. Returned 1.	

WAR DIARY or **INTELLIGENCE SUMMARY**

Army Form C. 2118.

(Erase heading not required.)

Instructions regarding War Diaries and Intelligence Summaries are contained in F.S. Regs., Part II and the Staff Manual respectively. Title pages will be prepared in manuscript.

Hour, Date, Place	Summary of Events and Information	Remarks and references to Appendices
BERNANCOURT		
Tuesday Oct 24 - 1916	Usual Routine.	
Wednesday Oct 25. 1916	Usual Routine. Rifle Inspection.	
Thursday Oct 26 1916	Admitted 2nd Supply Col. 1.	
Friday Oct 27 - 1916	Admitted 4th Hussars 7, 16 Lancers 3, 5th Lancers 17. 3rd M.S. Squadron 6. 1st Bat N.Z. F. Artillery.	
Saturday Oct 28 1916	3rd M.S. Squadron 2. 4th Inf Div 4.	
Sunday Oct 29 - 1916	Admitted 1st C. R.L. 4 Heavy 1, Mule 3rd R.S. Squad 1. Mo7 MVS 1. X Battery R.H.A. 5. J Battery R.H.A. 1. 1st Hamp Reg 1. Evacuated. 6 No 7 V.H. 50. To No 7 M.V.S. 16. To No 9 M.V.S. 8. Admitted Car Corps Squad 2.	
Monday Oct 30 - 1916	Received 2 remounts. Usual Routine.	
Tuesday Oct 31.	Destroyed 1 horse, Australian. Party returned from the base of ADVS visited the section.	T.7 Forstfield A.V.C Capt A.V.C OC No 8 M.V.S.

SECRET.

Vol 25

WAR DIARY

of

8th MOBILE VETERINARY SECTION.

NOVEMBER, 1916.

VOL. ~~XXVII~~.

Army Form C. 2118.

WAR DIARY
INTELLIGENCE SUMMARY.
(Erase heading not required.)

Instructions regarding War Diaries and Intelligence Summaries are contained in F. S. Regs., Part II. and the Staff Manual respectively. Title pages will be prepared in manuscript.

Hour, Date, Place	Summary of Events and Information	Remarks and references to Appendices
DERNANCOURT		
Wednesday Nov 1. 1916	Admitted 4th Hussars 2. 2nd Cav Res Park 1 horse + 1 mule 5th Lancers 3. 3rd Hs Gun Sqn 1. 16th Lancers 2.	
Thursday Nov 2	Admitted 16th Lancers 1. Evacuated through No.9 M.V.S. to No.7 V.H. 12 horses + 1 mule.	
Friday Nov 3	Admitted 3rd H.G.S. 1. 4th Hussars 1. Information received that three mules attached of T.4.Y.A.8.12.16 were left by Lieut Rankin A.S.C. 1st & 2nd Cav Res Park	
Saturday Nov 4	Admitted 2nd Cav Res Park 1 mule. 5th Lancers 1. 16th Lancers 1. Mobile supply Column 1.	
Sunday Nov 5	Admitted 16th Lancers 1. 5th Lancers 1.	
Monday Nov 6	Admitted 3rd Hs S. Sqn 1. 2nd Cav Res Park 1. 4th Hussars 2. 5th Lancers 3. H.Q. 5th Cav Bde 1.	
Tuesday Nov 7	Admitted H.Q. 2nd Cav Bde 1. Evacuated 13 horses + 1 mule to No.7 V.H. per No.7 M.V.S.	
BUSSY		
Wednesday Nov 8	Section moved to BUSSY arriving 4.30 p.m. bivouacked for the night. Axle of the top part of a G.S. limbered wagon broke on the journey + was left empty 1 mile N.E. of CORBIE.	

(73989) W4141—463. 400,000. 9/14. H.&J.Ltd. Forms/C. 2118/10.

WAR DIARY or INTELLIGENCE SUMMARY

Army Form C. 2118.

(Erase heading not required.)

Instructions regarding War Diaries and Intelligence Summaries are contained in F.S. Regs., Part II and the Staff Manual respectively. Title pages will be prepared in manuscript.

Hour, Date, Place	Summary of Events and Information	Remarks and references to Appendices
BOURDON Thursday Nov 9th 1916	Admitted 4th Hussars 1. 2nd Cav Field Amb 1. 5th Lancers 2. H.Q. 3rd Cav Bde 1. Saddler & Scholar 1. Lieut Beachlan not Captain left from the BOURDON.	
LE TITRE Friday Nov 10th 1916	On hopes left at BOURDON, moved off at 7.45 am Admitted 16th Lancers 3. 4th Hussars 1. H.Q. 2nd Cav Bde 1. On route evacuated 8 sick to No 22 V.H. St OMER arrived LE TITRE 5.20 pm	
TORTE FONTAINE Saturday Nov 11. 1916	Moved off 8am 8.25 Pte Dawson of Liver. ill on march & handed over to 2nd Cav Field Ambulance. OC proceeded on + found staff Capt in billeting area allotted a very unsuitable for 2000 yds from Bde H.A.	
Sunday Nov 12. 1916	Admitted H.Q. 3rd Cav Bde 1. Pte Matthews & Turner reported from Base.	
Monday Nov 13. 1916	Pte Turner reported sick + admitted to Rest Station Admitted Amm Col 1. 2nd F. Sq R.E 2.	
Tuesday Nov 14. 1916	Admitted of 1 Chargers Col Mullihed. 2nd F. Sq R.E. 1. H.Q. H.C.E Clipping machines put together + working.	

Army Form C. 2118.

WAR DIARY
or
INTELLIGENCE SUMMARY.
(Erase heading not required.)

Instructions regarding War Diaries and Intelligence Summaries are contained in F.S. Regs., Part II. and the Staff Manual respectively. Title pages will be prepared in manuscript.

Hour, Date, Place	Summary of Events and Information	Remarks and references to Appendices
TORTE FONTAINE		
Wednesday Nov 15. 1916	Admitted 3rd Sig Troop 1. Amp # Truax 2nd Cav Bde 1.	
Thursday Nov 16. 1916	Evacuated by road to No 22 V.H. 10.	
	Capt Faithfull proceeded to BOULOGNE on route for interp. board.	
	Elected 1 ZA left at ST REMY aux BOIS by 1st Fd Sqd R.E. Capt J Stow forming around for command of the section.	
Friday Nov 17. 1916	A.D.V.S. visited the section.	
Saturday Nov 18. 1916	Admitted from M.M.P. 3rd Cav Bde 1.	
	Interpret Robertson	
Sunday Nov 19. 1916	Admitted 1 (Bn Fanciers) # evacuated to No 22 V.H.	
	Admitted 16th Lancers 5, 5th Lancers 10. 2nd Sq R.E. 4.	
	Pte Truman returned from hospital.	
Monday Nov 20. 1916	Admitted 1 horse St Ethelin 2nd Cav Bde.	
Tuesday Nov 21. 1916	Pte Snowin returned from the rest station.	
	Returned to M.M.P. 1.	
	Admitted to No 22 V.H. Amp # T. 1.	
Wednesday Nov 22. 1916	Admitted 4th Hussars 6. M.M.P. 2nd Cav Bde 1. 2nd F.S. R.E. 3. (2 hrs)	
	Evacuated 28 to No 22 V.H. by road.	
	A/VS visited the section.	

Army Form C. 2118.

WAR DIARY
or
INTELLIGENCE SUMMARY.
(Erase heading not required.)

Instructions regarding War Diaries and Intelligence Summaries are contained in F.S. Regs., Part II. and the Staff Manual respectively. Title pages will be prepared in manuscript.

Hour, Date, Place	Summary of Events and Information	Remarks and references to Appendices
TORTEFONTAINE		
Thursday Nov 23. '16	Usual Routine	
Friday Nov 24	Rifle Inspection	
Saturday Nov 25	Clothing Parade. 1 Pony Cart 1 received in place of same.	
	Admitted 5th Lancers 9, 16th Lancers 3	
Sunday Nov 26	Admitted 2nd J.S.R. 2. Amm Col 2nd Cavalry Div 8. H.Q. R.H.A. 3	
Monday Nov 27	ADVS visited Section.	
	Admitted 3rd Dr. 5, Sy 6, Hazeled	
	Evacuated 2 8 6 No 22 V.H. 5, road	
Tuesday Nov 28	Col Harris DDVS Can Corps visited section with ADVS	
	Returned 1 horse to K. Hunnar for treatment	
	1 horse H.Q. 2nd Cav. Div. died strangulated bowel.	
	Capt Faulkfield returned to the section & took over command.	T.J. Faulkfield Capt MC
Wednesday Nov 29	G.O.C. 2nd Cav Div visited the section.	
	Admitted from Col R.H.A. 5	No 28 M.V.S.
Thursday Nov 30	Admitted 14 Cav. 1, 3rd Car Bde 4, K Hunnar 1 Sec. Evacuated 15 Cart & 6 road	No 30 11.16
	4.2.1 Sergt Hooper H.B. result 6 5.4.8 Troop Train MONTREUIL	
	to Latrigues for local commission in SVC.	
	During two months this N.C.O. has been with the section he has given entire satisfaction & I have a high opinion of his abilities	

(73969) W4141—463. 400,000. 9/14. H.&J. Ltd. Forms/C. 2118/10.

CONFIDENTIAL.

Vol 26

WAR DIARY

of

8th MOBILE VETERINARY SECTION.

DECEMBER, 1916.

VOL. XXVIII.

Army Form C. 2118.

WAR DIARY
or
INTELLIGENCE SUMMARY.
(Erase heading not required.)

Instructions regarding War Diaries and Intelligence Summaries are contained in F.S. Regs., Part II and the Staff Manual respectively. Title pages will be prepared in manuscript.

Hour, Date, Place	Summary of Events and Information	Remarks and references to Appendices
TORTEFONTAINE		
Friday Dec 1. 1916	Admitted 5th Lancer 1.	7/1ᵗ
Saturday Dec 2. 1916	Admitted 4ᵗʰ Hussars 1. Strayed 16ᵗʰ Lancer 1. 3916 S/Corp Wakerton. O. reported 6ᵗʰ rank to shave without authority (2nd offence). 3870 Pte Ivens. W. awarded 5 days F.P. No 2. for ditto.	1/1ᵗ 1/1ᵗ 1/1ᵗ
Sunday Dec 3. 1916	Usual Routine	
Monday Dec 4. 1916	Admitted 16ᵗʰ Hussars 1. from Col. 4. 4ᵗʰ Hussars 9. 5 Lancers 2. H.Q. 3rd Cav Bde. 2. A.S.C. Strg ref Fig Troop 1. Evacuated 21. 1 & 1 wark to No 22 V.H. Group.	1/1ᵗ 1/1ᵗ
Tuesday Dec 5 Wednesday Dec 6	Usual Routine.	
Thursday Dec 7	Usual Routine	
Friday Dec 8 9/16	Rifle Inspection	1/1ᵗ
Saturday Dec 9 1916	Usual Routine. Pte Hall sent to No 5 V.H. Etaples for range shooting.	1/1ᵗ
Sunday Dec 10 9/16	Medical inspection. Statement free from parasitic disease.	1/1ᵗ

Army Form C. 2118.

WAR DIARY
or
INTELLIGENCE SUMMARY.
(Erase heading not required.)

Instructions regarding War Diaries and Intelligence Summaries are contained in F.S. Regs., Part II and the Staff Manual respectively. Title pages will be prepared in manuscript.

Hour, Date, Place	Summary of Events and Information	Remarks and references to Appendices
TORTE FONTAINE		
Monday Dec 11. 1916.	Admitted 3rd M.G.Sqd 9. 4th Hussars 3. 16 Lancers 3. 5th Lancers 4. Arm. Col. 1.	71c
Tuesday Dec 12 1916	Evacuated 23. 6 horses including 4 Porophic Mange	71c
Wednesday Dec 13 1916	Admitted 5th Lancers 2 Porophic Mange. 494 Sergt Jordan attended for Eye School. 623 Sergt Brian granted 10 days leave to England.	71+
Thursday Dec 14. 1916	L/Cpl Pratt took charge of Capt Hermon Ambula A.G. Sy & Hotville. SS 14283 Pte. Hall S.H. despatched for Emp. duty at Car Cops HQ. SS 19562 Pte. Hatherly 47+ SS 7036 Pte. Corden 2. joined the section from No 1 Convalescent Horse Depôt.	71+ 71+ 71+
Friday Dec 15. 1916	Returned 1 mare to 4th Hussars.	71c
Saturday Dec 16. 1916	494 Pte. Capt Justin R. Epton P/A Except. I.E.O. orders No 59. (Station 1. 12. 16. 316.O. Pte Osborne A9. to Co. O/A Cops. (3. 12. 16.	71+
Sunday Dec 17. 1916	Une Routine.	
Monday Dec 18 1916	Admitted 4th Hussars 1. HQ 2nd Cav Bri. 1. Chargers 1. Arm. Col 2nd Cavdiv 1. 2nd Field Squad 1. 5th Lancers 6.	71+

(73989) W.4141—463. 400,000. 9/14. H.&J.Ltd. Forms/C. 2118/10.

Army Form C. 2118.

WAR DIARY
or
INTELLIGENCE SUMMARY.
(Erase heading not required.)

Hour, Date, Place	Summary of Events and Information	Remarks and references to Appendices
TORTE FONTEINE		
Thursday Dec 19. 1916	3670th Lucas W. returned from leave.	M?
	Evacuated to the train 9	
	Admitted 3rd Signal Troop 1.	M?
Wednesday Dec 20.	Unit Routine	M?
Thursday Dec 21	Inspection of horses & saddles.	M?
Friday Dec 22	— Unit Routine	
Saturday Dec 23	— Unit Routine	
Sunday Dec 24	Admitted Changeur (Capt Alexander) 9th Lancers	M?
"	Inspected skin	
Monday Dec 25	Admitted 8th Lancers 3. 3rd Signal Troop 1.	M?
Tuesday Dec 26	16th Lancers 11. 3670 wanted transfer.	M?
Wednesday Dec 27	623 Sergt Brown returned from leave.	
	623 Sergt Brown G. dispatched to No 13 V.H.	M?
	Admitted 4th Hussars 1.	
	Evacuate 10 by road to No 22 V.H. Abbeville.	
Thursday 28	Unit Routine	M?
Friday 29		
Saturday 30th	Admitted 8th Lancers 1. stores within the section	
Sunday 31st	Admitted 2nd F.S. R.R. 1.	F.J. Faithfull Capt.
		O.C. 8th MOBILE VETERINARY Sec.

CONFIDENTIAL.

Vol 27

WAR   DIARY

of

8th MOBILE VETERINARY SECTION.

JANUARY ~~1916~~ 1917 - VOL. XXIX.

Army Form C. 2118.

WAR DIARY
INTELLIGENCE SUMMARY.
(Erase heading not required.)

Instructions regarding War Diaries and Intelligence Summaries are contained in F.S. Regs., Part II and the Staff Manual respectively. Title pages will be prepared in manuscript.

Hour, Date, Place	Summary of Events and Information	Remarks and references to Appendices
TORTE FONTAINE.		
Monday Jan 1. 1917.	Admitted 16th Lancers 2. 3rd Vty-Sy.1. Div.h.2.P.1. 2nd F.S.R.E.1.	77*
Tuesday Jan 2. 1917.	Evacuated 8 to M.022 Vety Hos ABBEVILLE. Returned 2 to H.Q. 2nd Can Bde. Remount received for Inspection. Lecture to N.C.Os	77*
Wednesday Jan 3. 1917	Admitted 5th Lancers 2.	77*
Thursday Jan 4. 1917.	Admitted 20th Hrs. G.Sy.1.	77*
Friday Jan 5. 1917.	Rifle inspection. Lecture to N.C.Os.	77*
Saturday Jan 6. 1917	Admitted 2nd Field Sq R.E.1.	77*
Sunday Jan 7. 1917	Admitted 6th Lancers 1. Made arrangement with Horse slaughterer (M. Rualroy Normant) of HESDIN to take dead carcases & injured live horses. Submitted suggestion on the subject to the A.D.V.S.	77*
Monday Jan 8. 1917	Admitted 4th Hussars 6. 2nd Can F. Amb.1. Army H.T.1 mule. Instructions received from O.i/c Adv Records Base the S.S.8081 Re Worksheet & had been received from all/had come to England 25.12.16 to the No.72.3.1.17	10*

(73989) W4141–463. 400,000. 9/14. H.&J.Ltd. Forms/C. 2118/10.

Army Form C. 2118.

WAR DIARY
or
INTELLIGENCE SUMMARY.
(Erase heading not required.)

Instructions regarding War Diaries and Intelligence Summaries are contained in F.S. Regs., Part II. and the Staff Manual respectively. Title pages will be prepared in manuscript.

Hour, Date, Place	Summary of Events and Information	Remarks and references to Appendices
TORTE FONTEINE		
Tuesday Jan 9, 1917	Admitted M.M.P. collection 1. Evacuated 9 horses + 1 mule. The 2/2 K.H. Bde. wrote a letter (S.14) to ours urging the authorisation of additional horses for M.V.S. with Cavalry. Two more I.O. 5 men. Ridden also 1 more attd. C. drivers + 1 bugler. Pointed out that the men here to be mounted or given the have when they now went wanted they would have to be left with Echelon "B", but definite authority should be obtainable for their retention.	7/1 7/1
Wednesday Jan 10, 1917	Usual Routine.	7/1
Thursday Jan 11	Returned (horse tryst known admitted 8 Officers).	7/2
Friday Jan 12, 1917		
Saturday Jan 13, 1917	Usual Routine	
Sunday Jan 14, 1917		7/7

Army Form C. 2118.

WAR DIARY
or
INTELLIGENCE SUMMARY.
(Erase heading not required.)

Instructions regarding War Diaries and Intelligence Summaries are contained in F.S. Regs., Part II. and the Staff Manual respectively. Title pages will be prepared in manuscript.

Hour, Date, Place	Summary of Events and Information	Remarks and references to Appendices
TORTEFONTEINE		
Monday Jan 15, 1917	Admitted H.Q. H.Q. 1, Scout H.T. 1, 2nd Mr G. Sy. 1, 4 Whitman 1	7/4
Tuesday Jan 16, 1917	Admitted 5th Lancers 4. Returned 1. 62nd Sy R.E.	Nil
Wednesday Jan 17, 1917	Evacuate 7 horses + 1 mule E/16220 H.H. ABBEVILLE	7/4
Thursday Jan 18, 1917	Returned 18th Lancers 1. Admitted 16th Lancers 1	7/4
Friday	32 4/10 Corp. Gordon A + SE 7036 Lancer 8 evacuated to No 5 Hospital	
	2nd Lieut Orr on route to Hospital	
	32 165 Matthews J.C. granted 10 days leave of absence from	7/4
Saturday Jan 20, 1917	Annual Routine	
Sunday Jan 21, 1917	Admitted H.Q. 3rd Cav Bde 1.	7/4
	5th Lancers 1, H.Q. 2nd Cav Brig. 1, 4 Whitman 4	Nil
Monday Jan 22, 1917	Admitted 5th Lancer 1, H.Q. 2nd Cav Brig 1, 4 Whitman 4	7/4
	5th Car Res Park 1. A.S.V.S. visited Inspection	
	32 42 63 Mr Sgt T6144 found Unsection from No 5 MVS	
	authority A.G. Base letter 7/6/50/17 d. 16.1.17	

Army Form C. 2118.

WAR DIARY
or
INTELLIGENCE SUMMARY.
(Erase heading not required.)

Instructions regarding War Diaries and Intelligence Summaries are contained in F.S. Regs., Part II and the Staff Manual respectively. Title pages will be prepared in manuscript.

No. 8 MOBILE VETERINARY SECTION

Hour, Date, Place	Summary of Events and Information	Remarks and references to Appendices
TORTEFONTEINE		
Tuesday Jan 23 - 1917	Returned 1 E. of Horses. Admitted 5 Inponies. Evacuated 8 Horses 1 K.H. Base.	797
Wednesday Jan 24	Usual Routine	797
Thursday Jan 25		
Friday Jan 26 - 1917	Returned 16th Lancers 1. Admitted Horses Col 2. 1 horse H.Q.R.H.A. and 4th E.S.D.I.M. for destruction. Suggestions for alteration of War Establishment sent to Brigade H.Q.	797 part III
Saturday Jan 27 1917	Usual Routine	797
Sunday Jan 28 1917	1 horse H.Q. 2nd Cav. Bde. died removed to H.E.I.D.M.M.	797
Monday Jan 29 1917	Admitted 10th Lancers 7, 2nd of S. R.E. 1. Returned 4 Horses 1. 3rd M.G. Sqn 1.	797
Tuesday Jan 30 1917	Admitted Carb. 2 1 K.S.R.B. Inman Col 5 + Empules R.H.A. HR 1 1 797 HR 2-1 Carbs 1, other H.T. 1 mule. Evacuated 9 sick + 10 castrates + 1 mule to M.O.R.2 1/4. 5 ponies received for castration head to F. Carbs in Castrating.	797
Wednesday Jan 31 - 1917	Usual Routine	

F. Faulkhill Lt M.V.

CONFIDENTIAL.

WAR DIARY

of

8th MOBILE VETERINARY SECTION.

FEBRUARY, 1917.
VOL. XXX.

WAR DIARY or INTELLIGENCE SUMMARY.

Army Form C. 2118.

Hour, Date, Place	Summary of Events and Information	Remarks and references to Appendices
TORTEFONTEINE		
Thursday Feb 1. 1917	Admitted 5th Lancers 10 Cont. 10th 9 Cont. 4th Hussars 7	7/7
Friday Feb 2. 1917	Evacuated 30 Cul horses to No 22 V.H. Admitted 5th Lancers 2.	7/7
Saturday Feb 3	} Usual Routine	7/7
Sunday Feb 4		
Monday Feb 5. 1917	Admitted 3rd M.G. Sqn 3 Skin cases 2nd F.S. R.E. 1 Returned 2nd F.Sq R.E. 1.	7/7
Tuesday Feb 6. 1917	Returned 5 th Lancers 1.	7/7
Wednesday Feb 7. 1917	8/1286 Pte Pty M. 35-16108 Pte McKenzie J.T. joined Unit return from No 23 V.H.	7/7
Thursday Feb 8. 1917	Admitted 3rd M.G. Sq. 2	7/7
Friday Feb 9. 1917	Usual Routine	7/7
Saturday Feb 10. 1917	Admitted North Irish Horse 1. Rifle infection	7/7

Army Form C. 2118.

WAR DIARY
or
INTELLIGENCE SUMMARY.
(Erase heading not required.)

Instructions regarding War Diaries and Intelligence Summaries are contained in F.S. Regs., Part II and the Staff Manual respectively. Title pages will be prepared in manuscript.

Hour, Date, Place	Summary of Events and Information	Remarks and references to Appendices
TORTE FONTEINE		
Sunday Feb 11th 1917	Admitted 16th Lancers 1. 5th Lancers 1.	7A
Monday Feb 12th 1917	Returned 16th 1. Admitted 2nd Cav. F. Amb 1. Drill dismounted	7A
Tuesday Feb 13 1917	Kit inspection	7A
Wednesday Feb 14 1917	Admitted 1. 2 a.m. rifle section 4th Corps. Drill dismounted.	7A
Thursday Feb 15 1917	Smoke helmet drill & inspection.	7A
Friday Feb 16 1917	No 3670 a/c/Corps Troops W. reported to the ranks and SS 7849 Pt Woods G. awarded 14 days F.P. No 1. for drunkeness at DOMPIERE on Feb 14th. 1 horse 2 M.G. Squadron destroyed.	7A
Saturday Feb 17 1917	Admitted 5th Lancers 1.	7A
Sunday Feb 18 1917	" 5th Lancers 1. (for destruction).	7A
Monday Feb 19 1917	Returned 5th Lancers 1. 16th Lancers 2.	7A

Army Form C. 2118.

WAR DIARY
or
INTELLIGENCE SUMMARY.
(Erase heading not required.)

Instructions regarding War Diaries and Intelligence Summaries are contained in F.S. Regs., Part II and the Staff Manual respectively. Title pages will be prepared in manuscript.

Hour, Date, Place	Summary of Events and Information	Remarks and references to Appendices
TORTEFONTEINE		
Tuesday Feb 20, 1917	Usual Routine	
Wednesday Feb 21, 1917	Rifle drill	7.97
Thursday Feb 22, 1917	Usual Routine	7.97
Friday Feb 23, 1917	Admitted 16th Lancers 1. 5th Lancers 1. 2nd Cav. F. Amb. 2. Returned 5th Lancers 1. A.D.V.S. visited Section	7.97
Saturday Feb 24, 1917	Evacuated 16 horses to Chelers No 22 V.H. Admitted 5th Reserve Regt R. of Lancers 1.	7.97
Sunday Feb. 25th 1917.	Usual Routine	N.S.
Monday Feb 26th 1917	Admitted 4th Hussars 1. 3rd Machine Gun Squadron 2. A.D.V.S. visited Section	N.S.
Tuesday Feb 27, 1917	Admitted 16th Lancers/chargr. 1 Stray at 10.30 am on S.E. 3670 Private (acting L/Cpl) Lucas N. and S.E. 7849 Wood G.	N.S.
Wednesday Feb. 28th 1917	Usual Routine. Gas helmet drill. Private Capra V.C.	N.S. N.S.

(7989) W4141—263. 400,000. 9/14. H.&J. Ltd. Forms/C. 2118/10.

WAR DIARY

OF

8th MOBILE VETERINARY SECTION

MARCH 1917

VOL. XXXI.

WAR DIARY of No 8 Mobile Veterinary Section

Army Form C. 2118.

INTELLIGENCE SUMMARY.

(Erase heading not required.)

Instructions regarding War Diaries and Intelligence Summaries are contained in F.S. Regs., Part II and the Staff Manual respectively. Title pages will be prepared in manuscript.

Hour, Date, Place	Summary of Events and Information	Remarks and references to Appendices
TORTEFONTEINE		
Thursday 1st March 1917.	Usual Routine	
Friday 2nd March 1917.	Admitted 3rd Hussars 2.	T.W.S.
Saturday 3rd March 1917.	Usual Routine	T.W.S.
	Admitted 6th Dragoon Guards 1.	
	" 3rd Cav. Res. Park 3.	
	SE 3670. Pte Lucas W } Tried by F.G.C.M. on 27/2/17	
	SE 7849 Pte Hood G } Sentenced to 28 days F.P. No 1.	
	Sent to A.P.M. Today.	T.W.S.
Sunday 4th March 1917.	Admitted 2nd Cav. Bde M.2.1.	
	5th Ammunition Col. 1.	T.W.S.
Monday 5th March 1917.	Admitted 4th Hussars 2. } by order of A.D.V.S. who	
	16th Lancers 1. } visited Section at 10 am	
	2nd J. Squd. R.E. 2	
	12th Lancers 3	
	5th " 4	

Army Form C. 2118.

WAR DIARY
or
INTELLIGENCE SUMMARY.
(Erase heading not required.)

Instructions regarding War Diaries and Intelligence Summaries are contained in F.S. Regs., Part II. and the Staff Manual respectively. Title pages will be prepared in manuscript.

Hour, Date, Place	Summary of Events and Information	Remarks and references to Appendices
FORTS FONTEINE		
Tuesday 6th March 1917.	Evacuated 14 horses to No 22 Vety Hospital	7.17
Wednesday 7th " 1917.	Usual routine	7.17.
Thursday 8th " 1917.	Usual routine	7.17.
Friday 9th March 1917	Capt Truthfull took over command of section	7.17
Saturday 10th March 1917	Returned 8th Lancers 1. Admitted 2nd Can Infant 1.	7.17
Sunday 11th " "	Usual Routine	
Monday 12th March 1917	Admitted 5th Lancers 1. 10th Lancers 1. 5th Res Park 1. is the Hussars 1.	7.17
Tuesday 13th " 1917	Admitted H.Q. 3rd Cav Bde 1. Evacuated to No 22 V.H. 10.	7.17
Thursday 15th " 1917	5th Lancers 1. Medical Inspection of Unit.	7.17
Friday 16th " 1917	Sick men inoculated with T.A.B.	7.17
Saturday 17th " 1917	Admitted 4th Hussars 1. S.H.Q 2.	14.7.

Army Form C. 2118.

WAR DIARY
or
INTELLIGENCE SUMMARY.
(Erase heading not required.)

Instructions regarding War Diaries and Intelligence Summaries are contained in F.S. Regs., Part II and the Staff Manual respectively. Title pages will be prepared in manuscript.

Hour, Date, Place	Summary of Events and Information	Remarks and references to Appendices
TORTEFONTAINE		
Sunday March 18. 1918	Horse Parade	
Monday " 19 "	Admitted Army H.T. 1 mule M.M.P. 3 other Ranks 1	1/7
	St Francis 1. 4 returned 1. STOP washed the nature	7/17
Tuesday 20.4.18	Evacuated 10 to No 22 V.H.	
	Admitted 2nd Cav ft stud 1. 3 mth G. Sq 1.	
	3670 Pte Freen W. + 7849 Pte Woods G. returned to	
	duty the finding of the P.S.C.M. being granted by G.O.C. Cavalry Corps	7/7
	16.3.17.	
Wednesday March 21.4.18	Admitted 4th Res Park 3 5th Res Park 1	7/7
Thursday March 22. 917	Returned 1 4 Morg M.V.S.	7/7
Friday March 23.917	5 mm inoculated with T.A.B.	7/7
Sunday March 25.917	Box respirator inspection stud.	7/7
Monday March 26.917	1 Officer 1 Sister 4 hrs inoculated T.A.B.	
	Admitted 1 Veterinary 2. 5th Hanover 2. 6 Veterinary 2. 2nd F Sqn R.E. 1	
	3 mules sent to No 22 V.H.	7/7

Army Form C. 2118.

WAR DIARY
or
INTELLIGENCE SUMMARY.
(Erase heading not required.)

Hour, Date, Place	Summary of Events and Information	Remarks and references to Appendices
TORTEFONTEINE		
Tuesday March 27. 1917	Admitted 16 m Joneers 1. Evacuated 9 to No 2 E.V.H. 717	
Wednesday 28.	Bore Resperator drill. Admitted HR 2nd Canadal. 1. Q.H.Q. 1. 771	
Thursday 29. 1917	Rifle inspection. 4 men vaccinated 7KB 775	
Friday 30. 1917	Admitted 2nd Can Fd Amb 1. Limber wagon exchanged with HR 3rd Can Bde for a G.S. wagon. 776	
Saturday 31. 1917	Usual Routine 772	

T. J. Faithfull
Capt
O.C. 8TH MOBILE VETERINARY SECTION

CONFIDENTIAL.

WAR   DIARY

of

8th MOBILE VETERINARY SECTION.

APRIL, 1917.

VOL. XXXII.

WAR DIARY or INTELLIGENCE SUMMARY

Army Form C. 2118.

Hour, Date, Place	Summary of Events and Information	Remarks and references to Appendices
TORTIEFONTAINE		
Sunday April 1/17	Uneventful	
Monday April 2. 1917	Admitted 5th Lancers 1. G.H.A. 1. West Cheshire Ammn. Col. 2. Army H.T. 1. Mule.	
Tuesday April 3. 1917	Admitted 6th Hussars 1. 5th Lancers 1. Evacuated to No 22 Vet. Hospital 7 horses & 1 mule.	
Wednesday April 4. 1917	Returned from Col. 1. 5th Lancers 1. Admitted Kenilworth G.H.A. 2. 1 G.H.A. horse evacuated to Front zone for H.Q. 2nd Cav Bde.	
MACFEEKNOW OCCOCHES		
Thursday April 5.1917	Section moved at 9 a.m. & trekked to new billets.	
Friday April 6. 1917	Admitted 4th Hussars 1. 16th Lancers 2. 3rd M.G. Sq. 6. 5th Lancers 3. Rifle Inspection	
Saturday April 7. 1917	—	
GUDEAUT PRE		
Sunday April 8. 1917	Evacuated 14 from BOUQUEMAISON to No 22 V.H. Section moved to new billets at GUDEAUMPRE. Destroyed 1 horse 3rd M.G. Squadron.	
RIVIERE		
Monday April 9. 1917	Section moved out at 10.20 am & trekked to billets at ARRAS then returned to RIVIERE arriving at 2 a.m. Admitted 1st Hussars affiliated 16th Lancers 1. 3rd M.G.S.1. 10th Lancers struck down Major GRUDAUMPRE & 2nd Lieut. G.S. left at WAILY.	

Army Form C. 2118.

WAR DIARY
INTELLIGENCE SUMMARY.
(Erase heading not required.)

Instructions regarding War Diaries and Intelligence Summaries are contained in F. S. Regs., Part II and the Staff Manual respectively. Title pages will be prepared in manuscript.

Hour, Date, Place	Summary of Events and Information	Remarks and references to Appendices
RONVILLE Tuesday April 10. 1917	Section went from RIVIERE at 13 hours & billeted in field at RONVILLE at midnight. One horse evacuated through No 9 MVS.	
Wednesday April 11. 1917	Admitted 18 Fevers 3, 2nd D.G. 12, 5 R.H.G. Sq. 2, R.O. O.H. 1, 20th Hussars 1, 12 Lancers 5, 4 Hussars 3, 3rd H.G. Sq. 1, 5th Anthony 2, 5th Fevers 3, Btty 1. D troop 1. Sent a party up the trenches road which reports no live horses to be found.	
GAUDIEMPRE Thursday April 12. 1917	Evacuated 27 horses to No 27 MVS. Killed & 3 destroyed. Section moved out at 19 hours & travelled via the AMIENS DOULLENS Rd to GAUDIEMPRE arriving at 22½ hours.	
Friday April 13. 1917	Admitted 16th Lancers 16, 5th Lancers 11, 4 Hussars 1, 16th Lancers 1.	
Saturday April 14 1917		

Army Form C. 2118.

WAR DIARY
or
INTELLIGENCE SUMMARY.
(Erase heading not required.)

Instructions regarding War Diaries and Intelligence Summaries are contained in F. S. Regs., Part II. and the Staff Manual respectively. Title pages will be prepared in manuscript.

Place	Date	Hour	Summary of Events and Information	Remarks and references to Appendices
GAUDIEMARE	Sunday April 15 1917		Admitted H.Q. 2nd Lieut Lieu 2. 18th Reserve Park Dublin 10. 2nd Lt G. Griffin 6 2nd F.S. R.E. 3.	1/F
	Monday 16.4.17		Admitted 5th Lancers 2. 4th Hussars 1. 2nd Bg 82 2. 16th Lancers 1. Evacuated 42 hrs 16 miles to No 22 V.H.	7/F
	Tuesday 17.4.17		Admitted 16th Lancers 6. Returned to duty 1 18th Lancer Evacuated 6 through No 7 H.V.S.	7/F
	Wednesday 18.4.17		Admitted Hd Sec Can Bde 1. Returned 1 Gunner.	4/F
FROHEN LE GRAND			1 Officer + 1 Return of XX 1st Hussars.	
	Thursday April 19. 1917		1 horse left at XX O.S.H. N.C. particulars sent to No 7 17.H.S. Moved billets at 9.30 am.	7/F
LE PLANEY Farm AUXI LOCHATEAU	Friday April 20. 1917		Moved billets 13 hours.	7/F
	Saturday April 21. 1917		7/29.10.2.9 D. Wilson P & Hd C joined the section from MAURE.	
	Sunday April 22		Admitted 5th Lancers 12. 5 Battery R.H.A. 2. 15th Lancers 1. Evacuated to No 22 V.H. 17.	1/F
	Monday 23		Admitted 2nd H.g. 20. 4th Hussars 11. K Battery 1. Allchfarm NOEUX.	7/F

2352. Wt. W25141/1451. 500,000 5/15 D. D. & L. A.D.S.S./Forms/C. 2118.

Army Form C. 2118.

WAR DIARY
INTELLIGENCE SUMMARY.
(Erase heading not required.)

Place	Date	Hour	Summary of Events and Information	Remarks and references to Appendices
LE PLANTI FERM AUX LE CHATEAU			Evacuated to MG 22 # 17.	
	Tuesday April 24.17		Admitted 1 Horse received from 4th Hussars transferred to H.Q. 5 Cav Bde.	7/7
			R.O. 1195 a form indispensable.	
	Wednesday 25.17		Evacuated to M.O.72 V.H. 15 passed here H.Q. 5th Cav Bde	7/7
	Thursday 26.17		Admitted F. Battery R.H.A. 2.	7/7
	Friday 27.17		Admitted H.Q. 2nd Cav Bde 1. Wound Routine S1 2050 Pte WEBB P gained section from H.Q. V.H. M7	7/7
	Saturday 28.17		Received 1 grey mare from 2 M.G.Sq. transferred to No 2 Cav Res Park.	7/7
			no autopsy F.A.R. Cav Corps.	
	Sunday 29.17		Admitted Stationary 1.	7/7
	Monday 30.17		Admitted D Battery 1. 4th Hussars 2. 3rd Cav Bde 1.	7/7
			3rd M.G. Sq. S. 16th Lancers 8. 5th Lancers 13.	

U Turtleford
Capt/N

CONFIDENTIAL.

WAR   DIARY

of

NO. 8 MOBILE VETERINARY SECTION.

MAY, 1917 - VOL. XXXIII.

WAR DIARY
INTELLIGENCE SUMMARY
(Erase heading not required.)

Army Form C. 2118.

Place	Date	Hour	Summary of Events and Information	Remarks and references to Appendices
LE PLANTY FERME AUX LE CHATEAU	Tuesday May 1st 1917		Evacuated 3.2 by road to No 22 V.H. Attrequette. 7/4 233829 Sr HARRIS A.E.C. + 7/4 233434 GOODALL G.+S.C. arrived from Base depot HAV R.E.	7/4
	Wednesday May 2 1917		2 horses evacuated by ambulance to No 22 V.H. 1 afternoon admitted. 7/4 232434 St GOODALL G + S.C. transferred to HTD 2nd Car Bde.	7/4
	Thursday May 3 1917		Evacuated 64 cart horses to 22 Vety Hos. Admitted 5 horses.	7/4
	Friday May 4 1917		Wire Routine.	7/4
	Saturday May 5 1917		Kit Inspection	
	Sunday May 6 1917		Annual Routine.	7/4
	Monday May 7 1917		One horse cast to B. below + to 3rd No. 9 Squadron. Admitted 1 chestnut 1 16th Lancers D. + Krume 2 Sebrnaval 2nd Cav Rn Park 2 mules. Rifle Inspection	7/4
	Tuesday May 8 1917		Admitted 10 mules 1st Cav Rn Park. Evacuated 4 horses. 12 mules to M.O 2 V.H. One man put returned for 6 hrs on to No 2 Advanced Remount Squadron. Admitted 1 Veterinary.	J/3

Army Form C. 2118.

WAR DIARY
or
INTELLIGENCE SUMMARY.
(Erase heading not required.)

Instructions regarding War Diaries and Intelligence Summaries are contained in F. S. Regs., Part II. and the Staff Manual respectively. Title pages will be prepared in manuscript.

Hour, Date, Place	Summary of Events and Information	Remarks and references to Appendices
AUX LE CHATEAU Wednesday May 7. 1919	170 sent to hop M.V.S. 1 returned to 5th Lancers	7/7
Thursday May 8. 1919	Rifle inspection. admitted 16th Lancers 1.	7/7
Friday May 9. 1919	Destroyed one horse 16th Lancers	7/7
FROMEN LE GRAND Saturday May 10. 1919	S/S 3704 Pte Allen C. left on 10 days leave. Moved billets to FROMEN LE GRAND	7/7
WARMIES Sunday May 11. 1919	Section moved to WARMIES	7/7
QUTERIEU Monday May 12. 1919	Section moved to QUTERIEU	7/7
SUZANNE Tuesday May 13. 1919	Section moved to SUZANNE	7/7
HAMEL Wednesday May 14. 1919	Section moved to open ground outside HAMEL	7/7
Thursday May 15. 1919	Admitted 5th Lancers 2 (skin)	7/7
BOUCLY Friday May 16. 1919	Usual routine. 1S/S inoculation.	7/7
Saturday May 17. 1919	Evacuated 3 horses; through No.7 M.V.S. Moved to open ground S. of BOUCLY	7/7

Army Form C. 2118.

WAR DIARY
or
INTELLIGENCE SUMMARY.
(Erase heading not required.)

Instructions regarding War Diaries and Intelligence Summaries are contained in F. S. Regs., Part II. and the Staff Manual respectively. Title pages will be prepared in manuscript.

Place	Date	Hour	Summary of Events and Information	Remarks and references to Appendices
BOUELY	Sun May 20 1917		Admitted shoein K. Butt RHA Corps Commander visited the section and expressed to the horses being on the lines. Enquiry had already been ordered for spare	7JA
	Mon May 21		Admitted 10th Hussars 1k 1 mule. S Batt 2 horses. Whitmore & Stevenson of the Hussars to Battery (s). mf and Easton 1. Returned to "B" Echelon and Cpl Bolt.	7J
	Tues May 22		Evacuated from RO15TL 16 horses & 1 mule also B for N°7 MVS to N°7 VH. Ssad/Lt Pratt and on leave. S1 31 G/o Cpl Osborn ? returned from N°6 Vety Hos	7JL 7JK
	Wed May 23		Admitted 5th Lancers 1 (Army)	
	Thurs May 24		Rifle drill & inspection. Letters untakable we return	7J
	Friday May 25		Admitted 2 sick cases from N°7 MVS also RHA (Khiv) 5th Lancers 22. Sarcoptic mange perrash included.	7J

Army Form C. 2118.

WAR DIARY
or
INTELLIGENCE SUMMARY.
(Erase heading not required.)

Instructions regarding War Diaries and Intelligence Summaries are contained in F.S. Regs., Part II. and the Staff Manual respectively. Title pages will be prepared in manuscript.

Hour, Date, Place	Summary of Events and Information	Remarks and references to Appendices
BOUCH		
Saturday May 26.	Evacuated 25 sick cases to No. 7 V.Hos. S.T. 3160 Cpl Oldham J. not on leave to England. 7/2910 29 Dr Mahon R returned from Six Rest that Whither HBatt R.H.A.	7/L
Sunday May 27	Usual Routine	
Monday May 28	Admitted S/16018 Gr. 1 Stevens to 4 in Hunen. 3 HBatt R.H.A. 1	7/L
Tuesday May 29.	Evacuated 9 to No.7 V.Hos & Mog MVS.	
Wednesday May 30.	Usual Routine	T.R.
Thursday May 31st	Admitted S/Batt R.H.A. 1 Shoer Hewitt R.	7/L

O.C. 8TH MOBILE VETERINARY SECTION

CONFIDENTIAL.

WAR DIARY.

OF

8th. MOBILE VET. SECTION.

From 1st. JUNE — 30th. JUNE, 1917.

(VOLUME XXXIV)

Army Form C. 2118.

WAR DIARY
or
INTELLIGENCE SUMMARY.
(Erase heading not required.)

Army Form C. 2118.

Instructions regarding War Diaries and Intelligence Summaries are contained in F. S. Regs., Part II. and the Staff Manual respectively. Title pages will be prepared in manuscript.

8th Mobile Vet. Section.

June 1917

Place	Date	Hour	Summary of Events and Information	Remarks and references to Appendices
BOUCLY	1.6.17		Usual routine. Rifle drill	97
	Saturday 2.6.17		Rifle & Foot drill.	97
	Sunday June 3		St/4263 S/s Sergt T.Dill W.H. reported to P/a Corpl. for inefficiency. This N.C.O. shewed entire lack of control of men & rather than level allowed himself to be guided by his subordinates in carrying out of his duties.	
	Monday June 4.		SS/3621 Pte Retry. A. evacuated to No 36 C.C.S. SS/4267 P/a Corpl T.Dill W.H. sent to Base Depot. No 2 Vety. Hos. Admitted 16 th Lancers 4. 5 th Lancers 11. sent to sq. B "A" Battery H.A. RHA 1. A Bat R.H.A 1.	97
	Tuesday June 5.		Evacuated 24 horses to No 7 Vety Hos Base. Collected 5 floats 1 horse M.M.P. 2nd Cavdn. & 1 S Battery R.H.A.	97
	Wednesday June 6.		Usual Routine.	7/4
	Thursday June 7.		Satisfyed 1 horse "D" Battery R.H.A.	7/9
	Friday June 8.		Usual Routine	7/4
	Saturday June 9.10.		Usual Routine	7/4
	Monday Jun 11		Admitted 5 th Lancers 11. 4 th Hussars 2. I. Batt R.T.A. 16 th Lancers 1 3rd M.G. Sqn 2. 1 Charger returned to 16 th Lancers. T/33640 St McCabe P transferred to 4/4 a 3rd Cav Bde T/4 / 124012 St Findlay printed transfer from 4/4 3rd Cav Bde.	97

2353 Wt. W2541/1454 700,000 5/15 D.D.&L. A.D.S.S./Forms/C.2118.

Army Form C. 2118

WAR DIARY
or
INTELLIGENCE SUMMARY.
(Erase heading not required.)

Place	Date	Hour	Summary of Events and Information	Remarks and references to Appendices
BOUELT Thursday	June 12/17		Evacuated 18 to No 7 V.H. Base. S₂ 676 Pt BOWES A granted Leave to England. S₂ 10667 Serjt STANLEY W.J. joined the section from No 3 Convalescent Horse Depot.	W/
Blathony	Jun 13/17		Admitted 4th Cavalry Division Col 1.	W/
Thursday	June 14		1 Charger returned to 5th Lancers (Irish Cav Bde). B² 3702 Pt Allen O.J. regd from Chelsea Eye Hospital.	W/
Friday	Jun 15		O.C. attended conference at No 7 V.H. to discuss proposed working of MV.S. during active operations. The scheme proposed is roughly that arranged for this division in 1915. The three M.V.S are to be used in the form of a chain. In addition it is proposed at one Wry Post to formed out it is doubtful it in practice there will be a sufficient men are inexperienced & no men are available to being back not with wounded horses it will be impossible to have all wounded informed of the position of Bde Posts & have naturally look to	W/

Army Form C. 2118

WAR DIARY
or
INTELLIGENCE SUMMARY.
(Erase heading not required.)

Instructions regarding War Diaries and Intelligence Summaries are contained in F. S. Regs., Part II. and the Staff Manual respectively. Title pages will be prepared in manuscript.

Place	Date	Hour	Summary of Events and Information	Remarks and references to Appendices
BOVELY			"A" Echelon & HQ advanced M.U.S. The rumour that many units	
Arras	June 15	Coll	have went astray at ARRAS 1917 was that the portion at	797
			it & while was not known to exists.	
Saturday	June 16, 1917		Admitted 2 MG Sq 1.	797
Sunday	June 17, 1917		O.R. movement received instruction	797
Monday	June 18, 1918		Returned 1 to nump 2nd Canadian	
			Admitted 18th Lancers 5. 3 MG Sq 3. 2nd Sy Trp 1. 5 Lancers 1.	797
			Proposed Amendment to "Vety arrangements for 2nd Cavdn sent to C/DDVS 2nd Cav Dr & when required.	
Tuesday	June 19, 1919		Evacuated 13 to MOT V.H. Bazn.	797
Wednesday	June 20-911		S.I. 3160 a/p Corp OSBORNE # T bounded at/o knelt on offrontrast	
			to "C" Battery 178th Bde R.F.A.	797
Thursday	June 21, 1917		Admitted 1 horse 2nd Can L. Amb.	
			92-14782 Pte CYLE A.A. 513850 Pte CROSS MT 7m & water from JC	
			MOT V.H.	
Friday	June 22, 1917 2 P 21		Mr PENNN. C grand nation from MOT.2 V.H.	

[signature]

WAR DIARY
or
INTELLIGENCE SUMMARY.
(Erase heading not required.)

Army Form C. 2118.

Hour, Date, Place	Summary of Events and Information	Remarks and references to Appendices
BUCKLEY		
Saturday 23.6.17	S.E. 498 Pte TURNER R. to be transferred to No 2 V.H. being surplus to establishment.	
Sunday 24.6.17	S.E. 6671 Pte ADLER C. transferred to No 22 V.H. for Base duty, authority A.V. Base. Capt Faithfull handed over section 1 Septn J.S. Henry being on leave returned for duty with 7th Division.	
Monday 25.6.17	S.E. 2254 Pte Robinson J. to V.E. Joined section from 22 Vet: Hospital	
Tuesday 26.6.17	Inoculated 7 horses & entrained 24 cast horses to Vet: Hospital Admitted phone from 2nd E.C. F.A. for treatment.	
Wednesday 27.6.17	S.E. 6871 Pte Ewbank A. re Joined section from No 24 Vet Hospital.	
Thursday 28.6.17	Admitted 10 horses for Facostyn	
Friday 29.6.17	S.E. 14784 Pte Pyle A. Re transferred to No 6 Vet. Hospital on being granted 1 month Convalescent leave.	
Saturday 30.6.17	Evacuated 10 horses to Base. S.E. No 3494 Pte CROCKER W. H. posted to No 19 Vet. Hospt.	

Army Form W. 3091.

Cover for Documents.

Confidential

Nature of Enclosures.

War Diary
of
No 8 Mobile Vety Section
from
1/7/17 to 31/7/17

(VOLUME XXXV)

Notes, or Letters written.

Army Form C. 2118.

WAR DIARY

INTELLIGENCE SUMMARY.

(Erase heading not required.)

No 8 Mobile Veterinary Section

Place	Date	Hour	Summary of Events and Information	Remarks and references to Appendices
Bulley	1st July 1917		No 6760 Cpl. DUDLEY Returned from leave	ASS
"	2nd " "		S.E. PTE HATHERLEY W.J. transferred to 12 M.V.S. 7th Div. authority A.G. base	ASS
			Ordinary Routine	ASS
"	3rd " "		Sectn inspected by A.D.V.S.	ASS
"	4th " "		Ordinary Routine	ASS
"	5th " "		S.E. 719 S/S Compton A. returned from leave	ASS
"	6th " "		S.E. 6023 PTE WEEDS.W. transferred from 12th M.V.S. on relief Pte HATHERLEY	ASS
			admitted 4 horses for evacuation	—
			evacuated 5 horses to No 4 Vet. Hospital.	
"	7th " "			ASS
"	8th " "		on leave to England.	ASS
"	9th " "		S.E. 2004 PTE LLOYD F.T. proceeded on leave to England. A.D.V.S. visited section	ASS
			admitted 4 horses for examination + as for treatment by O.C.	ASS
"	10th " "		4 horses evacuated to base. Lieut R. Clarkstone AVC assumed command of section camp	
			from the 3rd Hump Th Brecon Rifles " Caithorpe.	NG
			No 10755 PTE H.G. Innes Eaton Mar. 5 Vet Hospital in relief of Pte Evinson Authority AVC	
"	11 " "		Reemp T6/462/17. Ordinary routine	NG
"	12 " "		Horse admitted from 252 A T C R C	NG
"	13 " "		Section Horses + Cappey area — Sectn Billeted in Poppa camp Cappy	NG

Army Form C. 2118.

WAR DIARY
or
INTELLIGENCE SUMMARY.
(Erase heading not required.)

Instructions regarding War Diaries and Intelligence Summaries are contained in F.S. Regs., Part II. and the Staff Manual respectively. Title pages will be prepared in manuscript.

Hour, Date, Place	Summary of Events and Information	Remarks and references to Appendices
July 14 1917	Brigade continued its march — Section encamped at Heilly — in same grounds as D" Battery R.H.A.	h.q
15 1917	Brigade continued its march — Section encamped at Hotel de Ville at Oisville. Chief-man reverse for 16" Division supplied for C.Div — was awaiting as he was reported to continue the march towards with 16" Sept blind.	h.q
16 1917	Brigade continued to march — Section encamped at Gran Somitz Brecourt Sur Canche. Have a hut to keep horses. Bay/Mar reserve Mar. 3 Machine gun. marge.	h.q
17 1917	Visit of A.D.V.S. — 2 no horses evacuated by A.D.V.S. for marge	h.q her
18 1917	Horse Routine	h.q h.q
19 1917	2 no horses admitted from No 7 M.V.S with sore pastern marge	h.q h.q
20 1917	Horse Routine	h.q
21 1917	Horse Routine	
22 1917	S.E. 200 to Pte Bray I certificate for leave.	h.q
23 1917	Previous orders Audit drafts at Stabling hospitals kent	h.q
24 1917	11 horses admitted — A.D.V.S studies Tents. 7 horses arr. ill — 1 horse brought from for Doullens in Amb.	h.q h.q
25 1917	Evacuated 20 horses from St Pol	h.q

Army Form C. 2118.

WAR DIARY
or
INTELLIGENCE SUMMARY.
(Erase heading not required.)

Instructions regarding War Diaries and Intelligence Summaries are contained in F. S. Regs., Part II. and the Staff Manual respectively. Title pages will be prepared in manuscript.

Place	Date	Hour	Summary of Events and Information	Remarks and references to Appendices
In the Field	July 26/1917		Two horses admitted from 5th Bugali Group with mange	W.D
	July 27/1917		Two M.V.S attached to 2nd Cavalry Div. for use of 11th Air Sqdn	W.D
			Two horses admitted from D. Battery	W.D
	July 28/1917		Two M.V.S attached to 2nd Cavalry Div. for use on sick — mange etc	W.D
			One horse brought in BELLANCOURT wants to be destroyed	W.D
			horse Rubb.	W.D
	July 29, 1917		Attended the march of horses by a Committee of the hospital & selected horses	W.D
	July 30, 1917		Canaries Sunlote for meat horse. Committee consisting of D. Burnett, Davis & Col Cope	W.D
			5 horses sent to Cope Sqn to be destroyed.	W.D
			One horse admitted at M.L. 5th Canners. Lent to LUCKBUR. Es-Assignment & manage of horse	W.D
	July 31/1917		from three Reserve Sqns.	W.D

R. CLARKE-GLOVER
Lieut.
R.V.C.
O.C. 8TH MOBILE VETERINARY SECTION

Vol 34

Confidential

War Diary

of

8th Mob. Veterinary Section

From 1st Aug. 1917   To 31st Aug. 1917

Volume XXXVI

Army Form W.3091.

Cover for Documents.

~~Confidential~~

Nature of Enclosures.

War Diary

of

8th Mobile Veterinary Section

for Month of

August 1917

(Vol. XXXVI)

Notes, or Letters written.

Army Form C. 2118.

WAR DIARY
or
INTELLIGENCE SUMMARY.
(Erase heading not required.)

August 1917
8th Mtd Bde Section

Instructions regarding War Diaries and Intelligence Summaries are contained in F.S. Regs., Part II and the Staff Manual respectively. Title pages will be prepared in manuscript.

Hour, Date, Place	Summary of Events and Information	Remarks and references to Appendices
In the Field August 1	Evacuated 10 horses - admitted 1 horse from 8" trailers & received on Remount list TS 131 Dumb tooth but in leave.	nil
2	Admitted one horse. HQ & 3" Bayone - Capt Young went on leave, OC of this Section took over 8" trailers during his absence	nil
3	Inspection by OC AVC of all transport at the Canteen - PREVANT. One horse admitted from 3" Signal Troop & 2 horses discharged cured KHOMC 2" Cav Div.	nil
4	Owing to continued hot weather, stables were found too warm for a number of sick horses.	nil
5	Conference at No 9 MVS believe the HORS 2" Cav Div & the OC No 7 & 9 MVS regarding provide active operations in the field	nil
6	Admitted 15 horses to DOVS (Major HOLMES) Canada "Cape" inspected.	nil
7	In Sector. Admitted two horses from 8" trailers	nil
8	Evacuated 26 horses from PREVANT, admitted charge property of General GREENLY for treatment, admitted 2 horses 2 Cav Brigade.	nil

Army Form C. 2118.

Continued

WAR DIARY
or
INTELLIGENCE SUMMARY
(Erase heading not required.)

Instructions regarding War Diaries and Intelligence Summaries are contained in F.S. Regs., Part II. and the Staff Manual respectively. Title pages will be prepared in manuscript.

Hour, Date, Place	Summary of Events and Information	Remarks and references to Appendices
August 8 — (continued)	T4.12012 Driver Lindsay forfeits 7 days pay for to following crime "When on active service making an improper reply to NCO" & "drunkenness"	h.q
— 9	Wounded 3 horses S" haves	h.q
— 10	Discharged 1 horse 3 Signal Troop, Discharges 2 horses to 2 Cav	h.q
	field Ambulance Admitted a C horse S" haves	
— 11	A.S. notes 1 horse Rifle amp. Bde (2 Cav Div)	h.q
— 12	Horse Rubric	h.q
— 13	Wounded 15 horses, receives 2 Remounts from No.15 field Remount	h.q
	Depot; ADVS 2"Cav Div visited Section — C.O of his Section	
	took him from Capt Smith (on leave) 3" M.G.S. & Divisional Troops	
— 14	TS 131 Driver WEST returns from leave, admits his horse from	h.q
	2"Cav Mobile Supply Col & HQ 3" Cav Brigade	
— 15	Receives 30 horses from PREVANT. Dispatch 1) D"Roy Squadron	h.q
	5" haves for Manzy by ADVS 2" Cav Div o VC of his Section	

Army Form C. 2118.

(continued)

WAR DIARY
or
INTELLIGENCE SUMMARY.
(Erase heading not required.)

Instructions regarding War Diaries and Intelligence Summaries are contained in F.S. Regs., Part II. and the Staff Manual respectively. Title pages will be prepared in manuscript.

Hour, Date, Place	Summary of Events and Information	Remarks and references to Appendices
August 16 — C In the Field	Admitted 2 horses Mobile Supply Col (2 [illeg])	nil
17	Admitted 6 horses 3" [illeg] Jun Spares & Accessories 9 Range [illeg]	nil
18	8 horses 9MD3 Issued Plaster	nil
19	76,20,12,40,12 Dvr LINDSAY — S accident. 14 days RPW (Jan. 1) Reformig	nil
20	8 Dog in orders. (2) being Orders for large for NCOs Admitted 4 horses — KAMS 2" [illeg] & 2 horses hi field. On	nil
21	LINDSAY out & 14 R 2 [illeg] for promotion. Sgt CARROLL Harriers having reported this course for 20,19 [illeg]	nil
22	PE 1067 Sgt STANLEY — W. J. left duty a Transfer M15 [illeg] — 26 horses Accessories 1 [illeg]	nil
23	Received 6 animals & no personnel (backups) 9 shall I place no in their [illeg] Califones — 8 men present for "A" Coding	nil

Army Form C. 2118.

WAR DIARY
of
INTELLIGENCE SUMMARY.
(Erase heading not required.)

Instructions regarding War Diaries and Intelligence Summaries are contained in F.S. Regs., Part II. and the Staff Manual respectively. Title pages will be prepared in manuscript.

Hour, Date, Place	Summary of Events and Information	Remarks and references to Appendices
August 24	6025 Pte Biggs W. admitted sick & 2 "Car Res Ambulance	M.G
25	Usual Routine	M.G
26	Another one horse HQ 3 "Car Brigade	M.G
27	Adds 2 Cars Res motor sect, another 6 horse.	M.G
28	Another one horse range — MM Pte Ayres Sgt. 2 "Car Div — 2 horse discharges 2 "Car Field Amb. at base discharges	M.G
	Res Park, 2 "Car Div	
29.	Errands 16 horse sick to base — another horse	M.G
	— Mounted Cellulitis fro "Staines	
30	C.O. holds dipping Park. B 6 Cups at L. his Tissu Faue	M.G
	near Montigcourt	
31	Receive 2 Cooper & 1 Rush remounts fro Base	M.G
	77065 Pte Penn C. to base & England	

R. Crawshaw Lieut
O.C. No 6 M.V.S.
M.C.

Army Form W.3091.

Nº 8 MOBILE VETY: SECTION

Cover for Documents.

Vol 35

Confidential

Nature of Enclosures.

War Diary
for Month of
September 1917

VOLUME NUMBER

XXXVII

Notes, or Letters written.

WAR DIARY
INTELLIGENCE SUMMARY

Army Form C. 2118.

Sept 1917

Vol No XXXVII   8th Mobile Vety Section

Hour, Date, Place	Summary of Events and Information	Remarks and references to Appendices
Sept 1	Usual Routine	h.s
2	ditto	h.s
3	ADVS 2 Cav Div visited the Section & inspected sick animals, also the 9 horses. ADMS Cavalry Corps inspected the Section. Driver LINDSEY admitted hospital.	h.s
4	Recovered into Section 8 horses of Mue "D" Battery RHA for treatment.	h.s
5	Admitted 10 horses & 3 B.S. horsecoovalus evacuated by rail from	h.s
	PRESENT & ABSENCE. Driver LINDSEY discharged from hospital & transferred to H.Q. A.S.C. 2 Cav Div. Driver GREGG. T.	
	received the Contribution of the Section from H.Q. A.S.C. 2 Cav Div.	
6	Usual Routine	h.s
7	ditto	h.s
8	ditto	h.s
9	ditto	h.s
10	ADVS 2 Cav Div visited the Section, inspected sick animals.	h.s
11	Charge proposed of Major TURNER A.P.V.J. 3rd Cav Div wounded for treatment	h.s
12	20 horses Pte PENN admitted from Cav level wounded 15 hours from	h.s
	PRESENT to rail to M.M.S.P/Vet L.O. GAS mill heel	h.s

WAR DIARY or INTELLIGENCE SUMMARY.

Army Form C. 2118.

Vol No 44 + 11

(Erase heading not required.)

Place	Date	Hour	Summary of Events and Information	Remarks and references to Appendices
Field	Sept 13		O.C. Stables near had PRESENT 5 new and draped 239 horses & mules sent up as repts for 2 Cav Div from ROUEN.	hq
	14		Time supplying for Remounts admin with Major Appleton 2 Cav Div.	hq
	15		210 horses suffering from mange belonging to 16 divisions admitted to Field hosp Horse Ruedin	hq
	16			hq
	17		Sec NOVS 2 Cav Div visited stables & inspected horses mules for Remounts. He also inspected the horses of the Field hosp 494 Coy & JOFFS. R. Sent to leave England. 210 horses & mules.	hqn.
	18		NOVS visited the stables & inspected sick horses for Remounts. These consisting of 3 cases of mange from 16 Lancers. C O visited ETREE MANIN & inspected his animals of the 2 Cav Monde Supp of Col & Rear Park.	hq

Sept 1917

WAR DIARY
or
INTELLIGENCE SUMMARY.

(Erase heading not required.)

Army Form C. 2118

Instructions regarding War Diaries and Intelligence Summaries are contained in F. S. Regs., Part II. and the Staff Manual respectively. Title pages will be prepared in manuscript.

Place	Date	Hour	Summary of Events and Information	Remarks and references to Appendices
Field	Sept. 19	—	As A.D.V.S. in charge of the Mobile Supply Coy – 2nd Cav. Div. – attended the inspection of the mobile Vet. S.O.C. 2 Cav. Div. at STREHHMIN.	
	20	—	Evacuated 11 horses from PREVENT & AGBEVILLE. Admitted a horse from 2 Queen's Spare R.E. Patch out.	
	21	—	DDVS Corps C.P.O. visited & inspected the section. Lieut R CLARKE RCVC SC.Q. Berlin went on leave to England. Capt J S Young A.V.C. take over section during absence. Pte WEEDS W. No Po to 23 transferred to No 2 Vet: Hospital.	
	22	—	A.D.V.S. mob section to see horses of 16th Lancers sent to section for skin disease.	
	23	—	Usual Routine.	
	24	—	A.D.V.S. mob section to inspect horses for evacuation – 4 horses + 3 mules taken over from 5th M.V.S. for sending to base.	
	25	—	Sanitary Officer 2nd Cav: Div: visits section – suggestions for improvement of sanitation being complied with.	
	26	—	admitted 11 horses evacuated 14 to base + 4 mules of 5th Mob. Vet. Sect.;	
	27	—		
	28	—	A.D.V.S. mob section & inspects camp – Section inspected by sanitary officer 2nd Cav. Div: who expressed approval of the way in which this suggested sanitary standing of system had been carried out. R.A. authority. DAG 6 H.Q. 3rd Echelon G.R. 67389/2 TT 655- Pte PENN G transferred dated W14/9 3/14/19 500/9/, 5/15. D.D. & L. A.D.SS/Forms/C.2145/ 1 horse admitted from 2nd C. Divs. Vetergn Psychus	

Army Form C. 2118.

WAR DIARY
or
INTELLIGENCE SUMMARY.
(Erase heading not required.)

Instructions regarding War Diaries and Intelligence Summaries are contained in F. S. Regs., Part II. and the Staff Manual respectively. Title pages will be prepared in manuscript.

Place	Date	Hour	Summary of Events and Information	Remarks and references to Appendices
[illegible]	29-9-17 30-		Two more Influenzas admitted for Treatment – Usual Routine	[illegible signature]

Vol 36

CONFIDENTIAL

WAR DIARY
OF
8th MOBILE VET. SECTION

From 1st October 1917 To 31st Oct 1917

(VOLUME XXXVIII)

Army Form W.3091.

Cover for Documents.

Confidential

Nature of Enclosures.

War Diary Volume N° XXXVIII
from
1st October 1917 to 31st October 1917
of
N° 8 Mobile Veterinary Section

Notes, or Letters written.

Army Form C.2118.

WAR DIARY
or
INTELLIGENCE SUMMARY.
(Erase heading not required.)

Vol 20 x x /11   8th Mobile Vety Sec.

Instructions regarding War Diaries and Intelligence Summaries are contained in F.S. Regs., Part II. and the Staff Manual respectively. Title pages will be prepared in manuscript.

Place	Date	Hour	Summary of Events and Information	Remarks and references to Appendices
G.V.Rly Sept 1916	1-10-17		A.D.V.S. Inst: section to inspect horses to ascertain 4 horses selected for evacuation	
	2nd		Usual routine. Inspected sick horses.	
	3rd		Evacuated 7 horses & 1 mule for evacuation. Received 11 horses 1 mule	
			Sent 1 horseshoer & 2 pioneers in charge of 8 sword horses to "D" Battery R.H.A. O.C. of section returned from Leave & Duties assumed by Lieut. A V. to Lieu.	
	4		Sanitary Officer visits section to inspect improvements in stables to pronounce his satisfaction.	
	5		A.D.V.S. 2 Cav Div visits section. Drainage for increase of number of animals provided. 8 horses & 4 mules received for treatment.	
	6		8 horses & 4 mules evacuated France.	
	7		Farriers Sergt Chopper Clark put hrs at Im'ace horn Hosp.	
	8		Section moves to new Billetting area - ROGELI COURT	
	9		A.D.V.S. 2 Cav Div. visits section.	
	10		D.D.V.S. Cavalry Corps & A.D.V.S. 2 Cav Div. visits section.	
	11		Pony Forest BELL-SMYTH visits section. 60 horses evacuated King 6 & 9 M.V.S.	
	12		Usual Routine.	

Army Form C. 2.

WAR DIARY
or
INTELLIGENCE SUMMARY.
(Erase heading not required.)

Instructions regarding War Diaries and Intelligence Summaries are contained in F. S. Regs., Part II. and the Staff Manual respectively. Title pages will be prepared in manuscript.

Place	Date	Hour	Summary of Events and Information	Remarks and references to Appendices
	Oct 17			
	13	—	Pte WEBB returned from leave — ENGLAND.	w.d
	14		Pte DAWSON G. on leave ENGLAND.	w.d
	15		Usual Routine	w.d
	16		A.D.V.S. 2nd Cav Div visited section. 6 horses re-evacuated.	w.d
	17		Pte FRY M. on leave ENGLAND. 6 horses evacuated Base	w.d
	18		Usual Routine. —	w.d
	19		Four horses evacuated Base.	w.d
	20		Section moves to rente new billeting area — Stays the night at HONVAL — Re-union horses lame horses from D° Battery. Corpl Mac charge of O.C Sect. Shd wing franchi, t'avoire.	w.d
	21		Section stay the night at DOMART —	w.d
	22		Section arrives at new billeting area at CROUSE (ANJERS-NAP B.2.) Pte MINTY ARRIVED	w.d
	23		A.D.V.S. 2nd Cav Div visited Section. Two lame horses returned to "D" Battery	w.d
	24		Usual Routine. Pte MINTY appointed Clerk Section vice Pte WEBB. Pte ALLEN arrives (?— not Sect Hosp.	w.d
	25		O.C. 1st Sect... visited H.Q 2nd Cav Div at St SAUFLIEU.	w.d
	26		D.D.V.S. Cavalry Corps visited section. Sh M.O.V.S 2 Cav Div. O.C of section visited FERRIERES with a view to moving the section there	w.d
	27		The Section moves press billeting area — FERRIERES — the section being billeted at Mr Clauffin.	w.d

Army Form C. 2118.

WAR DIARY
or
INTELLIGENCE SUMMARY.
(Erase heading not required.)

Instructions regarding War Diaries and Intelligence Summaries are contained in F.S. Regs., Part II. and the Staff Manual respectively. Title pages will be prepared in manuscript.

Place	Date	Hour	Summary of Events and Information	Remarks and references to Appendices
FIELD	Oct 28		Usual Routine	hut 8
	29		Usual Routine	hut 9
	30		Hrs 2 Coy Bn worked Scott taking a conference on the Pompon pit spraying on Anopheline lymphagoge -	hut 8
	31		7 horses mules inspected 5m/180H/h.b. Usual Routine	hut 9

J Anderson
Lieut
RMC
O.C. 205 M.V.S

Confidential

Vol 37

(6202 W 11186/M1151 350,000 12/16 McA. & W., Ltd. (Est. 781) Forms/W 3091/3. Army Form W. 3091.

Cover for Documents.

Nature of Enclosures.

War Diary Vol
8th Mobile Vety Sn
From 1st Nov 1917.
to 30 Nov 1917
(Vol XXXIX)

Notes, or Letters written.

Army Form C. 2118.

WAR DIARY
or
INTELLIGENCE SUMMARY. Vol No 3a.
(Erase heading not required.)

8th Mobile Vet. Sec.

Instructions regarding War Diaries and Intelligence Summaries are contained in F. S. Regs., Part II and the Staff Manual respectively. Title pages will be prepared in manuscript.

Hour, Date, Place	Summary of Events and Information	Remarks and references to Appendices
Full November 1st	Pte LUCAS. W. AVC left for Paris	
2	We have news from D'Bellay RHA for hitherto were RnK.	hq
3	Pte MINTY. L M admitted Sho 4.2 Stationary Hospt.	hq
	Pte BOWES A.E. admitted to 2 Cav. Fees Amb	hq
	RMS's Car with suspected measles.	hq
4	We have rendered 3 horses admitted from 3rd HBS with mange	hq
5	We have D' Battery admitted with mange	hq
6	Pte LUCAS.W. returns from leave. Pte MACKENZIE-T returns from	hq
7	leave. We have from 3 RGS 6 ae hue for & Horses admitted with mange. The O.C. 2nd 5 MVS having arrived we exchange the following units	hq
	We retain 1 Capt SMITH AVC. who lead gne Pte CHOUNDS - S cunde	hq
	D' Battery RHA - W Hussars + 3rd M.G.S.	
8	The Advd 2 Cav. Div. Index transporters live fetch	hq
9	11 horses evacuated Meaux.	hq
10	We have RnK	
11	Pte BOWES A.E. returns from Hospital (2 Cav Div Ay) Employed as...	hq
	6 Dr. HARRIS returns from leave. 3 horses admitted with mange	hq
12	We have and with fetch.	hq

Army Form C. 2118.

WAR DIARY
or
INTELLIGENCE SUMMARY. Vol 29
(Erase heading not required.)

Instructions regarding War Diaries and Intelligence Summaries are contained in F. S. Regs., Part II. and the Staff Manual respectively. Title pages will be prepared in manuscript.

Hour, Date, Place	Summary of Events and Information	Remarks and references to Appendices
2nd Jun 13"	The A.D.M.S. 2nd Can Div visits Headqrs & held a Conference with the D.O.S	ref
	The Brigade is in "Brigade Reserve".	
14"	6 horses arrived. Horse Parade	ref
15	Pte MINTY L.M. returns from sick Shel Hospital. Pte W BROWN sick	ref
	A leave System. have Rustin	
16	The Section left PERRIERS at 10.30AM & arrived at BRAY SUR	ref
	SOMME at 11 PM	
17	The Section left BRAY SUR SOMME at 4.30 PM & arrived at	ref
	TREFCON at 12.30 (night)	
18	The O.C. WS this chapter is Conference at the office of the A.D.M.S.	ref
	having future Trench Operation.	
19	Pte CHISM N.R. left a base at PERFERING. Pte ROBINSON Sick to	ref
	PERRIERES there had 3 sick horses. It has ceased to rain &	
	2.07 MVS.	
20"	At 1 AM the Section accompanies the 3rd Cav Bde on its march to	ref
	VILLERS- FAUCON. arriving there about 9 km. the section marchea	

(73989) W4141—463. 400,000. 9/14. H.&J.Ltd. Forms/C. 2118/10.

WAR DIARY
or
INTELLIGENCE SUMMARY.

(Erase heading not required.)

Army Form C. 2118.

Vol 24

Hour, Date, Place	Summary of Events and Information	Remarks and references to Appendices
Nov March 20 (cont)	"A" Echelon of the 2 Cav Bn at BOESART. Here the night was spent	WD
21	The section arrived at WEA (Pas-Neuvy Pau ignounati map) following	WD
	8 MEERS FAUCON here that night. Also reached at 1900, 3 men +	
	how Lanes. B.O of each Regu of the Bran.	
22	The section remain at VILLERS FAUCON all day.	WD
23	O.C. of the Bran attended a conference at the office of Brit Standard at	WD
	the Hotel of VILLERS FAUCON and at 4.30 pm the "A" Echelon arrived	
	at VRA (Pas-2 Brane Pau, ignounati map) & then 2000 yds a home	
	new EQUITEN COURT - PINS road. The night was spent here.	
24	At 5.30 pm the section proceeded to 2nd Cander Region at a place 2000	WD
	yds west of the 10 Cander Depot at the METZ-FINS road.	
25	The Section left the area at 9 am to the 3rd Cander Region (with the	WD
	Bran) stationed at RIBECOURT - here the Bran bivouacked shelling	
	for about 2 hours. & much of casualties occurred. Officer ran or horse	
	the Bran - the section reached the bivouac of the Bran but he was kept back	
26	moving	WD
27	tonic March.	WD
	town March.	WD

Army Form C. 2118.

WAR DIARY
or
INTELLIGENCE SUMMARY. Vol 29

(Erase heading not required.)

Place	Date	Hour	Summary of Events and Information	Remarks and references to Appendices
W	25		Work Routine	
"	29		Work Routine	
"	30.		Men of "A" Details & Boi. DSSSART in camp & picked up by French	

CONFIDENTIAL

WAR DIARY

OF

8th M.V. SECTION
FROM 1st DEC. 1917 TO 31st DEC 1917.

(VOLUME XL)

Confidential

(6202 W 11186/M1151 350,000 12/16 McA. & W., Ltd. (Est. 731) Forms/W 3091/3.   Army Form W. 3091.

Cover for Documents.

Nature of Enclosures.

War Diary
Volume XXX
1st Dec 1917
to
31st Dec 1917

8th Mobile Veterinary Section

Notes, or Letters written.

WAR DIARY
or
INTELLIGENCE SUMMARY.
(Erase heading not required.)

Army Form C. 2118.

Hour, Date, Place	Summary of Events and Information	Remarks and references to Appendices
FIELD. Dec 1st	Sectn-Sub w.h. "H" Echelon at BOIS - DESSART.	nil
Dec 2nd	Sectn rejoins 3rd Cavalry Brigade at FINS. 10 horses evacuated from his sectn to hospital. Sick 7 horses evacuated by sub off (Sick)	nil
Dec 3rd	24 horses received from units of the 2nd Cav. Bui for transfer to off sick.	nil
	6 horses sick suffering from fronts D.P. (sick) group	nil
Dec 4	Horse ambce - 4 horses received for transit.	nil
Dec 5	25 horses Gnd Eno 7 MVS evacuated. Sectn kemb? shelter	nil
Dec 6	had to move to posn. Sectn together w.h. 3rd Cav. Bui Porgare moves to BOUVET	nil
Dec 7	Sectn together w.h. 3rd Cav. Porgare moves from BOUVET to SAILLY-	nil
	LE-SEC	nil
Dec 8	Sectn moves from SAILLY-LE-SEC to FERRIERES - from	nil
	Billeting area. Both move Lf Sectn dud-evacuated	nil
Dec 9	Pte Embank returns from leave - horse ambce	nil
Dec 10	Horse R.mbie	nil
Dec 11	Horse Rmbie	nil
Dec 12	Horse Rmbie	nil
Dec 13	Sectn moves to MOLLIAUX	nil

Army Form C. 2118.

WAR DIARY
or
INTELLIGENCE SUMMARY.   Vol XXX

(Erase heading not required.)

Instructions regarding War Diaries and Intelligence Summaries are contained in F. S. Regs., Part II. and the Staff Manual respectively. Title pages will be prepared in manuscript.

Hour, Date, Place	Summary of Events and Information	Remarks and references to Appendices
Dec 14	O.C. visits Lithuanians - outlet had Behr at SALZUX	wef
Dec 15	Local India. O.C. attended Cooks. Parade of DDR Cav Cops	wef
Dec 16	The O.C. & Capt YOUNG ATC gave the Mallets Test & 42 horses	
	Rest of the following week of the Brigade - to Thursday Starving	wef
Dec 17	16 horses	
Dec 18	O.C. visits to Thursday & inspects mules & horses	wef
Dec 19	Horse Parade	wef
	The MDS D to Div. visits the sick & Greencarts, 10 horses	wef
	Sick.	
Dec 20	10 Sick horses (4 Deaths) Alluitis - 1 Periodic Ophthm.	wef
	(5 Men Sick) Greencarts & PM & ES-LSC-BAVX.	wef
	Remounts arrived to the Depot - 9.9 geldings, showing	
Dec 21	54 horses cases of DDR Cavalry Corps. Brownies & FOR??	wef
	LSC - BAVX.	wef
Dec 22	Horse parades of 115 horses sent to Vers Batch AN13113	wef

Army Form C. 2118.

WAR DIARY
or
INTELLIGENCE SUMMARY.

(Erase heading not required.)

Instructions regarding War Diaries and Intelligence Summaries are contained in F.S. Regs., Part II. and the Staff Manual respectively. Title pages will be prepared in manuscript.

Hour, Date, Place	Summary of Events and Information	Remarks and references to Appendices
Dec 23	Horse Routine	HQ
Dec 24	Horse Routine	HQ
Dec 25	Xmas Day	HQ
Dec 26	OC Of section notes AMT & SAA Cl RHA Batt. units of the 2"Cav	HQ
	Div. for the purpose of visiting their sick	
Dec 27	O.C. visits 4" Hussars & 2" Cav Reserve Park (for the purpose)	HQ
	Inspecting their sick	
Dec 28	Horse Routine. 302 huns of 2"d Cav Div sent Hq for Sp Force	HQ
Dec 29	Horse Routine	HQ
Dec 30	Horse Routine	HQ
Dec 31	OT visits L" Hussars, Horse Routine	HQ

N Cooper Swan
Lieut
RHC
O/C HQ NS

Army Form A. 2007.

CENTRAL REGISTRY.

Central Registry No. and Date.

Attached Files.

Confidential

SUBJECT, AND OFFICE OF ORIGIN.

8th/4 Mobile Veterinary Section

WAR DIARY

JANUARY - 1915 VOL XXIII

Referred to	Date	Referred to	Date	Referred to	Date

P.A.	Date

Schedule of Correspondence.

Inter-Office Minutes.

Note.—Inside sheets to be attached to this page.

NOT TO BE WRITTEN ON.

WAR DIARY
or
INTELLIGENCE SUMMARY.
(Erase heading not required.)

Army Form C. 2118.

VOC xxx
48
4

Hour, Date, Place	Summary of Events and Information	Remarks and references to Appendices
January 1st	Route Rouke - at violet 15 taken at BOUELLES & S' towns at ASSY	nil
" 2	Or ADVS 2nd Cav Dis looks the search for inspect reserves of Suite	nil
" 3	Scene (moopects) HAVGE D'Stance about us section to 6 other side road	nil
	S.M.HAVGE comes at 11 other side one routes Rhue (PORGES)	nil
" 4	V.P./A/Ket WEST activities sed to t soften. Hospl & stomk of to	nil
	Stugt auxiously, 6 side home admitted to Reclain.	
" 5	O.C. viole 4 Hussars. vised Pub Gs. O.C. hauts ase returning	nil
	Change of S & 15 cenemi of Capt Hill. A.V.C.	
" 6	vised Routes	nil
" 7	At case suspected HAVGE activities from S' Cinema HQ muselis	nil
" 8	vised Routes.	nil
" 9	O.C. violes S.A.A. of RHA, AHT Co & 4 Hussars Baunj	nil
	Samples HAV/GE received inspects f victualment	
" 10	POYS 2nd Cav Dis viscts & inspects serchi. S'H'ArGE of solten	nil
	Still have removed Rhue (PORGES). Pic woods left testing	
	line FENGLUND.	

WAR DIARY
or
INTELLIGENCE SUMMARY.

(Erase heading not required.)

Army Form C. 2118.

VC mm 44

Hour, Date, Place	Summary of Events and Information	Remarks and references to Appendices
January 11	OC visits 4" Hussars, 2" Cav Reserve Rd, SMO Oc RHA & AVTS – S heroes consulted the sick for parades for Pevensie OPHTHALMIA.	mG
" 12	All men in the section including NCOs report to MO NOIS 2 Tr On an Khin hiSical Calisym.	mG
" 13	Wore routine – Church Parade Service at Select SALISUR	mG
" 14	Horse Ridin	mG
" 15	OC Visits 4" Hussars – 2 cases Gonopicks range received from 4 Hussars	mG
" 16	MovS 2 Cav Div India's section for inspection & Inoculation of hours to PARIS ("14 days") 6 sick hereo received 9 mare. PURGES	mG
" 17	OC in the inspection trange at 2 Car Div Select. DUTY. Pte Luckori	mG
" 18	OC Visits 4" Hussars & work of Personel Troops at HQS	mG
" 19	2 cases Gonopick's Manos received from 4" Hussars	mG
" 19	Be here returned to 2 Car Res Qu H – OC 5 MRT Q & 2	mG
" 20	Revr 5 SRD Oc RHA – discharges cases. Pte Rohan Sorins ordered Horse Radius (Remarks, sick Pers Stat Hosp	mG

WAR DIARY
or
INTELLIGENCE SUMMARY.

Army Form C. 2118.

Hour, Date, Place	Summary of Events and Information	Remarks and references to Appendices
January 21	OC visits 4" Inspection + STAT.C.E.H.A + 2 Cav Res Park	AG
" 22	Horse Parade	AG
" 23	The ADVS Cavalry Corps + MOVS 2 Cav Div visits inspection	
	Lt Fisher OC visits inspects horses evacuated etc 2 Cav	AG
	Rly Siding at DURY	
	The OC visits inspects the following units for EPIZOOTIC	AG
24	LYMPHANGITIS - 2nd MVS, STAT C.E.H.A, AHT C + 3 Troop	AG
	HQ	
25	The OC visits inspects the following units for EPIZOOTIC	
	LYMPHANGITIS - 4 HUSSARS (2 Squadrons), The RSMS	
	2 Cav Div visits he returns on it. OC visits Lt SAGINAW	AG
	+ AHT G at HERS in connection with two suspicious cases	
	of EPIZOOTIC - LYMPHANGITIS.	
26	The OC visits inspects the following units for EPIZOOTIC	AG
	LYMPHANGITIS - Eskadron (1st Sqdn), 3 Co Full Arto + 2 Cav	

Army Form C. 2118.

WAR DIARY
or
INTELLIGENCE SUMMARY. Vol not 54

(Erase heading not required.)

Instructions regarding War Diaries and Intelligence Summaries are contained in F.S. Regs., Part II. and the Staff Manual respectively. Title pages will be prepared in manuscript.

Hour, Date, Place	Summary of Events and Information	Remarks and references to Appendices
January 27	Usual Routine.	
— 28	MOVS 2/Lt Orr Welch inspection Use Seter.	w.g
— 29	2/Lt Such Warcombe transfers S. FORCES, Pte hoods. G. admin p	w.g
	Pte Lucas W returns for leave (Paris)	w.g
— 30	Usual Routine. Pte Lucas W. returns for leave (Paris)	w.g
— 31	Sgt Juggs + 2 OR left for new billetting area. OR Weldi inspects	w.g
	4 H roard, SMACO + MHTG	

[signature]

Army Form A. 2007.

CENTRAL REGISTRY.

Central Registry No. and Date.

Attached Files.

8th Mobile Veterinary Section

SUBJECT, AND OFFICE OF ORIGIN.

WAR - DIARY -

FEBUARY - 1915

Referred to	Date	Referred to	Date	Referred to	Date
		(VOLUME 42)			
				P. A.	Date

Schedule of Correspondence.

Inter-Office Minutes.

Note.—Inside sheets to be attached to this page.

NOT TO BE WRITTEN ON.

Army Form C. 2118.

WAR DIARY
or
INTELLIGENCE SUMMARY.
(Erase heading not required.)

Army 1918   No 8 Mobile Vet. Section

Instructions regarding War Diaries and Intelligence Summaries are contained in F. S. Regs., Part II. and the Staff Manual respectively. Title pages will be prepared in manuscript.

Hour, Date, Place	Summary of Events and Information	Remarks and references to Appendices
February 1st 1918	Usual Routine	nil
" 2nd 1918	Usual Routine	nil
" 3rd 1918	The section moves into the 3rd Cavalry Brigade at MARŒUIL-CAUB area	nil
4	Hints live for the ngh	
	The section moved in from MARŒUIL-CAUB to St CHRIST being the road	nil
	area - taking over from the MASQUE Sq & COT Bergase Jkt 4 cavalry	nil
	Brown	
5	Usual Routine	nil
6	Usual Routine	nil
7	The MOVS 2 the Pmt inv the section - usual Routine	nil
8	OC visits & inspects SANCE RHA	nil
9	The OC visited MOVS 2 the CO by regret. Two sections from here to	nil
10	Starting to visit the officers Brigade	nil
	Usual Routine	nil
11	The MOVS 2 CavDiv visited inspected the section	nil
12	Usual Routine	nil
13	Usual Routine	nil
14	Usual Routine	nil

Army Form C. 2118.

WAR DIARY
or
INTELLIGENCE SUMMARY. N/42

(Erase heading not required.)

Instructions regarding War Diaries and Intelligence Summaries are contained in F.S. Regs., Part II. and the Staff Manual respectively. Title pages will be prepared in manuscript.

Hour, Date, Place	Summary of Events and Information	Remarks and references to Appendices
February 15 1918	Usual Routine. 26 NCOs on vacation. A Burt Butt & NC Rayburn proceeded on leave to England.	
February 16 1918	Usual Routine. Major N.G. Grant to report to Tulloch, NC reported for duty from No 2 Veterinary Hospital	T.W.S.
Feby 17, 1918	Major S.E. Hollwarth J proceeded to 209 MCS to duty. No 26897, Pt Cording A.V.C horse died 1405 2nd J Tetanus also A/CSgt NC to sick unit.	T.W.S.
February 18, 1918	A.V.S. carried out rifle and sword inspection & inspection of unit & bivvies.	T.W.S.
February 19, 1918	No horse were evacuated. One maxim gun required. Horse at the lines on admission by Sergt Tuttle	T.W.S.
February 20 1918	Usual Routine	T.W.S.
February 21 1918	Usual Routine	T.W.S.
Feby 22 1918	26 NCOs ever attended sick Parade.	T.W.S.
February 23 1918	Usual Routine. No 576 Pt Barnes & NC reported to duty from No 2 VCH Hospital. No 10536 Pt Snow reported back to England.	T.W.S.
February 24 1918	Usual Routine	T.W.S.

Army Form C. 2118.

WAR DIARY
or
INTELLIGENCE SUMMARY.   1/11/42

(Erase heading not required.)

Instructions regarding War Diaries and Intelligence Summaries are contained in F.S. Regs., Part II. and the Staff Manual respectively. Title pages will be prepared in manuscript.

Hour, Date, Place	Summary of Events and Information	Remarks and references to Appendices
Feby 25 1918	1:30pm 2nd Div noted action w/ 11 Bns & inverted informants. Divns prepared for evacuation	JWS
Feby 26, MK	Sick horses were evacuated from LA CHAPELETTE to 3rd Vety Hospital FOUQUESCOURT-EPPY. About 10 Mules & horses were evacuated daily. Capt J W Smith MC took temporary charge of section while Lt Col B.C. Kirkpatrick proceeded to instruction of NCOs and Capt L.M. Barton proceeded to instruction of NCOs & W of UTU DIVN Kept in Field for duty	JWS.
Feby 27 1918	Routine as usual. CAPT L.M.BARTON M.C. arrived 8pm reported to HQRS for duty	JWS.

Army Form A. 2007.

CENTRAL REGISTRY.

Central Registry No. and Date.

Nº 8 Mobile Vety Section

Attached Files.

SUBJECT, AND OFFICE OF ORIGIN.

War Diary for

Referred to	Date	Referred to	Date	Referred to	Date
		March	1918		
		Volume XXXI			
		Volume 43			

P. A.	Date

Schedule of Correspondence.

Inter-Office Minutes.

NOTE.—Inside sheets to be attached to this page.

NOT TO BE WRITTEN ON.

8th Mobile Vety Sn

WAR DIARY
or
INTELLIGENCE SUMMARY.
(Erase heading not required.)

March Volume 43.

Army Form C.

Instructions regarding War Diaries and Intelligence Summaries are contained in F.S. Regs., Part II. and the Staff Manual respectively. Title pages will be prepared in manuscript.

Hour, Date, Place	Summary of Events and Information	Remarks and references to Appendices
1st March 1918	Sundry sick many wounds Gun Mules. Visited St Lawrence	OnB
2nd March 1918	Routine as usual	OnB
3rd March 1918	Routine as usual	OnB
3rd March 1918	H.O.A. inspected section and horses reported for evacuation	OnB
4th March 1918	Routine as usual. Routine talk + Inspection 2pm-4pm	OnB
5th March 1918	Evacuated few animals. Work expedited to hurryly hospital	OnB
6th March 1918	all anxious cases sent. Transports pack & track Letters	OnB
7th March 1918	usual Routine	OnB
8th March 1918	usual Routine	OnB
9th March 1918	Noted Jm Mule Line evac + inspected with A.D.V.S etc.	OnB
10th March 1918	A.O.Q.d visited section + inspected animals reported for evacuation	OnB
11th March 1918	usual Routine	OnB
12th March 1918	13 sick animals evacuated from H.Q. HAPDETTE to M.V. Hospital Force. Preparations made for moving to Ubani	OnB

8th Mob: Vet: Sec:n March 1918
Vol. 43

WAR DIARY
or
INTELLIGENCE SUMMARY
(Erase heading not required.)

Army Form C. 2118.

Instructions regarding War Diaries and Intelligence Summaries are contained in F.S. Regs., Part II. and the Staff Manual respectively. Title pages will be prepared in manuscript.

Hour, Date, Place	Summary of Events and Information	Remarks and references to Appendices
13 March 1918	The Section moved at 7.30 a.m. to Einemann where it took up its position in the 8th Cav Bde order of march & arrived at GAMORY at 5 p.m.	ChB.
14 March 1918	Visited R.V.S. reference or matters relating to veterinary ammunition in wartime.	ChB.
15 March 1918	A.D.V.S. visited section inspected sick/starting field.	ChB.
16 March 1918	Normal routine	ChB.
17 March 1918	Usual routine	ChB.
18 March 1918	A.D.V.S. visited section. Pte Smith went on leave.	ChB.
19 March 1918	SS/14488 Pte Burgess reported for duty from 1st Cav. Field Amb: evacuated nine horses, and admitted two from 5th Lancers.	ChB.
20 March 1918	SS/24884 Pte Brickell E. returned from leave, two strayed animals admitted until claimed. Inspection of mens billets and sanitary arrangements by A.D.V.S.	ChB.
21st March 1918	Usual Routine	ChB.

Army Form C. 2118.

WAR DIARY
or
INTELLIGENCE SUMMARY.
(Erase heading not required.)

Instructions regarding War Diaries and Intelligence Summaries are contained in F.S. Regs., Part II. and the Staff Manual respectively. Title pages will be prepared in manuscript.

Hour, Date, Place	Summary of Events and Information	Remarks and references to Appendices
22nd March - (Friday)	Usual Routine	ChuB.
23 March	Section Moved from GRANDRU this and day and are now a few kilometres South-west from same, situated on the edge of a wood.	ChuB.
24 March	Section moved to ST LEDGER, 1 M.E.6. 4 Men detailed and to be attached 5 Lancers	ChuB.
25 March	Are following the division south west and now at COMPEIGNE.	ChuB.
26 March	Moved from COMPEIGNE this morning Men attached to 5 Lancers reported to report and several reports from Scouts	ChuB.
27 March		ChuB.
28 March	Admitted three horses	ChuB.
29 March	Moved to south west and a kilometre outside the village of LETOURCLET	ChuB.
30 March	The section is lying on edge of wood north of LE TOURCLET, and awaiting developments. Two to habile espion, in accordance with orders, several wounded horses have been admitted, and tactern to blazing station by 1 M.O. as arranged. Men being on patrol in further the village to collect horses, strayed and wounded, and aircraft each with scene to the section	ChuB.
31st March	Section moved to south of the village of LETOURCLET, on account of being under observation from enemy. 22 Wounded horses have been admitted	ChuB.

C.R. Burton Capt M.V.C.
8th V.S.

Army Form W.3091.

Confidential

Cover for Documents.

War Diary Vol 44

Nature of Enclosures.

8th Mobile Vety Sn

3 Cav Bde

Reference to A.V.C. Records letter 17:259.18
dated 3rd April 1918.

Date of Mobilisation 5th Aug 1918
Arrived in France 16th Aug 1918

Notes, or Letters written.

Rate of Mobilization? Can Rd
Signed in Frankein May 1916
Volume ? ?

WAR DIARY
or
INTELLIGENCE SUMMARY.

(Erase heading not required.)

Army Form C. 2118.

Instructions regarding War Diaries and Intelligence Summaries are contained in F.S. Regs., Part II. and the Staff Manual respectively. Title pages will be prepared in manuscript.

Hour, Date, Place	Summary of Events and Information	Remarks and references to Appendices
April 1st Monday	Evacuated 22 wounded horses to SALEUX. to Veterinary Clearing Station	C in R.
April 2nd	Evacuated 14 Horses to Clearing Station PICQUIGNEY.	C in R.
April 3rd	Inspection of Rifles and Respirators	C in R.
April 4th	Evacuated 14 Horses mostly wounded to Veterinary Clearing Station PICQUIGNEY	C in R.
April 5th	Station moved today and arrived here just after midday BELLOY-SUR-SOMME admitted two horses	C in R.
April 6th	Section moved with brigade this morning and billeted now at BELLANCOURT, in empty cottage, evacuated the two horses admitted last night, to Clearing Station.	C in R.
April 7th	The section has today been overhauled, so as to have efficiency and a brush up action. Uniform as nearly as possible. One horse admitted today. Horses Mondieu	C in R.
April 8th	Twenty three sick horses inspected by A.D.V.S. evacuated and to horse my Hospital A.C.H.? at BELLANCOURT at 3.30 P.M. not verified + turned out.	C in R.
April 9th	LABROYE?	

WAR DIARY or INTELLIGENCE SUMMARY

Army Form C. 2118.

Volume 44

(Erase heading not required.)

Instructions regarding War Diaries and Intelligence Summaries are contained in F.S. Regs., Part II and the Staff Manual respectively. Title pages will be prepared in manuscript.

Hour, Date, Place	Summary of Events and Information	Remarks and references to Appendices
12th April 1918	Left LA BROYE about 2 P.M. and arrived at ERBLINGHEM about 8 P.M.	C in B
13th April 1918	Left ERBLINGHEM about 2 P.M. and arrived with Bde at LYNDE 7 P.M.	C in B
14th April 1918	Nothing unusual. 16 horses evacuated by road to No 3	C in B
15th April 1918	During afternoon Staff Captain wounded. Horse to forward area. Party left in charge of Shoe Smith returned 6.30 for 7 Bulls.	C in B
16th April 1918	Warm turned mounted troops in charge N/O N/G A.V.C. leaving at 7 P.M. returning 7 P.M.	C in B
17th April 1918	Routine as usual. 17 sick horses evacuated to No 23 vet. Hospital. Stomer.	C in B
18th April 1918	Left LYNDE at 11 A.M. with Feld von 3 Cav Bde arrived at EECKE about 5 P.M. 1 horse evacuated on line of march	C in B
19th April 1918	General Routine	C in B
20th April 1918	Usual Routine	C in B
21st April 1918	21 sick horses evacuated to XII CCS	C in B

Army Form C. 2118.

WAR DIARY
or
INTELLIGENCE SUMMARY.
8th Motor MGSn VOLUME 44

(Erase heading not required.)

Instructions regarding War Diaries and Intelligence Summaries are contained in F.S. Regs., Part II and the Staff Manual respectively. Title pages will be prepared in manuscript.

Hour, Date, Place	Summary of Events and Information	Remarks and references to Appendices
22 April 1918	Usual Routine	ChS
23 April 1918	Usual Routine	ChS
24 April 1918	Left ECKE took Rochinoy & Curlohe at 10 A.M. – arrived at LYNDE about 12.30 P.M. Sommelled 12 and horses to XI Corps YET en route	ChS
25 April 1918	Usual routine	ChS
26 April 1918	Usual routine – evacuated 21 and P horses to VIII Corps	ChS
	NET	
27 April 1918	Left with Kellon and 3rd Cav. Patrol LYNDE at 9.30 A.M. + arrived at HEURINGHEM 3.15 P.M. Stationed outside HEURINGHEM & Rebecque on Neuschoolroad leading to BLESSY	ChS
28 April 1918	Usual Routine	
29 April 1918	Left HEURINGHEM at 9.30 A.M. and proceeded with Kellon to DOHEM. Stationed in a field attached to RO office.	ChS
30 April 1918	NOW 2nd Cav. Div. and Cav. Corps visited section. Usual routine	ChS

ChS
Jn. Benton Capt KR
8th MMGSn

Army Form W.3091.

Cover for Documents.

Nature of Enclosures.

CONFIDENTIAL

War Diary May
8th Mobile Vety Sn
From 1st May 1918   To 31st May 1918
Volume 45

Notes, or Letters written.

Nº 8 Mobile Vety Section

WAR DIARY
or
INTELLIGENCE SUMMARY.

May 1918
Volume 45

Army Form C. 2118

(Erase heading not required.)

Instructions regarding War Diaries and Intelligence Summaries are contained in F.S. Regs., Part II and the Staff Manual respectively. Title pages will be prepared in manuscript.

Hour, Date, Place	Summary of Events and Information	Remarks and references to Appendices
May 1st	Rifle competition held and Gas Drill.	CInB
May 2nd	Inspection of Saddles and Harness	CInB
May 3rd	40 cast Horses and 7 Sick evacuated to St. OMER	CInB
May 4th	No 28836 Pte FERGUSON, A.V.C. reported for duty from 14 Vety. Hos:	CInB
May 5th	A/St DOHEM at 9 A.M. this morning and arrived at our present billet at 5 P.M. Major Section Fm. Gm. the F. in LEFAUX (anous 13)	CInB
May 6th	Waggon and Limbet received perfect - 1st Painting - Veterinary Equipment overhauled, with a view of making good deficiencies, and ref: A/Nos Letter dated 5-5-18.	CInB
May 7th	A/C Cpl MINTY, L.M. reported to S.H.2 2nd Echelon for dest.	CInB
May 8th	A.D.V.S. visited Section, two horses admitted for evacuation. Arrangements made for latrines, refuse dumps, etc. reported & demanded with a view to make section efficient. ref: ADVS Letter N09 dated 8-5-17.	CInB
May 9th →	Evacuated 5 Horses (sick) to 15 Vety. Hos:	CInB

Army Form C. 2118.

WAR DIARY
or
INTELLIGENCE SUMMARY.
(Erase heading not required.)

Instructions regarding War Diaries and Intelligence Summaries are contained in F. S. Regs., Part II. and the Staff Manual respectively. Title pages will be prepared in manuscript.

Place	Date	Hour	Summary of Events and Information	Remarks and references to Appendices
ZEFAUX	May 10	6 P.M.	Rifles inspected and drill followed. Horse of Actg QM died this morning at A.O.M. through Ruptured Intestine	CnB
"	May 11	7 P.M.	A lecture given with a view of advancing the men in Veterinary work.	CnB
"	May 12	5.30 P.M.	Usual Routine.	CnB
"	May 13	8 P.M.	Mg instructed in Map Reading. The section paraded for Baths.	CnB
"	" 14	4.30 P.M.	Kit Inspection, and examination of mens clothing. One Horse admitted (Mich Style)	CnB
"	" 14	8.30 P.M.	Two Horses admitted for treatment. (Mange) of 16" Lancers.	CnB
"	May 15	7.20 "	Seventy Horses admitted this Morning, and inspected by A.D.V.S., Twenty Horses evacuated this afternoon by road to 13 Vet Hos.	CnB
"	May 16	6 P.M.	Riding School was held for the section following the lecture on "Dressing".	CnB
"		7 P.M.	One Horse admitted (Mange) of 5" Lancers	CnB
"	May 17	5.30 P.M.	Disinfection of Blankets and further instructions in the use of small Kit Respirators	CnB
"	May 18	11 P.M.	Section paraded to Baths. One Horse has been admitted from D&M A H.A. as a suspected Mange case 3 Horses were evacuated to 13 V.H. Rousbrugt	CnB
"	May 19		Usual Routine	CnB
"	May 20		Gas drill 2-30 P.M. Rifle drill 3-30 P.M.	CnB

Army Form C. 2118.

WAR DIARY 8th Mobile Vety Sn
INTELLIGENCE SUMMARY. 3 Cav Bde Vol 45

(Erase heading not required.)

Place	Date	Hour	Summary of Events and Information	Remarks and references to Appendices
Field May	21		NCOs & Vety Section at 11 A.M. to inspect horses & vaccination races were evacuated to 13 Vety Hospital Neufchatel. Gas drill at 3.30 P.M.	Cav B.
	22		Lecture on Trops Road & Vety men given at 3.30 PM by OC	Cav B.
	23		Usual Routine	Cav B.
	24		Gas drill & Inspection at 2.30 P.M. 10 sick horses were evacuated to No 3 Vety Hospital Neufchatel	Cav B.
	25		Gas drill at 2.30 P.M. A lecture on Sanitation was given by Sgt Annesland 3.30pm	Cav B.
	26		Continuation between 2 nd & 3rd Divisions standing confirmed.	Cav B.
	27		In the morning the NCOs 2Cav Div inspected its Sanitary arrangements of the divisions. 2-3.30 P.M. Gas drill Inspection of horses evacuated to No 13 Vet Hospital Neufchatel	Cav B.
	28		NCOs 2 Cav Div in the morning inspected the sick horses Neufchatel were evacuated to USVS Vet Hospital Neufchatel	Cav B.
	29		Pursuant to Divl Orders all ranks underwent tear and chlorine gas gas for 12 hours in their gas masks	Cav B.
	30		Usual Routine	Cav B.
	31		Gas Inspection at Drill N 2.30 pm	Cav B.

CW Bardin
Capt A/C
"not no 6 Nt M.Vet.Sn 31 May 1918

CONFIDENTIAL
WAR   DIARY.
       OF
8th. MOBILE VETERINARY SECTION

From 1st.June,1918. - To - 30th. June,1918.

       (Volume 46).

       -:- -:-:-:-:-:-:-

                    NOT TO BE WRITTEN ON.

Army Form A. 2007.

CENTRAL REGISTRY.

Central Registry No. and Date.

Confidential

8th Mobile Vety Sn

Attached Files.

SUBJECT, AND OFFICE OF ORIGIN.

War Diary Volume 46 June

Referred to	Date	Referred to	Date	Referred to	Date

P. A.	Date

Schedule of Correspondence.

Inter-Office Minutes.

NOTE.—Inside sheets to be attached to this page.

Army Form C. 2118.

WAR DIARY

or

INTELLIGENCE SUMMARY. 8th Mobile Vy Sn

Volume 46

(Erase heading not required.)

Instructions regarding War Diaries and Intelligence Summaries are contained in F. S. Regs., Part II. and the Staff Manual respectively. Title pages will be prepared in manuscript.

Place	Date	Hour	Summary of Events and Information	Remarks and references to Appendices
France	1 June		1 horse & 3 mules evacuated to No 13 Vety Hospital Neufchatel. During night an aerial torpedo was dropped from an enemy aeroplane among the horses of the Sutor. No casualties either to horses or men resulted.	CinB
France	2 June		Usual Routine.	CinB
France	3 June		Royal Bovine gas drill at 2.30 P.M.	CinB
France	4 June		7 horses evacuated to No 13 Veterinary Hospital Neufchatel. 89 horses inspected below at 3.30 PL	CinB
France	5 June		Usual Routine. No 27836 Pte Ferguson S.T.M.C. proceeded to No 13th in relief of No 691 Pte Chaplin Pte Ayliffe who reported for duty 4 June. 12 All ranks attended H.E. 2.30am. Horses now groomed through shell gas chamber by Mo gas NC	CinB
France	6 June		Section attended Genl Dais Gaylas at 2.30 P.M.	CinB
"	"		Gas Drill at 2.30 P.M.	CinB
France	7 June		Full Drill & Inspection at 2.30 P.M.	CinB
France	9 June		Usual Routine.	CinB
France	10 June		25 horses inspected below at 10.30 AM. 18 horses evacuated afters 1st afternoon	CinB
France	11 June		5 horses evacuated 6 No 13 V.H. mainly string inaimotion at 2.30 PM	CinB
France	12 June		Afternoon Grooming at 2.30 by Cpl Smith	CinB

WAR DIARY or INTELLIGENCE SUMMARY

Army Form C. 2118.

Volume 16

2nd Mobile Vety Sn

Place	Date	Hour	Summary of Events and Information	Remarks and references to Appendices
Lepine	13 June 18		Musketry Instruction firing at 2.30 P.M. O.C., N.C.O.'s and 21 leading Grades of Staff	Cn.B
	14 June 18		Musketry Instruction firing at 2.30 P.M.	Cn.B
	15 June 18		2 N.C.O. & 4 men accompanied O.C. to Zuhrevent where a demonstration was given	
			by 2nd Cav Officer both to men & horses.	Cn.B
	16 June 18		Usual Routine	Cn.B
	17 June 18		47 horses cast 13½ men evacuated to No 5/13 Vety Hospital Mutzbrul	Cn.B
	18 June 18		23 Horses evacuated No 5/13 Vety Hospital horses taken routine wk	Cn.B
	19 June 18		24 N.C.B. & O.R. returned 2nd Bath.	Cn.B
	20 June 18		Usual Routine	Cn.B
	21 June 18		Parade of doctors and 16 Horsen transfer as a measure against the	Cn.B
			spread of P.U.O. Influenza active at 2.30 P.M. by parade on Pressing	
	22 June 18		Usual Routine. Arrival of numerous horses noted with P.U.O. 6?	
			Auxqs PRostlyings. R .N.C. Recalled to Pm. 2.20 Hthland went P.U.O Influenza	Cn.B
	23 June 18		Usual Routine held adjustrantion Statishi chestmen men took urk	
			P.U.O Influenza	Cn.B
	24 June		Kit Inspection at 10 P.M. "made" rubs destin worked on and moved	Cn.B
			to bee dready by M equipment.	Cn.B

Army Form C. 2118.

WAR DIARY of 8th March W Yorks
INTELLIGENCE SUMMARY. 26 June 16

(Erase heading not required.)

Instructions regarding War Diaries and Intelligence Summaries are contained in F. S. Regs., Part II. and the Staff Manual respectively. Title pages will be prepared in manuscript.

Place	Date	Hour	Summary of Events and Information	Remarks and references to Appendices
Where	June 1916			
	25 June		Both sides rather quiet — enemy shells reported to evacuate	ClnB
	26 June		21 hours intermittent R.F. into by stop int	ClnB
	27 June		Usual Routine	ClnB
	28 June		OC C/82 Bn reconnoitred — next I conduct	
			STATHCAUGH. Lt Col Comd of 8th Bn Wyr on his of service	ClnB
	29 June		Usual Routine Echos attended seal Bath	NoS
	30 June		Usual Routine	NoS

Todd Smith
Capt AVC
for
OC
8th March W Yorks
30 June 1916
War Diary Volume 26

Army Form A. 2007.

CENTRAL REGISTRY.

Central Registry No. and Date.   Attached Files.

Confidential

SUBJECT, AND OFFICE OF ORIGIN.

No 8 Mobile Vety Sn

War Diary for July 1918
Volume 47

Referred to	Date	Referred to	Date	Referred to	Date

P. A.	Date

Schedule of Correspondence.

Inter-Office Minutes.

NOTE.—Inside sheets to be attached to this page.

NOT TO BE WRITTEN ON.

Army Form C. 2118

WAR DIARY of Mobile Vety Sec
or
INTELLIGENCE SUMMARY. Volume 47
(Erase heading not required.)

Instructions regarding War Diaries and Intelligence Summaries are contained in F.S. Regs, Part II. and the Staff Manual respectively. Title pages will be prepared in manuscript.

Place	Date	Hour	Summary of Events and Information	Remarks and references to Appendices
Rouen	July 1st		Usual Routine	TWS
	July 2nd		AOVS inspected the section and animals proposed for evacuation	TWS
	July 3rd		10 horses & 1 mule evacuated to No 13 Vety Hospital NEUFCHATEL	TWS
	July 4th		Usual Routine	TWS
	July 5th		Pte Sgt CARNELL CT, Pte GREEN CT, Pte COX PRATT PC & Pte BOWES AE presented for Regt 2 Cav Div with certificates in recognition of service rendered	TWS
	July 6th		Usual Routine	TWS
	July 7th		Usual Routine	TWS
	July 8th		R/Os still inspection w/r 30 Pul	TWS
	July 9th		AOVS inspected section, Horses prepared for evacuation	TWS
	July 10th		18 horses evacuated to No 13 Vety Hospital NEUFCHATEL	TWS
	July 11th		Gen inspection 11 AM, all ranks now inspection & continued their ordinary duties from 11 AM — 11.30 AM. 2 horses evacuated by MP 15 Tpt 4th S/R 13/H/T of ambulance hunt was carried out from 11 — 11.30 PM	TWS
	July 12		Usual Routine. Workshops hunt was carried out, TCAPT CP BARTON AVC returned from leave and took over command vice CAPT WJ SMITH AVC	TWS
	July 13		Usual Routine	TWS

WAR DIARY
or
INTELLIGENCE SUMMARY.

Army Form C. 2118.

Place	Date	Hour	Summary of Events and Information	Remarks and references to Appendices
	14 July		6 horses evacuated. Section accompanied Bde to LEPPOER arriving 7 PM	Church
	15 July		Usual Routine	Church
	16 July		Section moved from LEPPOER at 10-30 AM with Bde to AVVIN arriving at 5-30 PM	Church
	17 July		Section moved out unexpectedly at 10-30 AM from AVVIN to EPS. ADVS + O.C.US visited section at 2-30 PM	Church
	18 July		ADVS visited section and unused horses for evacuation	Church
	19 July		3 horses evacuated to VET HEVCHIN.	Church
	20 July		Gas Inspection 2-30 PM	Church
	21 July		Usual Routine	Church
	22 July		Proceeded with Bde id. 9 AM for PROER arriving at 1 PM.	Church
	23 July		Proceeded at 7 PM with Bn. from LEPOER to some fields at LEPPER x arriving at 2-30 PM	Church
	24 July		Usual Routine	Church
	25 July		Usual Routine	Church
	26 July		Usual Routine	Church
	27 July		Usual Routine	Church
	28 July		Usual Routine	Church
	29 July		Usual Routine	Church

WAR DIARY

Army Form C. 2118.

of No 1 Mobile Vety Sec
Volume 47

INTELLIGENCE SUMMARY.
(Erase heading not required.)

Place	Date	Hour	Summary of Events and Information	Remarks and references to Appendices
	30 July		Accompanied ADVS 2nd Cav Div on his inspection of 2074 & 3 Cav Bde Vet Sections which arrived at the centre at 11.30 am	Qu B
	31 July		18 AVR mange horses evacuated by road to No 13 Vety Hospital. Accompanied OC Vety 2 Cav Div marked return transport at Lemotte and then visited the F.A.	Qu B

CnBaxter Capt AVC
OC
1st Mobile Vety Sec

Army Form A. 2007.

CENTRAL REGISTRY.

Central Registry No. and Date.

Attached Files.

Confidential

War Diary

SUBJECT, AND OFFICE OF ORIGIN.

Volume 48

8th Mobile Vety Section

Referred to	Date	Referred to	Date	Referred to	Date
				August 1918	

P. A.	Date

Schedule of Correspondence.

Inter-Office Minutes.

Note.—Inside sheets to be attached to this page.

NOT TO BE WRITTEN ON.

Army Form C. 2118.

WAR DIARY of Volunteer P.

INTELLIGENCE SUMMARY.

(Erase heading not required.)

July 1918 for the Vilytin

Instructions regarding War Diaries and Intelligence Summaries are contained in F.S. Regs., Part II. and the Staff Manual respectively. Title pages will be prepared in manuscript.

Place	Date	Hour	Summary of Events and Information	Remarks and references to Appendices
	1 Aug 1918		defence moved fortino	Ou B
	2 Aug 1918		defence usual content	Ou B
	3 Aug 1918		defence usual routine	Ou B
	4 Aug 1918		defence	Ou B
			moved unit 8 Oct Bn to MAINTENAY, starting 9 PM arriving at 2-30 AM. 24 horses evacuated also B 20 PVH to & PVH	Ou B
	5 Aug 1918		maintenay moved at 9-30 PM to PICRUIGNY arriving at 3 AM 13 horses evacuated to No 19 VES.	Ou B
	6 Aug 1918		arrived at 11-30 PM with No Silhym to 2 kilos S of GLISY arriving at 8-30 AM. 9 AM moves 1 kilometer further forward 12 sick horses evacuated to 39th Mob Vet Sect. Mob transport party proceeded with seven silting regiments	Ou B
	7 Aug 1918			Ou B
	8 Aug 1918		Proceeded to 9 AM forward echelon attacking at 6.20 AM Mob transport lorries remained the night near HANGARD	Ou B
	9 Aug 1918		Proceeded independently to position not 1500 yards SE of horses evacuated to 20th and 32nd mounted Regt VES	Ou B
	10 Aug 1918		Proceeded independently to position 1000 yds W of reference to a position W of CAYEUX arriving at 6 PM where action reported to No 5 area	Ou B
	11 Aug 1918		moved at 4 PM to position W of CAYEUX arriving at 3.15 PM where water Staff	Ou B
	12 Aug 1918		Staff car connected to Mob Vet	Ou B
	13 Aug 1918			

WAR DIARY
or
INTELLIGENCE SUMMARY

Army Form C. 2118.

Volume HP. 5th Mobile Vety Sec

(Erase heading not required.)

Instructions regarding War Diaries and Intelligence Summaries are contained in F. S. Regs., Part II. and the Staff Manual respectively. Title pages will be prepared in manuscript.

Place	Date	Hour	Summary of Events and Information	Remarks and references to Appendices
	14 August		Usual Routine	
	15 August		Left Catz 9-30 AM and arrived at PERDONVET 7-30 PM 15th	Ch. B
	16 August		Left PERDONVET at 10-15 AM arrived at PERNOIS at 2-30 PM 17th	Ch. B
	17 August		Left Pernois at 9-15 PM and arrived at GREZAUCOURT at 11-45 PM 18th	Ch. B
	18 August		Section environs 10 mile radius in by reported action.	Ch. B
	19 August		Usual Routine	Ch. B
	20 August		Usual Routine	Ch. B
	21 August		Left with Section 4½ mile at 8 PM and arrived at OUILLEMONT at 3 PM. 12 sick horses evacuated by road to No 5 Vety Hosp RDS	Ch. B
	22 August		Left with 14 horses at 8 PM all proceed to BELLICOURT	Ch. B
	23 August		Left BELLICOURT at 5 PM. Proceed to HYETTE arriving at 7 PM and returned to SOUCHY-LEMETTE	Ch. B
	24 August		Section left SOUCHY-LEMETTE 6-30 PM & returned to OUILLEMONT arriving at 11 AM	Ch. B
	25 August		Usual Routine	Ch. B
	26 August		8 horses evacuated to No 5 Vety. GOUY-EN-ARTOIS	Ch. B
	27 August		Usual Routine	Ch. B

WAR DIARY or INTELLIGENCE SUMMARY.

8th Mobile Vety Sec   Army Form C. 2118.

Volume 46

(Erase heading not required.)

Hour, Date, Place	Summary of Events and Information	Remarks and references to Appendices
28 August COULLEMONT	usual Routine	Ans
29 August COULLEMONT	usual Routine	Ans
30 August COULLEMONT 6 sickhorses evacuated to II Corps Vet Mondicourt		Ans
31 August COULLEMONT	usual Routine	Ans

A.W. Barlow Capt AVC
OC
8th MVS
31/8

Army Form A. 2007.

CENTRAL REGISTRY.

Central Registry No. and Date. — Confidential — Attached Files.

SUBJECT, AND OFFICE OF ORIGIN.

WAR DIARY
of
9TH MOBILE VETERINARY SECTION
From 1st to 30th September 1918
Vol. No. 49

Inter-Office Minutes.

Note.—Inside sheets to be attached to this page.

NOT TO BE WRITTEN ON.

WAR DIARY Mobile Veterinary Army Form C. 2118.
of
INTELLIGENCE SUMMARY. Mumu 46

(Erase heading not required.)

Instructions regarding War Diaries and Intelligence Summaries are contained in F. S. Regs., Part II. and the Staff Manual respectively. Title pages will be prepared in manuscript.

Hour, Date, Place		Summary of Events and Information	Remarks and references to Appendices
Doullimont	1st Sept	Mural Routine	Club
	2nd Sept	8 sick horses evacuated to VI Corps Vet Mob Section	Club
	3 Sept	Mural Routine	Club
	4 Sept	Mural Routine	Club
	5 Sept	Mural Routine	Club
	6 Sept	Mural Routine	Club
	7 Sept	Proceeded at 10 p.m with the Brigade to Lattre St Quentin	Club
Lattre St Quentin	8 Sept	arrived at 3.30 A.M	Club
		9 sick horses evacuated to 17 Corps Vet Mob Section, Lestoffes	Club
	9 Sept	4 sick horses evacuated to 17 Corps Vet Mob Section, Lestoffes	Club
	10 Sept	Proceeded with Brigade to Dieval at 10 p.m returned at 5.30 P.M	Club
Dieval	11 Sept	Mural Routine	Club
	12 Sept	Mural Routine	Club
	13 Sept	Mural Routine	Club
	14 Sept	10 W. Mosquito sick	Club
	15 Sept	2 knees wounded to 1 Vet Bn S.H.N	Club
	16 Sept	Mural Routine	Club
	17 Sept	Mural Routine	Club

WAR DIARY
or
INTELLIGENCE SUMMARY.
(Erase heading not required.)

Army Form C. 2118.

Instructions regarding War Diaries and Intelligence Summaries are contained in F. S. Regs., Part II and the Staff Manual respectively. Title pages will be prepared in manuscript.

Hour, Date, Place	Summary of Events and Information	Remarks and references to Appendices
18 September DIEVAL	Usual routine. No 438 & 375 & 1st French Cyclists reported for duty vice H/2386 & 7 stricken who proceeded	CircB
19 Sept DIEVAL	to S.A., 2nd Army Rd.	
19 Sept DIEVAL	Usual Routine	CircB
20 Sept DIEVAL	Usual Routine	CircB
21 Sept DIEVAL	25 Horses & 1 W.O.R. mule evacuated near to Mob. Vet.	CircB
	Section	
22 Sept DIEVAL	Lieutenant A Travis from 7sth/2 Lawson TCAPT	MSH
	Harvour took out in relief of TCAPT CM Barton M/C	
	Command of the Section, Capt Barton M/C proceeding	
	on duty to No 7 Mobile Vety Section	
	(30 mm) & Lieutenant Shawn to 18th Bde. Retnh? R. DIEVAL	
23 Sept DIEVAL	usual Routine	MSH
24 Sept DIEVAL	usual Routine	MSH
24 Sept DIEVAL	usual Routine	MSH
25 Sept DIEVAL	usual Routine	MSH
26 Sept DIEVAL	usual Routine	MSH
27 Sept DIEVAL	18 sick horses evacuated to No 1 Vet. Ambulance	MSH

8th Mounted Brigade HQ

WAR DIARY Volume 49
or
INTELLIGENCE SUMMARY.
(Erase heading not required.)

Army Form C. 2118.

Hour, Date, Place	Summary of Events and Information	Remarks and references to Appendices
28 Sept DIEVAL	Proceeded at 6-30 pm with the Brigade to KERLIN to MILLY arriving about 11 pm. Their horses were evacuated to HUT VET. BARLIN two men who proceeded with them from the Union of MMHS 249th	M/ys [?]
29 Sept MILLY	Proceeded at 11 pm with a Column of the Brigade to INCHY arriving at 7-30 am.	Nil
30 Sept INCHY	Remained in camp at INCHY	Nil

A.D.J. Howard
Capt AVC
30/9/15
O.C. [signature]

Army Form A. 2007.

CENTRAL REGISTRY.

Central Registry No. and Date.　　　　　　　　　Attached Files.

SUBJECT, AND OFFICE OF ORIGIN.

War Diary　　8th Mobile Vety Sn

Volume 50
October 1918

Referred to	Date	Referred to	Date	Referred to	Date

P. A.	Date

Schedule of Correspondence.

Inter-Office Minutes.

NOTE.—Inside sheets to be attached to this page.

NOT TO BE WRITTEN ON.

WAR DIARY Volume 50 October
INTELLIGENCE SUMMARY. 85th Mobile Vety Sec'n

Army Form C. 2118.

(Erase heading not required.)

Place	Date	Hour	Summary of Events and Information	Remarks and references to Appendices
INCHY	1/10		Usual Routine	103H
INCHY	2/10	15 Horses evacuated sick to Canadian Bgo VET QUE ENT		103H
		5.2 Horses cast off as unfit for General service invalided to Lully Harness Repn Can Cav Dep		
INCHY	3/10		Usual Routine	103H
INCHY	4/10		Usual Routine	103H
INCHY	5/10		3 mules + 6 Horses evacuated sick to Canadian Bgo VET QUE ENT	103H
INCHY	6/10		Usual Routine	103H
INCHY	7/10		Usual Routine	103H
INCHY	8/10		10 sick horses evacuated sick to Canadian Bgo VET QUE ENT	103H
INCHY	9/10		Usual Routine	103H
INCHY	10/10		Usual Routine	103H
INCHY	11/10		World 2 Lyn Duty mostly sudden + inferred mk 16g Afprind	103H
			Prdry 15 Horses evacuated sick to Canadian Bgo VET.	
INCHY	12/10		Usual Routine	103H
INCHY	13/10		Parade C.O's service for all ranks at 9.15AM usual Routine	103H
INCHY	14/10		Usual Routine	103H
INCHY	15/10		Usual Routine	103H
INCHY	16/10		Usual Routine	103H

Army Form C. 2118.

WAR DIARY
or
INTELLIGENCE SUMMARY.
(Erase heading not required.)

Instructions regarding War Diaries and Intelligence
Summaries are contained in F. S. Regs., Part II.
and the Staff Manual respectively. Title pages
will be prepared in manuscript.

Place	Date	Hour	Summary of Events and Information	Remarks and references to Appendices
INCHY	17/10		Usual Routine	108#
INCHY	18/10		8 Horses 1 mule evacuated to 22 Corps Vet CAMBRAI	109#
INCHY	19/10		Usual Routine	110#
INCHY	20/10		11 Horses 1 mule evacuated to 22 Corps Vet CAMBRAI	111#
INCHY	21/10		Usual Routine	112#
INCHY	22/10		Usual Routine	113#
INCHY	23/10		11 Y.C.R Horses evacuated to 22 Corps Vet CAMBRAI	114#
INCHY	24/10		Usual Routine	115#
INCHY	25/10		Usual Routine toto mules sudden returned mob V.O.s	116#
INCHY	26/10		Moved independently to BARALLE	117#
BARALLE	27/10		Starting unit in mud in which section was billeted	118#
BARALLE	28/10		Usual Routine	119#
BARALLE	29/10		7 Horses evacuated to 22 Corps Vet CAMBRAI	120#
BARALLE	30/10		Usual Routine	121#
BARALLE	31/10		Usual Routine	122#

R.W. Henwood — Captain R.V.C
O.C. 9th MVS

(6339) Wt. W160/M3016 1,500,000 10/17 McA & W Ltd (E 1893) Forms W3091. Army Form W.3091.

Cover for Documents.

Nature of Enclosures.

Confidential

War Diary Volume 51 Nov 1918

8th Mobile Veterinary Section

VOLUME 51.

Notes, or Letters written.

WAR DIARY

8th Mobile Veterinary Sn   Volume 51

INTELLIGENCE SUMMARY.   Nov. 1918

Place	Date	Hour	Summary of Events and Information	Remarks and references to Appendices
BAIRALLE	1st Nov.	10 A.M.	R.V. arrivals evacuated to 22 Mobile Vet. Section Cambrai W.S.331. Phi service returned	R.S.H.
	2nd Nov.		10 p.m. Usual Routine	R.S.H.
	3rd Nov.		Usual Routine	R.S.H.
	4th Nov.		Section moved out to Brigade starting at 9.15 A.M. to ESTRUN arriving at 3.15 P.M.	R.S.H.
	5th Nov.		2 p.m. 9 animals evacuated to 22 Mobile Vet. Camden Killed myself at 9.15 P.M. with my aid to 7o5 H.T. Letter on map ref S.5-32 P.M.	R.S.H.
	6th Nov.		Usual Routine	R.S.H.
	7th Nov.		Usual Routine blank horse evacuated & 33 M.V.S.	R.S.H.
	8th Nov.		Usual Routine	R.S.H.
	9th Nov.		Usual Routine	R.S.H.
	10th Nov.		Usual Routine	R.S.H.
	11th Nov.		Usual Routine	R.S.H.
	12th Nov.		Usual Routine	R.S.H.
	13th Nov.		Moved out with Brigade to RECOURT arriving at 7 p.m.	R.S.H.
	14th Nov.		Sect. moved with Brigade to GRAND RENG arriving at 5 p.m.	R.S.H.

WAR DIARY
INTELLIGENCE SUMMARY

Army Form C. 2118.

Place	Date	Hour	Summary of Events and Information	Remarks and references to Appendices
	16	11.18	Usual Routine. 2 Officers and 89 O.R's joined Bn as Reinforcements.	109H
	17	11.18	Moved into bivouac at LANDAS arriving at 6 p.m.	104H
	18	11.18	Moved into bivouac at LD MOTTES arriving at 6.30 p.m.	105H
	19	11.18	Usual routine.	109H
	20	11.18	Usual routine. 3 Lieut. Adams transferred to Corps School.	104H
			ORDERS 60	101H
	21	11.18	Moved into billets at BUVRINES arriving at 3 p.m.	103H
	22	11.18	Moved into BAIVRE + CURGY arriving at 3 p.m.	R103H
	23	11.18	Brigade Route March. Brigade night to MONVILLE arriving at 2 p.m.	R109H
	24	11.18	Usual Routine.	R103H
	25	11.18	Usual Routine.	R103H
	26	11.18	Usual Routine.	R103H
	27	11.18	Usual Routine.	R103H
	28	11.18	Usual Routine.	R104H
	29	11.18	Moved with the Brigade at 9.30 a.m. to MENIL FAVRE arriving at 2.30 p.m.	109H
	30	11.18	Usual Routine.	

R.W. Newcombe
Capt/V.V.
O.C. 21st Bn R.W. Fus. Bn.

(6339) Wt. W160/M3016 1,500,000 10/17 McA & W Ltd (E 1898) Forms W3091.   Army Form W.3091.

Cover for Documents.

Nature of Enclosures.

Confidential

War Diary Volume 52

8th Mobile Veterinary Section,
3rd Cavalry Bde.   December 1918

8TH MOBILE VETERINARY SECTION
No.
Date.

Notes, or Letters written.

8TH MOBILE VETERINARY SECTION
Army Form C. 2118:

WAR DIARY
or
INTELLIGENCE SUMMARY. Volume 52 December 1918
(Erase heading not required.)

Instructions regarding War Diaries and Intelligence Summaries are contained in F. S. Regs., Part II. and the Staff Manual respectively. Title pages will be prepared in manuscript.

Place	Date	Hour	Summary of Events and Information	Remarks and references to Appendices
Marieux	1/12/18		Usual Routine	123H
	2/12/18		Usual Routine	123H
	3/12/18		Usual Routine. A.O.V.S. 2nd Cav Divn visited Section	123H
	4/12/18		Usual Routine	123H
	5/12/18		5 sick Horses evacuated to 6 6/7 VCHS VINEY	123H
	6/12/18		Usual Routine. A.O.V.S 2 Cav Divn visited Section at 15:30 hrs	123H
	7/12/18		1 sick Horse evacuated to 6 Co. No Vet S. VINEY.	123H
	8/12/18		Usual Routine	124H
	9/12/18		Usual Routine	123H
	10/12/18		Usual Routine. No. 10150 Pte D. Burke R.A.V.C. on Cho noted Section at 11:30 PM	124H
	11/12/18		No 8201 Pte Buckler R.T.R R.A.V.C returned from leave to England	124H
	12/12/18		Usual Routine	124H
	13/12/18		Usual Routine	124H

WAR DIARY
or
INTELLIGENCE SUMMARY

(Erase heading not required.)

MOBILE
VETERINARY SECTION
Army Form 2118.

Volume 52

Instructions regarding War Diaries and Intelligence Summaries are contained in F. S. Regs., Part II. and the Staff Manual respectively. Title pages will be prepared in manuscript.

Place	Date	Hour	Summary of Events and Information	Remarks and references to Appendices
French Farm	14th		Usual Routine	
	15th		Usual Routine. Visited rear lines 4th Aust. Division not cases of typhoid markasmy etc.	108/V
	16th		Usual Routine	108/V
	17th		Action amid mkt Peop. at stables at 8.30 AM & 4th AVH arriving at 2 PM.	108/V
	18th		RAVC visited sections + inspected horse + mules	108/V
	19th		Inspection of stables of all horses (H°2°) with regard to A.D.V.S. letter N° 261-1 Dated. 2-12-18	109/V
AWAN	20th	SF 12857 Pte Minty LM Left section to a/30 to DPM 2nd Army for Substitution duties.	110/V
	21st		Usual Routine	101/V
	22nd		Usual Routine	102/V
	23rd		Visited railhead with a view of mobilizing Portulation for evacuations.	103/V
	24th		6 Mange (bad cases) admitted from 4th Division	103/V
	25th		Usual Routine	
	26th		N° 165 Pte Mathews EL admitted to 2nd Cass. Cltg Camb.	108/V
	27th		Usual Routine. Visit of D.D.V.S. to sector.	109/V

WAR DIARY Volume 52
or
INTELLIGENCE SUMMARY.
(Erase heading not required.)

Army Form C. 2118

8TH MOBILE VETERINARY SECTION

Instructions regarding War Diaries and Intelligence Summaries are contained in F.S. Regs., Part II and the Staff Manual respectively. Title pages will be prepared in manuscript.

Hour, Date, Place	Summary of Events and Information	Remarks and references to Appendices
A.W.N. 28th-12-18	41 Sick Horses evacuated to 13 Vety: Hos: NEUF. CHATTEL, from 2nd Cav: Div Railhead.	R/H
" 29-12/18	POPERINGHE. Admitted 11 O.R.'s to Supernumary Strength.	R/H
" 30-12-18	Admitted one horse from 4th Hussars. Mange.	R/H
" 31st-12-18	Usual Routine. Conference of all V.O's 3rd Cav: B^{de} and A.D.V.S. arranged for Jan: 1st 1919.	R/H

A.B. Hansworth
Capt: R.A.V.C.
OC N° 8 Mobile Vety. Section.
3rd Cav: B^{de}

(6392) Wt. W6192/P875 1,500,000 4/18 McA & W Ltd (E 2815) Forms W3091/4.   Army Form W.3091.

Cover for Documents.

~~Secret~~   Confidential

Nature of Enclosures.

War Diary -

N° 8 Mobile Vety Section

Month of January 1919

Volume. 53.

Notes, or Letters written.

No 8 Mobile Vety Section
Volume 53

Army Form C. 2118.

WAR DIARY
INTELLIGENCE SUMMARY.
(Erase heading not required.)

Jan 1919

Hour, Date, Place		Summary of Events and Information	Remarks and references to Appendices
AWAN	January 1st 1919	Conference held by A.D.V.S. at 8 M.V.S. attended by Capt Young R.A.V.C. Capt. Boys R.A.V.C. Capt. Harcourt R.A.V.C.	ADM
"	2-1-1919.	Four Mange Horses evacuated to 9 M.V.S. in accordance with A.D.V.S. orders of 13 inst.	ADM
"	3-1-1919.	Usual Routine	ADM
"	4-1-1919	Horse brought from civilian at SPRIMONT to section.	ADM
"	5-1-1919	SE 3670 Pte LUCAS S. rel returned from leave. Inspection Y.O.B. of all Horses and mules on strength of H² & 1 S Signal Troop.	ADM
	~~4-1-1919~~		
AWAN	6-1-19	Usual Routine.	ADM
"	7-1-19	2 Horses admitted from 16 Lancers. Pte Matthews 66 evacuated through Re 165 to 50 C.C.S.	ADM
"	8-1-19	2" two field Amb. to 50 C.C.S.	ADM
"	9-1-19	Usual Routine	ADM
"	10-1-19	Inspection by Vety Board of Horses and Mules 4" Hussars for classification Vety Board composed of A.D.V.S. Capt. Boys R.C. A/Capt 4" Hussars and 06 N°8 MVS	ADM
"	11-1-19	Classification of all animals of 4" Hussars completed.	ADM

WAR DIARY or INTELLIGENCE SUMMARY.

Army Form C. 2118.

No 8 Mobile Veterinary Section
Volume 53
(Continued)

Place	Date	Hour	Summary of Events and Information	Remarks and references to Appendices
A.W.A.N.	12/1/19	6 P.M.	Horse destroyed at exibitions at ROMESHAMPS. Left by 6 M.V.S.G Batty. for No 4 Jnt. M.V. as the animal was useless from a veterinary point of view.	R.S.H
"	13/1/19	5 P.M.	Usual Routine. Two reinforcements arrived from No 2 Vety Hos. No F/10395 Pte DAVIES. T.F. No 15015 Pte DELL J.F	R.S.H No H O.S H R.S.H
"	14/1/19	6-30 P.M.	Inspection of rifles and equipment / Men of section.	
"	15/1/19	7 P.M.	Classification for Demobilization of all animals of 5 Lancers by Vety Board comprising O.C. and O.D.M.S 2" Inn. Div.	
"	16/1/19	9 P.M.	Classification of 5 Lancers completed. Admitted 56 horse tempt K. from 4th Hussars.	R.S.H
"	17/1/19	6/30 P.M.	S.F. No 8389 Pte CROSS. W.R. granted leave to England from 19-1-19 to 2-2-19	R.S.H
"	18/1/19	7 P.M.	Admitted 1 Horse (mange) from 16th Hussars. Arrangements made by O.C. for Shipment of horses for England. U.S.H	R.S.H
"	19/ "	6 P.M.	Admitted 50 horses sick for evacuation on 20" inst.	R.S.H
"	20/ "	7 P.M.	Evacuated 47 sick Horse from X Corps Divn. Railhead PERNSTEP.	O.S H
"	21/ "	6 P.M.	Usual Routine.	R.S.H

War Diary (cont.) N° 17 Mob. Vety Section

WAR DIARY
or
~~INTELLIGENCE SUMMARY~~
(Erase heading not required.)

Army Form C. 2118.

Instructions regarding War Diaries and Intelligence Summaries are contained in F.S. Regs, Part II. and the Staff Manual respectively. Title pages will be prepared in manuscript.

Hour, Date, Place	Summary of Events and Information	Remarks and references to Appendices
AWANS 22 January 1919 7 P.M.	Classification of 16 Lancers. Pte Birkhill transfd Leave to England.	RSH
" 23 Jan: 6 P.M.	All animals of 16 Lancers Mallein'd, also for instructions 9 Mange. admitted from 16 Lancers.	RSH
" 24 Jan: 5 P.M.	Further arrangements made for disposal of all classified "D" animals to home slaughters. LIEGE during the coming week.	RSH
" 25 Jan: 7 P.M.	One Mange admitted from 3rd Lancers.	RSH
" 26 Jan: 5.30 P.M.	2 Mange cases admitted from D.Bn/T.	RSH
" 27 Jan: 7.10 P.M.	SF 13151 Pte Bell E. granted special leave to England on compassionate grounds. SF 891 Pte Chaplin left section to be attached to Div. H"2° for Educational course. D. Batt R.H.A. animals Malleing by Co.	RSH

(cont)

War Diary of WAR DIARY 1918 Mobile Vety Section Army Form C. 2118.

Volume 5·3 (cont)

INTELLIGENCE SUMMARY.

(Erase heading not required.)

Instructions regarding War Diaries and Intelligence Summaries are contained in F.S. Regs., Part II. and the Staff Manual respectively. Title pages will be prepared in manuscript.

Hour, Date, Place		Summary of Events and Information	Remarks and references to Appendices
AWAN January	28" 6PM	O.C. Mobilised Horses of section. 6 Marye horses admitted from "A" Hanovers	MVSH
"	29" 7PM	All Horses and Mules Brigade H" 2" Mobilised by O.C.	MVSH
"	30 6PM	15 "D" Horses sold to Horse Builder LIÈGE.	MVSH
"	31 4·30PM		MVSH

W. Henwood
Cpl RAV

Army Form W.3091.

Cover for Documents.

Confidential

Nature of Enclosures.

War Diary

(Secret)

N⁰ 8 MVS

Notes, or Letters written.

Volume 54
Month of February 1919

Army Form C. 2118.

WAR DIARY
or
INTELLIGENCE SUMMARY.

(Erase heading not required.)

Instructions regarding War Diaries and Intelligence Summaries are contained in F. S. Regs., Part II and the Staff Manual respectively. Title pages will be prepared in manuscript.

Feb. 19

Volume 54 A.M.V.S.

Hour, Date, Place	Summary of Events and Information	Remarks and references to Appendices
AWANS. February 1st 1919 6 P.M.	One horse collected from inhabitant Offremont.	AV94
" 2nd " 7 P.M.	Two animals collected from inhabitant HOTTEN.	AV94
" 3rd " 5 P.M.	Inspection of Men's equipment re demobilisation.	AV94
" 4th " 4-30 P.M.	Reclassified the Manges (J.L.B.) 3 Mange admitted from 4th Hussars	AV94
" 5th " 7 P.M.	1st Fag. 1/4 section for leave to England. (SE No. 959)	AV94
" 6th " 8 P.M.	15 Class "D" animals destroyed and sold to H.D. LIEGE.	AV94
" 7th " 7-30 P.M.	Mutual Routine.	AV94
" 8th " 6-0 P.M.	No. 261142 Pte Doig F reported for duty from No. 2 Vety Hos.	AV94
" 9th " 10 P.M.	Evacuation of sick and Class "D" animals from BANSTER (2 Cav Div) Rowbied) to 15 advanced Vety Hos.	AV94
" 10 " 8-0 P.M.	6 Horses admitted from 5 Lancers.	AV94

WAR DIARY or INTELLIGENCE SUMMARY

Army Form C. 2118.

(Cont'd)

Volume 54

Hour, Date, Place	Summary of Events and Information	Remarks and references to Appendices
AWANS. Feb 11-1919 6 P.M.	Usual Routine.	109H
" 12 " 7 P.M.	P⁺ Birchill reported from leave.	109H
" 13 " 6-10 P.M.	P⁺ Cross 2⁻⁸⁸⁸⁰ reported from leave.	109H
" 14 " 7 P.M.	Inspection of Rifles.	
" 15 " 9 P.M.	N⁰ 753 Cpl Tatham two horses admitted. AFZ22 received for both Tatham, 109H	109H
" 16 " 6-30 P.M.	N⁰ 753 Cpl Tatham proceeded to concentration camp for demobilization.	109H
" " "	Usual Routine	109H
" 17 - 1919 5 P.M.	N⁰-1949 P⁺ Woods left section for leave in England	109H
" 18 - 1919. 7 P.M.	Evacuation of sick animals from PRINSTER to 15 advanced depots.	109H
" 19 - 6 P.M.	Reclassification of 2 animals	109H
" 20 - 5 P.M.	P⁺ Bowes admitted to 2ⁿᵈ Nov: Field Amb:	109H
" 21 " 4 P.M.	One Horse 16 Jemima reclassified "D"	109H

WAR DIARY *Volume 54*

or

INTELLIGENCE SUMMARY.

(Erase heading not required.)

Army Form C. 2118.

Instructions regarding War Diaries and Intelligence Summaries are contained in F.S. Regs., Part II. and the Staff Manual respectively. Title pages will be prepared in manuscript.

Hour, Date, Place			Summary of Events and Information	Remarks and references to Appendices
AWAN. Feb. 22 - 1919.	5 PM.		Annual Kit inspection of men.	109 H
" 23 "	7 PM.		Usual Routine.	129 H
" 24 "	4:30 PM.		Usual Routine.	129 H
" 25 "	5 PM.		7 L.D. despatched to SERAINS.	129 H
" 26 "	7 PM.		Usual Routine.	129 H
" 27 "	8 PM.		Usual Routine.	129 H
" 28 "	9 PM.		Usual Routine.	129 H

R.C. Hammond Captain RAMC
O.C. No. 3 MVS

(6302) Wt. W6192/P875 1,500,000 4/18 McA & W Ltd (E 2815) Forms W3091/4.   Army Form W.3091.

Cover for Documents.

Nature of Enclosures.

Secret 1 Confidential
War Diary
Volume N° 56
1/3/19 — 31/3/19
N° 8 Mobile Vety Section

Notes, or Letters written.

No 8 Mobile Vety Sect.   Volume No 5

Army Form C. 2118.

WAR DIARY
or
INTELLIGENCE SUMMARY.   S.O.
(Erase heading not required.)

Instructions regarding War Diaries and Intelligence Summaries are contained in F.S. Regs., Part II and the Staff Manual respectively. Title pages will be prepared in manuscript.

Hour, Date, Place	Summary of Events and Information	Remarks and references to Appendices
1st March 1919	Action Nil	
to 9th March 1919 at AWAN		
		N/H
10th March 1919 1800 hours	Section moved to ENSIVAL (CADRE AREA) N/H	
11th March to 18th March ENSIVAL	Action Nil	N/H
19th March 1900 hours ENSIVAL	10 Privates despatched to 13 Vety Hos. for duty pending demobilization. 8 Privates transferred to 1 M.V.S. 1st Cav. Res. Section is now at cadre strength. viz 1 Officer sergt 104th 7 Other Ranks.	N/H
20th March to 31st March	Action Nil	

A.J. Henwood
O.C. No 8 Mobile Vety Sect

Army Form C. 2118.

WAR DIARY
or
INTELLIGENCE SUMMARY.
(Erase heading not required.)

Instructions regarding War Diaries and Intelligence Summaries are contained in F. S. Regs., Part II. and the Staff Manual respectively. Title pages will be prepared in manuscript.

Hour, Date, Place	Summary of Events and Information	Remarks and references to Appendices
June 1915	Hondeghem	
13th	20 horses evacuated to Base	
14th "	1 horse A echelon admitted - hand routine	
15th "	J Reg A Section temporarily taken over by D.S.S. Young A.V.C.	
16th "	2 horses admitted for evacuation. Sent to 13 ave	
17th "	Rifle drill & target practice the Parade two teams ordered each for one hour. hand Routine	
18th "	"	
19th "	"	
20th "	11 horses evacuated	
21st "	A/Sgts Gedday & Wats posted to DDI.S. & D.I.S.	
22nd "	Pte Butler admitted IR to J.R.S.S. hand Routine - Purged horses of Section	
23rd "	"	
24th "	Purged horses of Section	

WAR DIARY
or
INTELLIGENCE SUMMARY.

(Erase heading not required.)

Army Form C. 2118.

Hour, Date, Place	Summary of Events and Information	Remarks and references to Appendices
25th June 1915	Kon dixfleur.	
26th June	Usual Routine.	
27th "	Conducted party to Keyenock stables & enforcement of Remounts from & mined. hoved conduc sick etc	
28th "	Conveyed veterinary supplies to D Battery R.H.A.	
29th "	1 Horse B echelon 3rd co. 13th Bde " attended	
30th "	1 " D battery R.H.A " " hoved constant